JORD

BEERSHEBA

Negev

EL AUJA

NIRIM

EL ARISH

EGYP

EILAT

AQABA

35

36

31

30

SYRIA

IR

SAUDI ARAB

JORDAN

LEBANON

Mediterranean Sea

ISRAEL

CYPRUS

EGYPT

PICTORIAL HISTORY
of ISRAEL

PICTORIAL

HISTORY of ISRAEL

JACOB A. RUBIN
and
MEYER BARKAI

New York · THOMAS YOSELOFF · London

© 1958 BY THOMAS YOSELOFF, INC.
© 1961 BY A. S. BARNES AND COMPANY, INC.
LIBRARY OF CONGRESS CATALOGUE CARD NUMBER: 61-9625

THOMAS YOSELOFF: PUBLISHER
8 East 36th Street
New York 16, N. Y.

Thomas Yoseloff Ltd.
18 Charing Cross Road
London W. C. 2, England

First printing October 1958
Second printing December 1960
Third printing December 1963
Fourth printing September 1965

CONTENTS

To
EDNA RUBIN
born in the year of
the birth of the State,
NIRA RUBIN,
and
FRANCES BARKAI

1 UNTO THY SEED...

This was the Covenant: "And I will give to thee and to thy seed after thee the land of my abode, all the land of Canaan, for an everlasting possession" (Genesis, 17: 8)..

This was the beginning, the beginning of the bond between the people of Israel and the land of Israel. From time immemorial this sacred attachment of the people to their land has never weakened, never been forgotten. Thousands of years have passed, tens of generations have vanished, civilizations have been created and have disappeared, nations have been lifted to heights of influence and have vanished from memory, but the people of Israel have remained ever faithful to the strip of land on the Eastern shores of the Mediterranean. The land had changed its name, its rulers, and, by force, its inhabitants, but it still remained the Promised Land.

There was no mystery involved. A people of shepherds and peasants gave birth to a unique idea of monotheism and gave a moral code to humanity—and still withstood the pressure of worldly affairs. After centuries of complete anarchy, which knew the lordship of executors of justice only, a growing need for authority culminated in the first monarchy. The State was born with boundaries, security problems, peace treaties, friendships, and enemies.

No great historic event of ancient times failed to touch the land of Israel. Great autocracies and mighty powers never overlooked the little land and its people. When others accepted foreign rule, assimilated, and lost their identity—the people of Israel refused to compromise. The "people of prophets" would not acquiesce. They revolted against the mighty, withstood endless attempts to destroy their sovereignty, and were dispersed and finally exiled only to appear again on the historic scene as an independent nation. The Kingdom of David and of Solomon, who built the Temple in Jerusalem, was organized and later split into the Kingdom of Judah and the Kingdom of Israel;

This mural, depicting Israel's bondage in Egypt, was found in the Theban tomb of Rechmire, governor and vizier at the time of Thutmose III, about 1450 B.C.E.

And the Egyptians made the children of Israel to serve with rigor. And they made their lives bitter with hard bondage, in mortar, and in brick, and in all manner of service in the field (Exodus 1:13,14).

Moses *(sculpture by Michelangelo).*
Then the Lord said unto Moses, Go in unto Pharaoh and tell him, Thus saith the Lord God of the Hebrews, Let my people go (Exodus 9:1).

The Exodus from Egypt.
Now the sojourning of the children of Israel, who dwelt in Egypt, was four hundred and thirty years. And it came to pass at the end of the four hundred and thirty years, even the selfsame day it came to pass, that all the hosts of the Lord went out from the Land of Egypt (Exodus 12:40,41)

The Holy of Holies, from a model of King Solomon's Temple.
I purpose to build an house unto the name of the Lord my God, as the Lord spake unto David my father, saying, Thy son, whom I will set upon thy throne in thy room, he shall build the house unto my name (I Kings 5:19).

Jeremiah at the fall of Jerusalem.
Zion shall be plowed like a field, and Jerusalem shall become heaps, and the mountain of the house as the high places of the forest (Jeremiah 26:18).

The destruction of Jerusalem.
And Nebuchadnezzar king of Babylon came against the city, and his servants did besiege it (**II Kings 24:11**).
And he carried away all Jerusalem, and all the princes, and all the mighty men of valor, even ten thousand captives, and all the craftsmen and smiths (**II Kings 24:14**).

The Wailing Wall in Jerusalem *(from an old print).*

Rachel's Tomb. Located near Bethlehem, it is a shrine revered by Jews, Christians, and Moslems alike.

Thus said the Lord; a voice was heard in Ramah, lamentation, and bitter weeping; Rahel weeping for her children refused to be comforted for her children because they were not (Jeremiah 31:15).

the two kingdoms were faithful to their great heritage until 586 B.C.E. when Nebuchadnezzar seized Jerusalem and destroyed the Temple, carrying a vast number of the people into captivity. So started the long history of Jewish exile, which was to last with one interruption for almost twenty-five hundred years. The fervent prayers and lamentations of the exiles were recorded for posterity. "On the river of Babylon we sat and wept when we remembered thee, O Zion." They uttered their pathetic oath of loyalty: "If I forget thee, O Jerusalem, let my right hand forget her cunning."

These people could not, did not, forget their land. At the first opportunity they left their homes of exile and went to the land of their fathers. Another Temple was built, national life was reconstructed, and new vistas were opened for the continued development of the Jewish way of life. Once again foreign countries probed into the internal life of Judea, and once again the people revolted —this time their heroic upsurge of devotion for Jewish independence was met with the success which assured Jewish independence for centuries to come. The Maccabean revolt of 166 B.C.E., against the Seleucids' attempts to Hellenize Judea was turned into a symbol of the Jewish fight for freedom, and has become an example worthy of emulation to all freedom fighters, through all centuries and in all nations.

The little nation, now free, attracted the rising power of Rome. Even the humanitarian Roman conception of overlordship, which allowed all captive nations to remain autonomous, and offered Judea the most generous treatment, was rejected by the free men of Zion. The little country put up a sturdy fight against the Roman legions and the Romans suffered more than one defeat at their hands. Even the destruction of the Second Temple by Titus in 70 C.E. did not stop the revolts. Again and again the people rose. These historic facts are a magnificent tribute to the faith of these people who withstood the might of a great, world-conquering empire. When, after three revolts, the Jews were finally conquered during the rebellion of Bar Kochba, the Roman emperor staged a prolonged celebration of victory, and proudly inscribed on great monuments and on the covers of State documents: "Judaea Victa, Judaea Capta." Judea subdued, Judea captured. The intensity of the Roman anger was reflected in the numbers of Jews who were exiled and enslaved, and the attempt to erase the very name of their little country from memory by changing it from Judea to "Syria Palestina." Nevertheless, the Romans still felt that the Jews were a threat to their entrenched political and social institutions, for the Jews openly proclaimed their adherence to spiritual values and rejected the Roman way of life.

The Roman philosopher, Seneca, bitterly attacked these strange Judeans who were responsible for the loss of one-seventh of the working time of

A fragment of a letter written by Bar Kochba (died 135 C.E.), leader of the Jewish revolt against the Romans during the rule of Hadrian.

Maimonides (1135-1204), the outstanding Jewish rabbi, philosopher, and physician of the Middle Ages, a staunch believer in the return to Zion.

men by their observance of the Sabbath, and wrote: "The customs of this criminal nation are gaining ground so rapidly, that they already have adherents in every country, and thus the conquered force their law upon the conqueror."

These mighty oppressive powers banished masses of Jews from their country, and though there is some historical proof that a great Jewish population was still in existence in Judea during the fifth and sixth centuries C.E., the fact remains that successive exiles left few Jews in Judea.

But Jewish hearts yearned for their homeland with a deep and lasting love. Almost every prayer was a plea for the return to Zion. On the holiest of days, Yom Kippur, the Day of Atonement, Jewish congregations throughout the world repeated no less than seven times: "Next year in Jerusalem."

Through the ages, this belief, this hope, united the Jewish masses in their dispersion. The so-called "false Messiahs" gathered about them a people full of human passion and endeavor, longing for a sign from God. Sabbatai Zevi, in the seventeenth century, was responsible for setting tens of thousands of Jews on the move to the Promised Land, to Eretz Israel. They symbolized the collective heart of a people striving for the country of their origin.

No epoch in history was without some kind of Jewish movement for the return to Zion. The Jewish people would never abandon their title to the ownership of the land of Israel, which they would never call by its Roman-given name, Palestine. Poets and leaders, from Judah Halevi and Maimonides to Don Joseph Hanassi (Duke of Naxos), though hundreds of years separated their lives, reflected the enduring love the Jewish people felt toward their land. Napoleon issued an appeal to the Jews to rise against the Turks, promising them in return the restoration of Jerusalem. The anti-Semites in Europe who wanted to destroy the Jewish people, but who could not conceive of Hitler's slaughter, used as their slogan: "Jews back to Palestine."

The Jews longed for that return. They remembered the words of Jeremiah: "The Lord shall set His hand again the second time to recover the remnants of His people, and He shall assemble the outcast of Israel and gather together the depressed of Judah from the four corners of the earth." They believed that the country waited for them to redeem it from the wilderness and desolation into which it had grown through the neglect of centuries of transient inhabitants. To the Jews, the neglected land represented their future independent, sovereign State.

The modern movement for the return to Zion

Sabbatai Zevi (1626-1676), the "false messiah" who promised to lead the Jews back to the Promised Land.

13

had its foundation in this belief in the necessity for uniting, once again, the country and its chosen people. It is not enough to attribute the return to the land of Israel to an escape from persecution and a need for a haven for refugees. Though one cannot ignore the vital importance of Israel as a haven for exiled Jews everywhere, the *raison d'être* for this return, for reestablishment of Jewish national independence after nineteen hundred years, is implied in the genuine right of every people to have a place where it can live as a nation, create as a nation, and develop its specific abilities for their own good and for that of mankind in general.

The people who gave the world two great universal religions—Judaism and Christianity—and decisively influenced the third, Islam, once again come to the end of years of wandering, once again approach the shores of their ancient land, and are once again able to renew their collective share in men's search for progress and brotherhood. The ancient Romans regarded the "Golden Era" as a matter of the past, but, according to basic Jewish belief, it is the future that harbors in it the secret of "better days to come." Israel in its land, free and independent—this is the new instrument through which the Jews can strive and labor for the *achrit hayamin*—the "last days"—the end of man's journey to perfection.

Detail from the Arch of Titus, erected in commemoration of the Roman victory over Judea.

2 FROM PROMISE TO FULFILLMENT

But, before the fulfillment, were the years of promise—of waiting. The promise was never forgotten. It was harbored in the hearts of millions dispersed all over the world. It was repeated daily in prayers and at solemn occasions in the lives of Jewish communities and individuals. The destruction of Jerusalem was remembered at the most joyous feasts.

This was the nationalism of passivity—faithfulness to a country about which only dreams, but no real picture, remained. With the ascendance of nationalist movements in nineteenth-century Europe, this ancient belief in Zion started its transformation from prayers and pious beliefs to practical efforts. As in all national movements of that epoch, books heralded the change. *Rome and Jerusalem* by Moses Hess, *Self-Emancipation* by Leo Pinsker, both classics of modern Zionism, were the most eloquent and influential expressions of thoughts and feelings which were nurtured by Jews in those times. The time was ripening for some dramatic expression of this Jewish will for redemption, for had it not been recorded that "the Almighty helps only those who know to help themselves"?

It was therefore only a dream of expectation when the word, one may say the "battle cry," came: "We Jews, too, along with all other nations, have a right to self-determination, to a place where the Jewish race, those who want it, can govern themselves and reinstate the national independence that once prevailed." That the man who sounded this modern expression of Jewish faithfulness to Zion was, in fact, a stranger to Jewish traditions; that it was the destiny of a brilliant and worldly journalist of Jewish descent to become the revered and recognized prophet, creator, and leader of a political movement; that, as historical implications indicate, it was a shocking demonstration of anti-Semitism in a most modern, freedom-loving nation like France, which prompted the mighty movement of man's will are but secondary causative factors. Nevertheless, these secondary elements strengthen the basic assumption—that it was the intense need of the time which was to turn Dr. Theodor Herzl, the renowned writer and journalist of Vienna (assisted by the renowned writer and critic Max Nordau), into the man who would actively change the destiny of the most ancient of peoples.

Herzl's call to action was the mightiest, the most decisive, accompanied by measures appropriate to the epoch and task, but it was not the first and only one. When Herzl threw into the life of the Jewish communities of Europe the truth "that the Jewish question is first of all a national question and has as such to be solved," he revealed a truth already known, the latent political implications of which were as yet unrecognized.

In 1840, Sir Moses Montefiore, the Jewish philanthropist in Great Britain, negotiated with Lord Palmerston on Jewish agricultural colonization in Palestine. This was soon followed by practical

Theodor Herzl (1860-1904), founder of the World Zionist Organization, leader and prophet of political Zionism.

steps. Settlers from the ranks of BILU,* which mushroomed in Russia, arrived to put their feet on the soil of their forefathers and the first Jewish agricultural settlements in Palestine came into being. In 1870, the Alliance Israelite Universelle established the first agricultural school near Jaffa which they called Mikveh Israel (The Well of Israel). In 1880, the desire for the return to the soil found its expression in the establishment of

Conference of Chovevei Zion held in Katovice, Poland, in 1884.

the first agricultural settlement, Petach Tikvah (the Opening of Hope).

In 1897, the first Zionist Congress was held in Basle where the delegates endorsed the Basle Program which defined the aims of the Zionist movement as follows: "The aim of Zionism is to create for the Jewish people a publicly recognized and legally secured home in Palestine." The Zionist World Organization laid the foundation for the development of political, practical, and administrative activities in Israel. Herzl's enthusiastic enunciation at the first Zionist Congress—"Here we have started to build the Jewish State"—was representative of the feeling of all the participants. They felt that they had started a movement which would bear fruit and lead to the realization of the unending dream of sixty generations of Jews—that a day would come when all who wished might start their journey back to Zion.

The Jewish national movement finally had its instrument for national policy. Within a few years it not only received the recognition of almost all Jews, but also received recognition in the highest circles of world diplomacy. In his quest for a

_____
*A mnemonic for *Bet Yaakov Lechu Venelcha*, "Come, O house of Jacob, let us go up" (II, Isaiah).

"charter," international recognition of the right to organize an autonomous Jewish community in Palestine, Herzl received an audience with the Sultan of Turkey (ruler of Palestine at that time), with Kaiser Wilhelm of Germany, and with a number of ministers and ambassadors. It was only a few years before the Zionist movement achieved the stature of a recognized and respected political body.

Under the influence of Herzl, the British Colonial Secretary, Joseph Chamberlain, proposed that the highlands of Uganda in East Africa serve as a Jewish homeland with a "Jewish official to serve as chief of the local administration." The offer was tempting, opinions were divided, but it was finally decided that the implementation of Jewish national aspirations could take place only in Zion.

The first political successes were accompanied by a concerted effort to organize all the machinery of the national movement to facilitate the rebirth of the ancient homeland. A banking institution for colonization, the Jewish Colonial Trust, with its subsidiary—the Anglo-Palestine Bank, was established. A fund for the acquisition of land for the settlement of the repatriated Jews, Keren

Sir Moses Montefiore (1784-1885), British philanthropist, who devoted most of his life to aiding persecuted Jews throughout the Diaspora.

Kayemet le-Israel (Jewish National Fund), introduced a new concept in the principles of land ownership, which was to be in the hands of the nation and not the individuals. The rejuvenation of the Hebrew language was decided upon along with a

16

firm avowal that a Hebrew university had to be created in Eretz Israel, in Palestine.

THE ALIYOT BEGIN

The political structure of the Zionist movement, conceived and implemented by Herzl, had as its basis the Jewish community in Palestine. Immigrants from Russia and Rumania, as well as from other lands, had laid the foundations for agricul-

Baron Edmond de Rothschild *(right)* with Sir Herbert Samuel, the first British High Commissioner in Palestine.

tural settlements. Baron Edmond de Rothschild's efforts to have Palestine settled again by Jews had placed into the hands of the people who wanted to return to Zion the practical means by which their dreams could be realized. Colonies of settlers began to emerge throughout Palestine—Gedera, Rehovot, Rishon-le-Zion, Zichron Yaakov, Rosh Pinah, and Yesod Hamaaleh. The colonies of the Jews who came to live and build in their new-old land were scattered all over the country.

The so-called *aliyot* (in Hebrew, *aliyah* means "ascent," and is the term used for the return of Jews to settle in the land of Israel) incited the new period of immigration to Israel. They were not the first to come, for during no period of history was Palestine completely without Jewish inhabitants. Continuity of Jewish life, no matter how inconspicuous, prevailed without exception through the ages. Jews lived in Jerusalem as guardians of the Wailing Wall, the last remnant of the Second Temple. Jews lived in Hebron, in Safed, in Tiberias, and in Gaza. In addition, there were a number of devoted, pious Jews who came to Palestine, often to assure their burial in the Holy Land.

The period that can be counted as a real mass movement of repatriation, however, started with the rise of the BILU movement, which preceded the rise of the Chovevei Zion (Lovers of Zion), which gave new impetus, new meaning, and new dimensions to the Jewish emigration to Palestine. The new era of Jewish repatriation can more accurately be dated from that time. Since then, several waves of immigration, of *aliyot,* occurred.

In 1880, when the first wave of repatriation began, the entire population of Palestine consisted of thirty-five thousand Jews and one hundred and ten thousand Arabs who had been in the country for at least one generation. This first *aliyah,* which established the initial Jewish agricultural settlements, was composed of repatriates who came with their whole families. The second *aliyah,* which started in 1904, although animated by the great love of Zion, as the name of their movement (Chovevei Zion) indicated, was driven to a great extent by the anti-Semitic pogroms in Russia. They brought with them a completely new type of settler. They were mostly young people who saw themselves not only as redeemers of Palestine and rebuilders of the Jewish State, but as bearers of social justice, freedom, and equality. These people were the founders of a new type of agricultural

Settlers at Zichron Yaakov (1915), one of the first colonies in Palestine.

settlement—a collective effort in which no private ownership prevailed, in which the classic formula of socialism, "to each according to his needs, from each according to his ability," was not only theory, but an ideal put into practice. The cornerstone for the whole *kibbutz* movement was laid with the experiments in Sedjera, in Lower Galilee, and the establishment in 1909 of the first full-fledged collective settlement, Dagania, on the banks of Lake Kinneret.

When World War I broke out in 1914, there were nearly eighty thousand Jews in Palestine, who, though living in about fifty centers in various parts of the country, were conscious of themselves as a national entity. They had even established the nucleus of an armed force for self-defense, The Hashomer (The Watchmen or Guardsmen).

Small as this community was, it was a factor with which to reckon. The Turks looked with an unsympathetic eye at the process of Jewish repatriation for they instantly recognized the threat to their absolute rule in the Holy Land. The persistence with which the Jewish repatriates clung to their land and penetrated the wall of isolation with which the Turks had surrounded the country was sufficient proof that here was the most formidable type of opponent—the pioneer with an idea and an ideal from which he could not be deterred by force or by threat.

The repatriates vocalized their contention that they were the legitimate owners and inhabitants of the country, openly indicating that the Turks were foreign invaders with no rights of possession. The intense national aspirations of the Jews seemed sufficient reason for the Turkish authorities to impose harsh restrictions upon them. The Jewish settlers in Palestine had many reasons to look upon the defeat of the Turkish Empire in World War I as the beginning of their national redemption.

The house in Mamillah Street, Jerusalem, where Theodor Herzl stayed while visiting Palestine in 1898.

THE BALFOUR DECLARATION

The Zionist movement did not miss the historic hour. Political activity was accelerated and contacts were made. There was no hesitation in the early years of World War I, when the odds of war were far from clear. When the Central Powers, Germany and Austria, with whom Turkey was allied, seemed to be winning, the World Zionist Organization came out in support of the Allies.

Within twenty years after the inception of the Zionist movement a new phase in the secularization of pious prayers for the return to Zion started. Some of the top leaders of the Zionist movement reached the conclusion that to realize their aim a contribution had to be made to the fighting forces of the Middle Eastern-Palestine front. The dream of a Jewish military unit, with its own symbols and insignia, fighting officially for the Jewish national cause of freeing Palestine from the yoke of Turkey, became reality. The Jewish Legion, conceived and fought for by the Zionist leader Vladimir Jabotinsky, came into being as a unit within the Army of Field Marshal Allenby and was organized in Great Britain. Immediately after, the first Judean Regiment, another battalion of the Jewish Legion, was organized in the United States by David Ben Gurion and Yitzhak Ben Zvi. These, together with a third battalion which consisted of a military force of a few thousand Palestine Jews, comprised the first Jewish military unit, known and recognized as such, since the fall of Judea. Thus, two of the elements of a sovereign nation were on the verge of fulfillment—a political organization and a military arm. Only one, but the most important and basic, link was missing: the

BILU pioneers (1882).

land, the territory in which the political organization could act and which the military arm could protect. After long and detailed negotiations between the Zionist leadership (headed by Chaim Weizmann and Nahum Sokolow) and the British, French, and Italian governments, the British War Cabinet decided to accept certain fundamentals of the "outline of program for Jewish resettlement of Palestine in accordance with the aspirations of the Zionist movement." This acceptance took written form in a letter, dated November 2, 1917, from the Secretary of State for Foreign Affairs, James Balfour, to Lord Rothschild, whom Dr. Weizmann had suggested as addressee. The text of the letter read:

I have much pleasure in conveying to you on behalf of His Majesty's Government the following declaration of sympathy with Jewish Zionist aspirations, which was submitted to and approved by the Cabinet:

"His Majesty's Government view with favor the establishment in Palestine of a National Home for the Jewish people, and will use their best endeavors to facilitate the achievement of this object, it being clearly understood that nothing shall be done which may prejudice the civil and religious rights of existing non-Jewish communities in Palestine, or the rights and political status enjoyed by Jews in any other country."

I should be grateful if you would bring this declaration to the knowledge of the Zionist Federation.

The implications of this document were clear: the Zionist movement was accorded international

Leading Zionists at the Sixth Zionist Congress in Basle (1903). 1. Israel Zangwill; 2. Herzl's mother; 3. Max Nordau; 4. Theodor Herzl; 6. Nahum Sokolow; 7. David Wolffsohn.

Members of Hashomer (Watchmen), the first Jewish defense organization in Palestine.

recognition and deemed a fitting body to make contracts with the leading powers. The consideration given to the Zionist movement and Zionist aspirations was very soon seconded by the adversaries of the Triple Alliance. The Turkish Government, with the concurrence of the German Government, issued, after the Balfour Declaration, a similar statement promising self-government in Palestine and free immigration of Jews to that country.

The unbelievable became actuality. The two great power blocs competed in achieving Zionist-Jewish cooperation and sympathy as one of their means in the deadly struggle for victory. The Central Powers and the Triple Alliance sought to enlist not only the assistance of the Palestine Jewish community but of all Jews who were sympathetic to Zionist aims. They knew that the Zionists could render practical services such as the Jewish Legion had done. Lloyd George, the wartime Prime Min-

A group of young pioneers of the second *aliyah*.

ister of Great Britain, testified many years later, in 1936, before one of the Royal commissions appointed to "inquire into the Palestine problem" that the publication of the Balfour Declaration at that particular time was dictated by "propagandistic reasons." Lloyd George stated that "the Zionist leaders gave a definite promise that, if the Allies committed themselves to giving facilities for the establishment of a National Home for the Jews in Palestine, they would do their best to rally Jewish sentiment and support throughout the world to the Allies' cause. They kept their word."

On the other hand, the British started to retract, but not before the Balfour Declaration became international law. The Allied Powers carried on detailed negotiations on the subject of the Balfour Declaration until parallel statements were issued in February and March, 1918, by the French and

Firing a "last salute" over the graves of soldiers of the Jewish Legion who died in action to liberate Palestine during World War I.

Italian governments. President Wilson followed these negotiations, encouraging the issuance of the Declaration, and later insisted on having a hand in the drafting of the Mandate, the international document which presented, in legal form, the obligations toward Zionism and entrusted Great Britain with the implementation of its provisions. In April, 1920, at a meeting in San Remo of the Supreme Council of the Allied Powers, the Balfour Declaration was unanimously adopted and embodied in the Mandate for Palestine which was offered to Great Britain. On July 24, 1922, the Council of the League of Nations unanimously ratified the British Mandate with the incorporated Balfour Declaration as an integral part. That same year, the Congress of the United States adopted a resolution which read:

Resolved by the Senate and House of Representatives of the United States of America in Congress assembled, that the United States of America favors the establishment in Palestine of a National Home for the Jewish people, it being clearly understood that nothing shall be done which may prejudice the civil and religious rights of existing non-Jewish communities in Palestine or the rights and political status enjoyed by Jews in any other country.

What the authors of the Mandate intended was explicitly defined in the Preamble which read:

. . . Whereas recognition has thereby been given to the historical connection of the Jewish people with Palestine and the grounds for reconstructing their national home in that country. . . .

The intention of the authors of the Mandate, and the aims of those Jews who worked for it, were therefore clear. They recognized the historic bonds between the people of Israel and the land of Israel with the clear understanding that these bonds would be reaffirmed through the reconstruction of Israel's independence. The word "reconstituting" left no doubt about the intentions of the signers of the Mandate. By definition, the word "reconstitute" presupposes former existence—in this case the existence of the independent Jewish Commonwealth of antiquity, which fell under the overwhelming might of the Roman conquerors.

That this was the real meaning of the Mandate —to prepare for the restoration of the Jewish State in Palestine—was manifested by many other important statements. On March 3, 1919, President Wilson stated that "the Allied Nations, with the fullest concurrence of our own government and people, are agreed that in Palestine shall be laid the foundations of a Jewish Commonwealth." Lloyd George wrote in his memoirs:

It was not their (The British Cabinet's) idea that a Jewish State should be set up immediately by the peace treaty without reference to the wishes of the majority of the inhabitants. On the other hand, it was contemplated that, when the time arrived for according representative institutions to Palestine, if the Jews had meanwhile responded to the opportunity afforded them by the idea of a national homeland and had become a definite majority of the inhabitants, then Palestine would thus become a Jewish Commonwealth.

General Smuts, the Prime Minister of the Union

Vladimir Jabotinsky (1880-1940) in the uniform of the Jewish Legion which he founded in World War I. Jabotinsky was imprisoned by the British for organizing the Hagana during the riots of 1920. Later, he founded the Zionist Revisionist movement (New Zionist Organization) and the Irgun Zvai Leumi.

of South Africa, who was a member of the Imperial War Cabinet in 1919, stated that he had envisaged an increasing stream of Jewish immigration into Palestine and, in generations to come, a great Jewish State rising there once more. And Winston Churchill, when he was Secretary of State in 1920, declared:

If, as may well happen, there should be created in our lifetime by the banks of the Jordan a Jewish State under the protection of the British Crown, which might comprise three million or four million Jews, an event will have occurred in the history of the world which would from every point of view be beneficial.

These are only a few of the many statements and declarations made by the leading personalities of the World War I and postwar era with reference to the Balfour Declaration and, later, the Mandate. These interpretations were fully translated

Field Marshal Edmund Allenby's official entry into Jerusalem on December 11, 1917, after capturing the city from the Turks.

into the language of practical political rules. The Mandate stated clearly that the Mandatory power, Great Britain, had the responsibility "to place the country under such political, administrative, and economic conditions as will secure the establishment of the Jewish National Home." But the Mandate went even further; it recognized instantly that in the endeavor of national redemption, the Jews should have a direct voice, a decisive influence. The Mandate recognized "an appropriate Jewish Agency as a public body for the purpose of advising and cooperating with the administration of Palestine in such economic, social, and other matters which may affect the establishment of the Jewish National Home."

The Mandatory power was also charged with the duty of "facilitating Jewish immigration into Palestine" and of encouraging "in cooperation with the Jewish Agency" close settlement of Jews on the land, including state land and waste land not required for public purposes. It explicitly provided for the facilitation of the acquisition of Palestinian citizenship by Jews making their permanent residence in Palestine.

The basis for the Jewish State was laid. The highest international authority of those days, the League of Nations, had taken upon itself the legal task of supervising the creation of the Jewish National Home. Appropriate rules were formulated for supervision of the conduct of the Mandatory power, Great Britain. The Zionist movement became internationally recognized. In the words of the Mandate: "The Zionist Organization was invited to secure the cooperation of all Jews who are willing to assist in the establishment of the Jewish National Home." The dream of Theodor Herzl became reality.

Joseph Trumpeldor (1880-1920), initiator of the *chalutz* movement and symbol of the Zionist Revisionist Youth Movement.

Professor Boris Schatz *(bearded man in coat at left),* founder of the Bezalel School of Art in Jerusalem, observes young artists at work in the school's courtyard (1920's).

Herzl Street and the synagogue in Rishon-le-Zion (1915).

Lord Arthur James Balfour in Tel Aviv (1920). To his left are Chaim Weizmann and Nahum Sokolow.

Allenby Road, now the main street of Tel Aviv, as it appeared in 1921.

Distinguished visitors to the *Hassidic* colony, Nachalat Yaakov. Center, the Yabloner Rabbi, leader of the colony; seated near him, Achad Ha-am, essayist and philosopher; standing at his left, I. Ch. Ravnitzky, eminent Hebrew writer; on Ravnitzky's left, Chaim Nachman Bialik, great Hebrew poet.

Nahum Sokolow and Menachem Mendel Ussishkin in the Herzl Room of the Jewish National Fund Building in Jerusalem.

The Voluntary Fire Brigade of Tel Aviv (1935).

Street scene in Tel Aviv, about 1910.

THE BREACH OF FAITH

These were the "honeymoon" days of victory—days of satisfaction in the British Foreign Office, for the policy which dictated the promulgation of the Balfour Declaration did bear the expected fruits: Palestine came under British rule.

There were many influential people in the Foreign Office and the Colonial Office who thought that the implementation of the provisions of the Mandate was of secondary importance. And in Palestine, many of the highest officials, who were in direct charge of Government policy, were actively unsympathetic with the idea of the Jewish National Home.

A series of detractions from the basic provisions of the Mandate began. The presence of Sir Herbert Samuel, of Jewish descent, who had been appointed first High Commissioner, became detrimental to the cause of the Jewish National Home because Samuel did his best to avoid any suspicion of partiality.

The first Mayor of Tel Aviv, Meir Dizengoff *(fourth from right)* with the municipality's Council (1930).

The relations between the Jewish community and the British officials were strained from the beginning. The fact that this administration was staffed with people with colonial experience contributed greatly to the deterioration of Anglo-Jewish relations. Unlike the Arab population, the Jews would not be treated as "natives." It was obvious that the British administration did not intend to be replaced by Jewish officials at any time.

In this atmosphere of open enmity, Arab agitators had an easy task. Though the Arab national leaders welcomed, as they termed it, "the return of the Jewish cousin to his land," the

Abraham Isaac Kook (1864-1935), Chief Rabbi of Palestine under the British Mandatory Government, who was revered by Jews throughout the world.

political activity of the *effendis* displayed a somewhat different feeling. The landlords saw in the Jewish settlers a seed of a revolution which could put an end to their feudal rule. Countless lies were spread to incite the Arab masses—the most dangerous being the rumor that the Jews intended to desecrate the holy El-Akza Mosque in Jerusalem.

The British administration took unending advantage of the situation. The disturbances in 1920 and 1921 were followed by immigration restrictions in direct violation of the provisions of the

Arab rioters attacking Jewish shops in Jerusalem.

Mandate which encouraged Jewish immigration. Starting in 1922, a series of White Papers appeared, the purpose of which was to reduce the possibilities for the development of the Jewish National Home. The 1922 White Paper stated: "The terms of the Balfour Declaration do not contemplate that Palestine as a whole should be converted into a Jewish National Home, but that such a home should be established in Palestine."

As a result, the initial dissection of Palestine followed. The Palestine referred to in the Mandate, which provided for the "reconstitution of the Jewish National Home" in the land where it had once existed, included Trans-Jordan and Cis-Jordan. In 1922, Trans-Jordan, three times the area of Cis-Jordan, was closed to Jewish immigration.

The acts of British policy in Palestine demonstrated how official international obligations could become no more than a host of meaningless words on paper. New Arab disturbances in the summer of 1929 provided excellent opportunity for the de-livery of an additional blow to Jewish national aspirations. A "Commission of Inquiry" was selected to justify this breach of international faith. Only one member of the Commission, Dr. Harry Snell, dared to place the responsibility for the disturbances on the "religious propaganda" of the Grand Mufti of Jerusalem, an arch-enemy of Western ideology who was later to become a close collaborator of Hitler. Nevertheless, the end result of the inquiry was a decision to moderate the original provisions of the Mandate, allegedly to avoid future Arab uprisings.

The report was considered inadequate. More substantial justification for the behavior of the administration and the enmity of the Arab was needed. The amount of cultivatable land was considered. A special land expert, Sir John Hope Simpson, arranged for an air survey, and arrived at the somewhat hasty conclusion "that there is no room for a single additional settler." The validity of this statement was soon proved questionable. When the British administration in Palestine re-

A unit of the all-Jewish Police Force of Tel Aviv (1935).

quired all landless Arabs to register, only 664 heads of families qualified, and of these 347 took advantage of the Government's offer of resettlement. The British Palestine Royal Commission admitted that: "The Arab charge that the Jews have obtained too large a proportion of good land cannot be maintained. Much of the land, now carrying orange groves, was sand dunes or swamp and uncultivated when it was purchased."

Nevertheless, the British Government pursued its unofficial policy of liquidation of the Jewish National Home. Land purchases were restricted, immigration came to a standstill, the term "economic absorptive capacity" was invented, with the supplementary provision that the administration was to determine the extent of this "capacity." It became apparent that all problems of Jewish immigration would become subject to Arab approval. The fact that Jewish initiative and development was drawing throngs of Arab immigrants into Palestine from neighboring countries was not considered in the analysis of immigration problems and in establishing the "economic absorptive capacity" of the country.

The inevitable pattern began to emerge. In 1936, a series of Arab disturbances, this time assisted, financed, and armed by the Fascist powers, brought chaos to the tiny area of Palestine. The British administration blindly refused to recognize this armed Arab action as, perhaps, directed more against British presence in the Middle East than against the Jews. The fate of the Jewish National Home hung in precarious balance. The White Paper (which was labeled the "black paper") of May, 1939, concluded almost twenty years of planned, though gradual, liquidation of all solemn international obligations assumed by Great Britain in the Balfour Declaration and the Mandate of the League of Nations. The White Paper blatantly stated that the promises contained in the Balfour Declaration had been fulfilled. The Jewish immigration into Palestine was to be prohibited after a period of five years during which a maximum of seventy-five thousand Jews would be permitted to enter the country; land purchases by Jews were outlawed in practically all of Palestine; the Jewish community was condemned to the status of a permanent minority; and the Arabs were promised an independent Arab State. The interlude of the Royal Commission, headed by Lord Peel, which recommended the division of Palestine into a Jewish State and an Arab State, with a portion retained as a British Mandate, was completely ignored.

The situation was clear. Great Britain had decided to shelve the Jewish National Home idea. Ironically, this appeasement of the Mufti faction, this complete surrender to Arab extremist demands, did not change the attitude of the Arabs toward Britain; they remained ever-faithful to the Fascist axis.

For the Jews in Palestine there remained the

Arabs burning and looting Jewish homes in Haifa (1938).

Hagana riflemen training for defense against Arab attacks before World War II.

Chief Rabbi Isaac Halevi Herzog is presented to Field Marshal Lord Gort, High Commissioner of Palestine (1944).

British soldiers attempt to arrest a Jewish youth during a demonstration against British rule (1945).

A unit of the Jewish Brigade on maneuvers during World War II.

obligation to fight for the right they had once more been denied. This struggle was to be not only a fight for national survival but for the survival of Jews everywhere. The terrible plight, the slaughter of millions of Jews in Europe, came at a time when the gates of Palestine were closed. Ships on the way to Palestine with escapees from the Nazihell were compelled to wander on the open seas until a deadly mine relieved them of all worldly burden. These ships, such as the *Struma,* became symbols of the tragedy brought about by the destruction of the Mandate.

In spite of these severe conditions, the Jewish community in Palestine responded to the call for assistance in the fight against Hitler. In the first week of World War II, one hundred thirty thousand Jews registered for service. Only a fraction of them had been called. Thirty thousand Jews volunteered for active service though the British authorities refused to recognize them as a national

unit, with its own insignia and flag. In the campaign of the Western Desert of North Africa, at the El Alamein push which became the decisive turning point in the Allied fight against Hitler, Jewish units often played a decisive role. The Chief of the Royal Engineers in Marshal Montgomery's Eighth Army, who fell in action, was Brigadier Frederick Kisch, former head of the political department of the Zionist Organization (Jewish Agency) in Jerusalem.

In 1944, a slight concession had been made and the Jewish Brigade Group was established. A Jewish fighting force came into being with its own symbols and flag. It saw action on the Italian front, and was an integral part of the Allied occupation forces. But the only Middle East nation which actively participated in the Allied war effort through its men and the total mobilization of its resources, skills, and productivity was entirely ignored, while the Arab states, of which none had contributed to the war effort, and some even served the enemy as a fifth column, were actively courted.

The echo of the guns of war still resounded as the British Government returned to its prewar policy. The fact that the Permanent Mandates Commission of the League of Nations disapproved of the White Paper of 1939 as inconsistent with the provisions of the Mandate was not a deterrent factor. The smoldering gas chambers, where millions of Jews perished, was surely an atrocity of enough force to open the gates of Palestine to the remnants of European Jewry. Yet they remained closed, a barrier that doomed hundreds of thousands of innocent people to death.

The struggle for the opening of these gates was

Services held in the field for a unit of the Jewish Brigade.

motivated by the intense need of these persecuted Jews, driven from their homes, pleading for admittance to the shores of their fatherland. The *Aliyah Bet,* the immigration conducted in opposition to the restrictions of the British rulers of Palestine, which had achieved considerable dimensions prior to World War II, became once again, almost the only avenue of escape for camp inhabitants. It was a curious situation. The British army and navy continued to "repulse" the people coming to Palestine to rebuild their broken lives. Ships were intercepted on the open seas, concentration camps for the repatriates were set up in Cyprus, and in Palestine itself a military regime suppressed any attempt to oppose the illegal policy of the perversion of Mandatory power.

The Jewish National Movement was prepared

Civilians break through barbed-wire barriers as they celebrate lifting of martial law in Jerusalem at conclusion of World War II.

to fight for independence. An armed revolt started. The underground forces took up arms. The Irgun Zvai Leumi, an offspring of the Revisionist party and Betar youth organization, organized by Jabotinsky, began to attack British military outposts and to defy British rule. Lechi (Fighters of Freedom of Israel), a smaller military organization, carried on its own war against the British. The Hagana, its shock units, the Palmach, the armed force of the organized Jewish community, in spite of its reluctance to fight directly against the British, decided to go into action. An army of one hundred thousand British soldiers could not pacify the people.

World public opinion had declared itself on the side of the Jewish national cause. The United States Government offered its services. In 1946, a joint Anglo-American Committee of Inquiry conducted a thorough investigation of the problem.

"Illegal immigrants" in a British detention camp.

31

At the graves of the Irgun fighters.

This epilogue of Anglo-Jewish relations which ended in the submission of the Palestine Mandate to the United Nations, was preceded by many chapters of practical Jewish achievements. The news of the Balfour Declaration, and later of the League of Nations Mandate, filled Jews everywhere with joy. Youth organizations to prepare youngsters to go to Palestine as participants in the reconstruction of the Jewish Homeland mushroomed. A new type of Jewish youngster was formed: a *chalutz*, a pioneer, who was a hearty combination of explorer, frontiersman, and adventurer, ready to sacrifice and fight. Joseph Trumpeldor, hero of Port Arthur, and later legendary figure of the defense of Palestine, was the central figure in the beginnings of the *chalutz* movement. The *chalutzic* immigrants constituted the third *aliyah*. Young people, mainly from Eastern and Central Europe, worked to turn swamps and sand dunes into arable land, to build roads, and to establish permanent settlements. So began the romantic, heroic era of peaceful conquest of the arid desert land.

It was peaceful if judged in light of the intentions and will of the *chalutzim*, the pioneers of the third *aliyah*. But, in reality, British policy made an acquaintance with arms indispensable. The fact that the British administration permitted Arab attacks upon the Jews compelled the Jewish community to provide for its own defense. The picture of the worker with the plow in one hand and his rifle in the other became a common sight on the Palestine landscape.

They visited Palestine, the Arab capitals, the Jewish displaced persons camps, and prepared a unanimous report suggesting the immediate opening of the gates of Palestine to one hundred thousand Jews from Europe, the abolition of land-purchasing restrictions, and a series of long-range recommendations. Though this did not satisfy the need for a Jewish State, it completely repudiated the British policy as formulated in the White Paper of 1939.

The British Government refused to consider these suggestions. Even the decision of the Jewish fighting forces in Palestine to discontinue their struggle at the admission of one hundred thousand Jews did not prompt a British acceptance. Again, conferences were called with Jewish and Arab leaders, with no results. On February 2, 1947, at the last meeting of the Palestine Conference in London, the British Secretary of State, Ernest Bevin, announced that "since no proposals put forward by His Majesty's Government had proved acceptable as a basis for further discussion, His Majesty's Government had decided to refer the whole problem to the United Nations."

This was only a part of the autonomous national life which came into being. The Jews of Palestine took the provisions of the Mandate for the upbuilding of a Jewish National Home very seriously. They did not wait for the British to start to build the nuclei of each new phase of national life. A framework for a parliamentary representative institution was set up in form of the *Asephat Hanivcharim*, or Elected Assembly, and an executive organ, the Vaad Haleumi, or National Council, which took over practical tasks of a government. Education, the absorption of immigrants, the development of the country, the establishment of new settlements and of lines of communication were problems handled and financed by the Jewish Community (*Yishuv*) assisted by the World Zionist Organization. Two administrations functioned simultaneously, one of the Mandatory power, which administered chiefly to the affairs of the Arab population, and the other, the National Council, which administered to the Jewish National Home.

A community with almost all the attributes of self-government grew rapidly. The General Federation of Jewish Labor, Histadrut, had in those circumstances to maintain a great deal of responsibility which was outside of the purpose and aim of a purely professional labor union. It was active in building settlements, in founding cooperatives and social institutions, and in inaugurating a country-wide health program.

The fourth *aliyah* began to make its entrance in 1924, bringing mainly Jews from Poland, Lithuania, and emigrants who had escaped from Russia. These were people of the Jewish middle class, unaccustomed to physical work. The economy of the country was not yet capable of absorbing so many merchants, artisans, and industrialists.

The policy of the Mandatory Government contributed quite considerably to the developing crisis. Palestine was the only country in which there were no duties on imported goods to pro-

tect the local industry. But these depression years did not last long. In the years of the world-wide economic depression, in the thirties, Palestine manifested its uniqueness not only in spirit, but in its economy as well. While the rest of the world suffered in the depression, an upsurge of economy began in Palestine. In spite of Government restrictions, Arab riots, and laws conceived to limit the growth of the Jewish community, the country entered a phase of rapid development.

With the fifth *aliyah* came people with skill, with economic experiences in Western Europe, who sought refuge and a national home in Palestine. New industries were developed; an atmosphere of boom and prosperity spread through the country. The intense need of the wandering German Jews compelled the Mandatory power to relax the immigration restrictions. The number of Jews in Palestine rose from 190,000 in 1929 to 375,000 in 1935. The national economy of the closely knit Jewish community was diversified, covering new fields and progressing toward a self-sufficient unit.

This economic growth was accompanied by a growing political dichotomy. Discussions of politi-

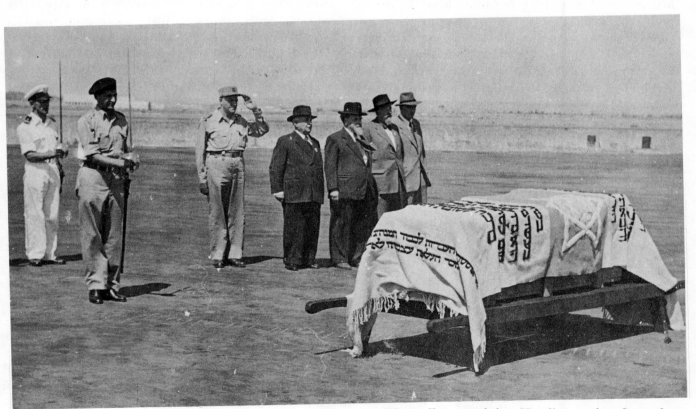

The coffin containing Herzl's remains, flown from Vienna, rests on Israel soil (August, 1949).

33

Herzl's grave on Mount Herzl, a national shrine where soldiers who have fallen in the defense of their country are buried.

cal and practical as well as cultural Zionism of Achad Ha-am's type were renewed. The violation of the basic provisions of the Balfour Declaration and the Mandate by the British generated a deepening rift in Zionist ranks. It was not easy to accept the "British breach of faith." The end result was the organization of a party to fight for the "revision" of the standing policy of leadership in the Zionist movement. The Zionist Revisionist Party headed by Vladimir Jabotinsky also devised a policy of retaliation to put a stop to the Arab riots. The official policy of the Zionist Executive and the Hagana forces had been one of self-restraint and self-defense only under attack.

The Revisionists, who later left the World Zionist Movement and created the New Zionist Organization, considered the reestablishment of the Jewish State as their immediate goal. During this period of change the World Zionist Organization underwent a metamorphosis of its own. The labor movement had become the ruling party in the Jewish Community of Palestine. Names like Arlosoroff (murdered in 1933), Ben Gurion, and Berl Katznelson achieved national fame. An attempt was made to afford representation to non-Zionists throughout the world. The creation of the extended Jewish Agency, which enlisted the enthusiastic support of Louis Marshall, the dean of non-Zionist Jewish leaders in the United States, was a failure but nevertheless provided the impetus for the creation of a permanent political body to handle all international affairs in lieu of the Zionist organization.

As time passed, especially during the years of World War II, the need for a re-definition of Zionist goals became imperative. The "Biltmore Program," formulated in 1942 at a Zionist Conference in New York, proclaimed that the Zionist movement would strive for, fight for, and settle for no less than a Jewish State.

The Zionist movement was again united by the basic definition of its goal, though dissension as to procedure continued to exist. One thing became increasingly clear to both the Zionists and the Mandatory Power—that with the conclusion of the war there would be no room for bickering for positions, for vague definitions, for evasive promises. After a quarter of a century of growth—a growth impaired by British opposition and obstructionist tactics—the political body of the National Jewish Home was ready for the delivery of an independent nation. The dream of sixty generations of Jews—of settlers, pioneers, toilers, and workers, of soldiers and revolutionists—was to become fact.

The hour of fulfillment was nearing. When the United Nations General Assembly voted for the establishment of the Jewish State, it provided only formal approval to a reality that was already in existence.

3 THE INGATHERING OF THE EXILES

The Jewish settlement in Palestine was small and played only a minor role in the destiny of the country in the years after the Roman conquest. However, after the Moslems overran the Middle East, it played a tremendous part as a link between the past and the future of the Jewish Homeland, a living reminder of the people who had impressed their character upon the land.

In the first half of the nineteenth century, most of this small group of Jews, known as the Old *Yishuv* (Old Settlements), lived in the four Holy Cities—Jerusalem, Hebron, Safed, and Tiberias—and were dependent upon the money (*chaluka*) provided by the Jews of the Diaspora. In the years following 1840, Sir Moses Montefiore became interested in the advancement of Jewish agriculture in Palestine. He attempted to lease two hundred villages in the Galilee and established a bank to subsidize the project, with a capital of one million pounds, but his negotiations with the Turkish Government came to naught. In 1865, Montefiore bought an orange plantation near Jaffa in order to introduce Palestinean Jewry to agricultural training.

In 1870, the Alliance Israelite Universelle established an agricultural school at Mikveh Israel. The Jews of Jerusalem began to move outside the walls of the Old City and others began to settle the countryside around Safed. In 1878, several Orthodox Jews from Jerusalem bought a plot of land on the banks of the Yarkon River and founded the first Jewish colony in Palestine—Petach Tikvah. The malarial swamps and Arab hostility compelled the colonists to abandon their land, but they heralded the rebirth of the Jewish settlement in Palestine. In 1880, at the inception of the *Chibat Zion* (Love of Zion) movement, there were approximately thirty-five thousand Jews in Palestine.

The New *Yishuv* (New Settlements) started in 1881. This New *Yishuv* was composed of five *aliyot* (waves of immigration) between 1881 and the establishment of the State of Israel. The first *aliyah* began in 1881, the second in 1904, the third in 1919, the fourth in 1924, and the fifth in 1929.

THE FIRST ALIYAH

The catastrophes which hit Russian Jewry in the 1880's brought in their wake a desire to evacuate the Diaspora and a renewed interest in Zion. Members of the BILU movement turned eastward to Palestine; other emigrants turned westward, across the Atlantic Ocean. The return to Zion was crystallized in an organized national political movement—Zionism.

The BILU immigration, the first *chalutzic** *aliyah*, actually comprised too small a part of the total immigration to Palestine to be called the first *aliyah*. But it infused new life into the Old *Yishuv*, expanding beyond the four Holy Cities to Jaffa and Haifa. The real significance of this era lies in the birth of the new agricultural settlement.

In 1882, ships began to bring destitute immigrants from Russia and Rumania to the port of Jaffa. That year Rishon-le-Zion was founded, Petach Tikvah was strengthened, Zichron Yaakov rose in Samaria, and Rosh Pinah in the Upper Galilee, and in the years that followed, Mishmar Hayarden, Ness Ziona, and Yesod Hamaaleh were established.

Hardship and suffering visited these early colonists. Gradually, new *chalutzim* followed these pioneers. The wealthier Jews began to participate in the national renaissance, notably Baron Edmond de Rothschild whose generous and wholehearted participation earned him the title, "the father of the New *Yishuv*." Today, forty-five settlements comprise an everlasting memorial to the work of the Baron and his successors.

Immigration to Palestine mounted in 1890 when the Jews were banished from Moscow. Rehovot, Gedera, and a number of small colonies were established, but the Turkish Government began to restrict the immigration of Russian Jews and the influx of settlers declined.

_____
*Pioneers from the Chibat Zion movement.

A boatload of desperate illegal immigrants is pushed ashore in a night landing.

THE SECOND ALIYAH

Herzl's appearance and the founding of the Zionist Organization wrought no profound changes in immigration to Palestine. The situation remained static until the beginning of the second *aliyah* in 1904. The second *aliyah,* like the first, came at the height of a wave of anti-Jewish outbreaks; in 1903-1904, as in 1882, most of the Russian fugitives went to America and only a small portion to Palestine. The immigrants to Palestine included the rich and the poor, the aged and the young, but this wave of immigration was characterized mainly by the youths who came, determined to start a new life. The second *aliyah* could not have achieved what it did had not the courageous first *aliyah* preceded it, but it has more than earned its own place of honor as it brought into being the concept of the conquest of land, the new type of Jewish laborer, the collective form of settlement, the new urban settlement, the crystalliza-tion of the Jewish educational system, and the revival of Hebrew culture in Palestine.

News of the return to the ancestral homeland reached the ancient Jewish settlements in Arabia. These devout Jews had lived in Yemen, according to their own tradition, since the destruction of the First Temple. In Yemen they lived in absolute misery, enjoying no rights whatever, sustained only by their belief in the Messiah. In the days of the first *aliyah,* when the songs of Zion were once more on the lips of Jews everywhere, the Yemenites began to stir. Between 1882 and 1887 a small number of Yemenite Jews migrated to Palestine, where they readily established themselves. Immigration from this country increased during the period of the second *aliyah* when hundreds of families came to settle on the land.

The second *aliyah* also included some middle-class merchants who settled in the towns, chiefly in Jaffa. Some sixty of them, finding the ancient homes of Jaffa inadequate, organized into a group which laid the foundation of the new city of Tel Aviv.

In 1914, on the eve of World War I, Jewish Palestine was flourishing. 73,000 people dwelled in towns, and 12,000 lived in the country's 43 colonies.

Of the more than two million Jews who left Europe—especially Czarist Russia, Rumania, and Austrian Galicia—during the declining days of the Turkish empire from 1882 to World War I, only some seventy thousand, or 3 per cent, went to Palestine. A portion of these failed to adjust to the difficult economic conditions in Palestine and migrated back to the Diaspora. But one small stream of immigration differed from the others of the time in that it comprised a substantial number of Jews who left their homes for religious, national, social—that is, ideological—reasons rather than for economic reasons or to find personal security.

THE THIRD ALIYAH

During World War I, Jewish Palestine was visited by privation and epidemics. Many Jews who were Russian citizens were expelled by the Turks. In 1918, when the war ended, there were some 56,700 Jews in Palestine. On November 2, 1917, the British Government issued the historic Balfour Declaration which recognized the right of the Jewish people to establish a national home in

Refugees at the Latroun Detention Camp strain at the barbed wire that barricades them from freedom and their Homeland.

Carrying 470 illegal immigrants from Europe, this small vessel, captured by a British destroyer, reaches Haifa after fifteen days at sea (June, 1946). The refugees were interned at the Athlit Detention Camp.

Palestine. As a result of the Balfour Declaration, immigration to Palestine assumed an entirely new aspect, that of nationalism. When Palestine became a British Mandate in 1920, Jewish immigration was legalized. However, the Mandatory Government established the principle of the "absorptive capacity" of the land, that is, unrestricted immigration would be allowed only to people of means; people without capital would be admitted only according to the capacity of the land to support them.

Even before the end of World War I, thousands of Jewish youths in Eastern Europe began to organize themselves into the *Hechalutz*, (Pioneer) movement whose guiding spirit was Joseph Trumpeldor. These *chalutzim* or pioneers, trained themselves as laborers, farmers, and craftsmen. At the end of the war, before the Zionist Organization had even given official approval to immigration to Palestine, thousands of youths set out from Russia, Poland, and Galicia. Penniless, they hiked for weeks and months over untracked areas and poor roads where danger lurked at every step, smuggling themselves across sealed borders, crossing land and sea until they reached Palestine.

The third *aliyah*, which in four years brought almost 35,000 Jews to Palestine, was composed partly of people of means who settled in the cities, but largely of these *chalutzim*, the laborers who undertook every difficult chore—road building, swamp drainage, clearing and settling the land. They organized the Labor Brigade which contracted road building and other public works, and founded the great communal settlement—the great *kibbutz*.

In 1921, together with members of the second *aliyah*, the members of the third *aliyah* laid the foundations of the *chalutzic* settlements in Emek Yezreel, the *kibbutzim* Tel Yosef and Ein Harod, and the workers' cooperatives Nahalal and Kfar Yehezkeel.

THE FOURTH ALIYAH

In 1924, when the Polish Government issued decrees restricting the economic activity of the Jews, tens of thousands of Jews left the country, many of them for Palestine. Within two years some sixty thousand Jews came to Palestine, most of them business men, manufacturers, and laborers from Poland. Many settled in Haifa, Jerusalem, and, principally, in Tel Aviv, where some of them opened factories. The Jewish residential areas in the cities expanded; large oil, salt, and textile works were established; electric power plants were built to supply home and factory. During this, the fourth *aliyah*, Jewish agriculture continued to

This overcrowded ship is typical of the small craft that ran the British blockade to bring thousands of immigrants into the Holy Land.

A small refugee girl has "dinner" aboard the *Exodus 1947*.

grow as immigrants settled on the land and founded new colonies whose principal product was the orange. Many *Hassidim* came from Poland, some of whom founded the settlement of Kfar Hassidim. The return to Zion found many enthusiastic adherents even among the Orthodox Jews who did not belong to, or accept the authority of, the Zionist Organization.

Many of the immigrants who turned to manufacturing were ignorant of conditions in Palestine and had little capital. In 1926, after a series of failures, depression and unemployment set in. Immigration to Palestine decreased and emigration from the land increased. In 1929, the balance of the economy recovered and the tide of immigration slowly began to turn again, gaining considerable momentum when the Nazis came to power in Germany. At the close of the fourth *aliyah*, there were approximately 159,238 Jews in Palestine.

THE FIFTH ALIYAH

In 1921, the Arabs fell upon the Jews and massacred more than a hundred. Despite this outbreak of violence, immigration to Palestine gradually increased. Between 1926 and 1939, after Hitler had consolidated his power, the tide of new settlers reached major proportions as the German immigration began. In these years more than one hun-

dred thousand German Jews came to Palestine. They quickly adjusted to their new life in town and village. The major cities, Jerusalem, Haifa, and Tel Aviv, grew and improved socially and economically thanks to the initiative and the cultural level of the German Jews. German immigrants founded settlements near the cities; people who had never before tilled the land or planted seed now raised poultry and fruit trees.

During the period of the fourth and fifth *aliyot*, the working population of Palestine increased. New workers' settlements of various sorts were founded. Even during the Arab outbreaks the pioneers established new settlements in remote regions.

Some 80 per cent of the Jews lived in the towns where they engaged in labor and the crafts, in commerce and industry. Side by side with private enterprise, which launched so many important economic ventures, new cooperative groups sprang up, as small capitalists joined together to organize manufacturing, transportation, and construction cooperatives. The balance of the population settled on the land where breaking with the tradition of

Women and children leave the illegal immigration ship, *Exodus 1947*, which had been intercepted by British warships and rammed during a fierce battle at sea. The 4,500 refugees aboard the ship were returned to France.

Jewish detainees on Cyprus, protesting their exclusion from Palestine, are restrained by British military police (October, 1946).

A temporary shelter for a few of the thousands of exiles who were finally able to enter the Holy Land after the new State was established.

Yemenite Jews await flight from Aden to Israel via "Operation Magic Carpet" (April, 1950).

Preparing food for new arrivals in a *maabara*.

Maabara, built of wood and corrugated metal sheeting, to house new immigrants in 1952.

Oriental and North African Jews in one of the first *maabarot* or transitional camps.

Young people in a *maabara* keep physically fit while awaiting transfer to permanent settlements.

private farming, they continued to develop the *kvutzah* and the *kibbutz*—forms of agricultural settlement which are without parallel in the world.

From 1919 to 1948, while the country was under British rule, some 453,000 Jews came to Palestine. This immigration varied in size and character from year to year according to the turn of events in the Diaspora and the political and economic conditions in Palestine.

From 1932 on, Palestine played a most important part in the Jewish exodus from Europe. From 1932 to 1936 it received almost two-thirds of the refugees. At the beginning of this period, the immigration was still more or less organized, bringing with it a considerable amount of capital and making a substantial contribution to the technical and economic development of the land. After 1939, when the White Paper restricted Jewish immigration into Palestine, and after the outbreak of World War II, fewer people came to its shores. From 1946 to 1948, the final years of the British

Mandatory Government, immigration was as low as two thousand per month. With the termination of the British Mandate on December 31, 1947, there were 650,000 Jews in Palestine.

ILLEGAL IMMIGRATION

The impending catastrophe in Europe so aggravated the need to break the "iron curtain" of British restrictions on Jewish immigration that unofficially some Zionists organized the so-called "Illegal Immigration" which made it possible for thousands of Jews to be rescued from Nazi persecution. This unprecedented activity was all the more remarkable since it succeeded despite opposition, both within and outside Palestine, from those who feared British reprisal. Hitler's plan to end the Jewish "problem" once and for all by extermination, made "Illegal Immigration" an accepted, official Zionist activity.

Vladimir Jabotinsky's famous evacuation program to convince European Jewry to exit *en masse* for Palestine proclaimed: "Either the Jews will liquidate the Diaspora or the Diaspora will liquidate the Jews." He called upon Jewish youth to make "Illegal Immigration" successful.

In May, 1939, the British Government decreed that only fifteen thousand Jews might immigrate annually for a period of five years. Thousands of Jews fleeing Europe were prevented by the British from landing in Palestine; 250 refugees lost their lives in an explosion aboard the *S.S. Patria* in the harbor of Haifa; 769 passengers among them many women and children were drowned in the Black Sea on the *S.S. Struma*. These tragedies shocked the world. The Jews of Palestine were inflamed as never before and the British were warned by the Jewish Agency for Palestine that the treacherous policy of the Mandatory Government would not be tolerated. The Hagana performed great rescue work and dozens of ships brought illegal immigrants to the shores of Palestine, despite all the difficulties and the British bayonets. By 1947, 113,000 defiant "illegals" had entered the country. In retaliation, the British started a manhunt for "illegals," with mass arrests, and deportation to internment camps in Cyprus.

The fight over immigration became the struggle for the Jewish State. In 1945, for the first time in the history of the New *Yishuv* of Palestine, a combined force of the Hagana, the Irgun Zvai Leumi, and its offshoot, the Stern Group, waged guerilla raids against the British and struck at the installation that had been built to prevent illegal immigrants from entering the country. The Jewish community in Palestine helped in every way to shatter the closed gates of the Homeland and admit the children of Israel.

YOUTH ALIYAH

A most brilliant achievement in the growth of Israel resulted from the efforts of the Youth Aliyah. This began as the voluntary effort of individuals, but is now an administrative agency seeking out and rescuing lost, displaced, and orphaned children. Its objectives and purposes are: to bring Jewish boys and girls to Israel; to educate them; and to prepare them for pioneer work, especially in agriculture.

Jewish children by the tens of thousands were torn by the Nazis from their homes and parents, and were left to linger in filth and disease. In November, 1932, Rachab Friar of Berlin assembled a group of children between the ages of fifteen and seventeen and helped them to leave Germany and settle in Ben Shemen. In 1933, an American woman, Henrietta Szold, took on the leadership of the Youth Aliyah and devoted her entire life and energy to the project.

The new system of education and rehabilitation assumed its formal pattern with the arrival of a group of boys and girls who were settled at Ein Harod. As the Nazis spread over Europe, the project extended to many countries where the lives of Jews were menaced, and it soon received the aid and support of educational and social organizations everywhere.

Throughout World War II, Youth Aliyah enlarged its scope to include children in lower age brackets. About ten thousand boys and girls were rescued from impending death and brought safely to Eretz Israel. At the end of the war, the emissaries of Youth Aliyah went to Europe to seek out Jewish children who might have survived in the Displaced Persons camps, the forests, and in orphanages and convents. Some of these were children of families who had escaped from Soviet Russia to Poland. Thousands were traced and cared for until they could leave for Israel in the groups organized by Youth Aliyah. They still had to make their way through the corrupt immigration boards, travel on leaky ships, and then smuggle themselves into Israel, or make forced stop-overs in the internment camps on Cyprus. The personnel of Youth Aliyah were with them *en route,* instructing them, preparing them spiritually for their life in their new homeland, and restoring their faith in humanity.

Ten years after the declaration of Israel's statehood, Youth Aliyah can report with pride the rescue, rehabilitation, and resettlement of seventy-five thousand children—a humanitarian and social achievement without parallel in history.

ISRAEL OPENS ITS DOORS

Simultaneous with the proclamation of the Jewish State, at a time when Israel was in the midst of a struggle for survival against six invading Arab armies, the gates of Israel were flung wide open to Jewish immigration. In the first years of the State the "Ingathering of Exiles" assumed tremendous proportions. Between May, 1948, and the end of 1951, 687,000 people entered the country.

A ninety-year-old immigrant from Morocco is helped down the gangplank of the S.S. *Jerusalem* at Haifa.

The great stream of immigrants was composed mainly of three groups. First survivors from the concentration camps in Germany, mostly Jews from Central and Eastern Europe, including 24,000 people who had attempted to enter Palestine illegally but were stopped by the British authorities and interned in camps on Cyprus, and 75,000 inmates of Displaced Persons camps in Germany, Austria, and Italy. The second group was made up of survivors of Nazi persecution in Eastern Europe and the Balkan countries. This group included almost the entire Jewish population of Bulgaria. Approximately 40,000 out of the 43,000 Jews who at that time lived in tiny Bulgaria left *en masse* for Israel.

Immigrants from Jewish communities of many countries in the Middle East and North Africa made up the third group. Through "Operation Magic Carpet" almost all the Jews of Yemen, about 45,000 people, were air-lifted to Israel. The exodus from the oldest land of exile, Babylon, was accomplished by "Operation Ezra and Nehemia." The government of Iraq compelled the Jews to emigrate, depriving them of Iraqi citizenship and forcing them to leave behind all their possessions. Despite this harsh stipulation, 123,000 Jews returned to Zion. This airborne immigration started in March, 1951, with 14,326 people. In April, 20,340 and, in May, 22,000 arrived, the monthly total thereafter reaching a peak of about 30,000.

One planeload of the forty-five thousand Yemenite Jews who were flown to Israel.

Immigrants from Yemen are taught how to write.

Large contingents of Jews from Tripolitania, Libya, Iran, Egypt, Turkey, and North Africa also arrived.

This return to the ancient homeland by hundreds of thousands, primarily motivated by the two-thousand-year-old dream of seeing Zion liberated, was reinforced by the desire to leave both the blood-soaked soil of Europe, where life had become economically and socially intolerable, and to flee the mounting anti-Jewish hatred and persecution in Arab and Moslem countries.

Immigrants were quartered in reception centers for a period of two to four weeks, after which they were diverted to permanent dwelling places. Later, as a result of the growing need for housing, these reception centers were turned into camps where the immigrants had to stay for several months before they could be relocated.

Immigrant camps were established mainly in former Army installations which had been converted for this new purpose. The new Israelis lived in tents, buildings, and huts. The Jewish Agency did its best to improve conditions in the camps, but even with its substantial financial resources from world Jewry, it could not prevent serious overcrowding. There were just too many people to be accommodated in the few readily available quarters.

The Agency, however, did institute a number of programs to compensate for the physical surroundings and to help make the adjustment of the new settlers easier. Although the meals served in the camps were made up of the customary Israeli diet and were prepared in accordance with the in-structions of the Nutrition Committee, in camps where there was a preponderance of Oriental communities separate kitchens were opened so that foods could be prepared to their taste.

With the active help of women's organizations, infant and baby centers, as well as kindergartens and schools, were opened in every camp. Although the infant and baby centers and the kindergartens were run by the Absorption Department of the Jewish Agency, in cooperation with the women's organizations, the schools were operated by the Ministry of Education and Culture.

The Immigrants Medical Service of the Ministry of Health operated a clinic in every camp and, in addition, opened eight children's hospitals, eleven hospitals for adults, and one maternity hospital. On leaving the camp every immigrant was insured with the Sick Fund of the General Workers' Federation for three months, at the expense of the Jewish Agency.

In most camps, committees were formed to represent the various communities and work in close cooperation with the camp authorities. The camp administrations made a special point of employing a great number of workers of Oriental and Yemenite origin so that closer contact could be established with those groups. Unskilled labor in the kitchens and the camp yards was provided mostly by the immigrants themselves. In addition, workshops were opened to supply the camps' needs and offer a number of immigrants the opportunity to learn trades.

The serious lack of clothing of the immigrants from the Oriental countries was an unexpected problem. A countrywide collection for winter clothes was launched to supply part of the need

New settlers learning Hebrew in a *Ulpan* (language school) operated by the Jewish Agency.

A North African mother and her child find a new home in Israel.

of the Yemenites, who had arrived virtually empty-handed. The remaining need was filled by shipments from abroad and the purchase of new clothing by the Jewish Agency.

The prolonged stay in these camps was extremely trying, entailing difficult living conditions and enforced idleness. Unfortunately, these harsh conditions were an unavoidable counterpart to the unprecedented mass immigration which flowed into the little nation. In the winter of 1950, when torrential rains flooded many of the camps, the entire population of Israel once again came to the aid of the new settlers and over two thousand children were taken into homes in towns and villages for the winter.

By the end of April, 1950, there were thirty-five camps with a population of ninety thousand. The stay of each immigrant averaged roughly six months. The Government and the Jewish Agency introduced the first *maabarot* (transit camps) which they designed as a means of expediting the integration of the newcomers into the economic life of the country. These *maabarot* were actually small villages of tents, huts, and barracks supplied free of charge.

Several types of *maabarot* were established. There were urban and rural transit camps in the vicinity of towns and villages where the new immigrants could find employment. They sprang up around Jerusalem, Haifa, Beersheba, Afuleh, and their inhabitants slowly merged into the life of these cities. Pioneer *maabarot* were set up in development regions, far from the settlements, where the immigrants were employed in public and development work. In many cases large

maabarot were established with a view to their later use as administrative and economic centers.

In the beginning the immigrants lived in tents which were gradually replaced by corrugated-iron shacks and wooden huts. In many cases the dwellers constructed their own houses. The development of the *maabarot* was carried out in accordance with a master plan for the distribution of population, possibilities of employment in the area, facilities for water, and availability of land. The general tendency was to channel the new immigrants to the more sparsely populated areas, thus promoting the development of the country and strengthening national security. With this in view, 27 per cent of the *maabarot* dwellers were set up in Galilee and the Emek Yezreel, and 18 per cent in the South and the Negev.

From July, 1950, all new immigrants were directed to *maabarot* with the exception of those who were beyond working age or physically unfit. A great part of the population of the immigrant camps was also transferred to *maabarot*. By May, 1951, the number of immigrant camps had dropped to thirteen, whose population of thirty-four thousand consisted mainly of the sick and chronically ill, the aged, and the widowed with children too young to work. Invalids were hospitalized, older people unfit for work were accommodated in special homes, invalids and chronic patients, or the aged still capable of taking care of themselves, were given licenses to open shops or street kiosks. Those who were skilled or capable

An immigrant from Bulgaria.

46

A young immigrant receives training as a metal-worker in a _maabara_.

of acquiring a skill were given the opportunity to set up protected workshops (the raw material and marketing guaranteed by the agency concerned).

PERMANENT HOUSING

While the various stages of integration were being carried out, the construction of large-scale permanent housing projects was underway. The program, however, did not gain real momentum until July, 1949, when the endless flow of new immigrants could no longer be housed in the insufficient number of quarters left vacant by the fleeing Arabs.

These permanent housing projects fell into several distinct categories. Some were of concrete cast or block construction, others were of wood. Many of these were pre-fabricated imports (from Sweden), or domestic "pre-fabs." Both provided good, quickly constructed housing, since it was possible to work on the foundation and structure simultaneously—but they involved a great deal of money. The small concrete block buildings were

single or two-family houses which cost approximately the same per unit as the wooden houses. Labor constituted the main expense since the raw materials were available in Israel.

New houses were either rented or sold to the immigrants on several allotment bases: size, seniority, and location. Small families were allowed one dwelling unit which consisted of a room, a kitchen or alcove for cooking purposes, and the necessary conveniences. Families of five or more members were entitled to either two units or a two-room house. Housing was allotted to immigrants in accordance with the date of their arrival and, more important to the future of the country, an attempt was made to place the newcomers in locations suited to them, with the object of forming settlement nuclei as the bases for self-contained municipal communities.

In every group of dwellings a special area was set aside for the shops, restaurants, kiosks, and small trades of the social-welfare cases. Seven per cent of the buildings was kept for public use (kindergartens, schools, synagogues, and clinics). Unmarried men and women were not provided with permanent housing. They lived in hostels established by the Jewish Agency and operated by labor or women's organizations.

Before the proclamation of the State, the relatively small number of new settlers was easily absorbed into their new Hebrew-speaking environment. However, the mass immigration created vast new population centers where Hebrew was hardly

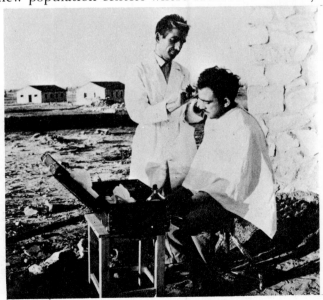

An outdoor barber shop in a _maabara_.

47

Members of Hapoel Hamizrachi take turns in reciting their morning prayers as they build their settlement in the Judean hills.

spoken. An intensive drive was launched to propagate the Hebrew language among the immigrant population. Evening classes were instituted in the *maabarot* and immigration centers. *Ulpanim,* classes in which Hebrew was studied intensively for a period of several months, were established in towns and agricultural settlements for professional people who were prevented from using their skills because of the language barrier. Special daily newspapers, using the most common Hebrew words and idioms, were translated from many languages for the benefit of newcomers. The children, who learned their Hebrew in school, proved an invaluable aid in bringing the new language to their parents.

Many efforts were made to help the backward

immigrants. Compulsory education, youth clubs, and hygienic centers were supplemented by communal centers in an attempt to create a homogeneous society out of large groups of varied national origin. The Defense Forces, in which every young man and woman must serve, exposed the young immigrant to the language and the country, enabling him to understand and appreciate the values of his new homeland.

By 1952, the integration of the immigrants was

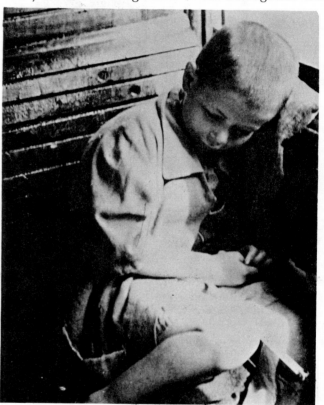

One of the children, orphaned by Hitler's tyranny but saved from the fate of their parents by Youth Aliyah, who reached Eretz Israel via Teheran in the midst of World War II.

Two boys from Morocco gather vegetables in an agricultural settlement.

well on its way, but the strain on the economy was becoming critically severe. A new policy was needed—selective, not mass, immigration. This new policy limited immigration to groups which could be most easily absorbed. The rate of immigration began to decrease and, in 1952, 1953, and the first eight months of 1954, only twelve hundred immigrants entered the country each month. Of course, the temporary exhaustion of immigration sources was an additional factor contributing to this decrease. The Jews of the free world were reluctant to settle in a country which was laboring under so many economic problems. Then, too, there were the prohibitive emigration laws in countries behind the Iron Curtain which made it impossible for the Jews of Eastern Europe to leave.

At the end of the summer of 1954, increasing anti-Jewish feeling brought about a change in the political status of Jews in North Africa which caused a renewal of large-scale immigration from Morocco, Tunis, and Algeria. These new immigrants were brought directly from the port of arrival to prepared settlements in various parts of the country. In the second half of 1956, immigration from Poland and Hungary was resumed when the anti-Soviet revolts in those countries temporarily forced open the gates.

By the end of 1957, Israel, which at the time of its establishment in 1948 had a Jewish population of 650,000, had welcomed nearly a million new immigrants. They came from all parts of the world and the most distant corners of the Diaspora. No longer was any one of them "a wandering Jew."

IMMIGRATION RATE FROM 1948

The 1957 influx reflects the first big immigration wave set off by the establishment of the State.

Immigration by Years

Year	Arrivals	Per Cent	Jewish Population at end of the year
1948 (from May 15)	102,000	11	758,701
1949	239,000	26	1,014,000
1950	169,000	18	1,203,000
1951	174,000	19	1,404,000
1952	23,000	2	1,450,000
1953	10,000	1	1,484,000
1954	18,000	2	1,526,000
1955	36,000	4	1,591,000
1956	55,000	6	1,667,000

1957
January-May 42,000   Estimate to end of May
June-December   Jews: 1,720,000
(estimate) 58,000   Total 1,930,000

	100,000	11	
Total	926,000	100	

FROM THE FOUR CORNERS OF THE EARTH

Nearly all countries with Jewish communities have been represented in the migration to Israel. Numerically the most striking contingents came from Africa, Rumania, Poland, and Iraq.

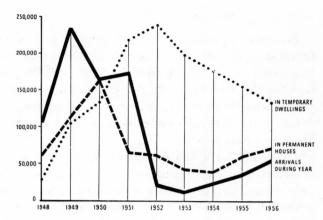

Immigration by Countries
May, 1948–April, 1957

Countries of Origin	Arrivals	Per Cent
Europe		
Rumania	124,000	14
Poland	120,000	14
Others (including D.P.'s)	118,000	14
Asia		
Iraq	123,000	14
Yemen	46,000	6
Turkey	37,000	4
Iran	32,000	4
Others	16,000	2
North Africa	200,000	23
Others	40,000	5
Total	856,000	100

The above figures show that more than half of the immigrants since the formation of the State came from countries other than Europe.

EUROPEAN JEWS ON THE MOVE

Half of the arrivals in the first eight months of 1956-1957 budgetary year came from Europe. Together with immigrants from Egypt, they account for over two-thirds of the influx during this period.

Immigration by Areas and Months, October, 1956–May, 1957

	Oct.	Nov.	Dec.	Jan.	Feb.
Europe	920	1,171	2,184	2,308	3,147
Egypt	102	34	370	2,953	1,513
North Africa	7,060	2,742	1,497	1,478	898
Others	430	315	421	289	253
Total	8,512	4,262	4,472	7,028	5,811

	March	April	May	Total	
Europe	4,468	6,935	9,160	30,343	51
Egypt	2,836	800	2,329	10,937	18
North Africa	772	466	827	15,740	26
Others	376	431	220	2,735	5
Total	8,452	8,682	12,536	59,755	100

Eventual liquidation of the *maabarot* and other temporary quarters is a social challenge of the first order. From an all-time high of 245,000 persons at the end of 1952, the population in non-permanent dwellings had been brought down to 130,000 by the end of 1956—despite the rising stream of new arrivals.

Up to 1952, the full impact of the housing problem was not felt because of the large number of abandoned houses in which newcomers found accommodation. Since then intensified building activities have progressively reduced the population in temporary dwellings. At the beginning of 1957 there remained 52,000 persons in *maabarot* and 82,000 in quarters of wooden huts.

IMMIGRANT HOUSING

About four-fifths of the arrivals received permanent housing in public building projects. Since 1953 when *maabarot* began to be liquidated, there has been a marked trend away from the cities to agricultural settlements and development areas.

Distribution of Housing 1948—1956 (in per cent)

	1948-49	1950	1951	1952	1953	1954	1955	1956
Public Housing Projects in towns and plantation villages	25	16	4	53	56	44	38	27
in agricultural settlements and development areas	23	24	19	16	12	36	38	48
elsewhere	5	3	9	5	3	2	6	2
	53	43	32	74	71	82	82	77
Other Arrangements abandoned houses	37	27	23	—	—	—	—	—
private arrangements	10	30	45	26	29	18	18	23
Total	100	.100	100	100	100	100	100	100

SURGES OF IMMIGRATION

The Jewish immigration into Israel has a cosmopolitan character for there is not one Jewish community in the world which is not represented among the immigrants.

The Balkan countries were already sending immigrants during the time of the British Mandate in Palestine, but since the independence of Israel, about three-quarters of the Jewish population

entered Israel. A substantial number of Jews reached the Holy Land from Asia during the British Mandate. The emigration from Eastern Europe was quite substantial during the British Mandate, but increased to 43 per cent of the Jewish population after Israel's independence. Of course, this excludes Soviet Russia which denies emigration to its citizens. Jews from Central Europe started to emigrate in small numbers in 1932, but their number increased until they constituted 9 to 10 per cent of the Jewish population in Israel during the period between 1948 and 1951. Emigrants from Africa entered Israel only after the establishment of the Jewish State, and 15 per cent of the African Jewish communities settled in Israel during the years between 1948 and 1951.

These five regions which had a Jewish population of 7,788,000 in 1925, 50.3 per cent of all the Jews in the Diaspora, now number only 1,365,000 or 13.4 per cent of all the Jews in the Diaspora, as a result of the Nazi persecution and mass emigration to Israel. It must be stressed that a part of this number lives in Communist-controlled countries where emigration is virtually forbidden. However, in 1955 it was estimated that half a million Jews still live in French North Africa, some of whom have emigrated to Israel since then.

Soviet Russia, Northern and Western Europe, and the Americas also have large Jewish communities, with a total population of 8,799,000 or 86.6 per cent of all the Jews in the Diaspora. The emigration of Jews from Soviet Russia before the borders were closed was substantial, but was very small from Northern and Western Europe and especially small from the Americas.

Future emigration will depend upon many factors: the possibility that Soviet Russia will open its doors to the Jewish population which numbers 19.7 per cent of the Jews in the Diaspora, contributing only 8.3 per cent to the Jewish immigration at the time of the British Mandate and 1.2 per cent after the establishment of the Jewish State, and increasing immigration from Western countries. These countries which in 1925 had 30 per cent of all the Jews in the Diaspora and in 1954, 67 per cent contributed only 3.7 per cent of the immigrants to Palestine when it was still a British Mandate and 2.3 per cent when Israel became established as an independent State.

In order to complete the picture of Jewish

A North African family's first act before moving into their new home—nailing a *mezuza* to the doorpost.

Rifles close at hand in the event of Arab attack, members of the Poale Agudat Israel *kibbutz* at Yesodot study the Talmud.

In the early hours of the morning the *S.S. Israel* arrives at Haifa with refugees from Egypt and Hungary (1956).

An elderly Iraqi returns to Zion.

Danny Kaye visits the Hadassah Mother and Child Welfare Center in Kastel.

An aged father and his son pick watermelons in the fields of Yashresh which have been settled by North Africans.

Youth Aliyah boys join in song before a portrait of Henrietta Szold.

Settlers in the Negev are taught how to use rifles to protect themselves.

A Youth Aliyah girl on a dairy farm in Kiryat Anavim.

A group of Youth Aliyah children leave Berlin on the first stage of their journey to Palestine (1935). In all, seventy-five thousand children have been rescued by Youth Aliyah.

New immigrants from Europe.

A wistful immigrant from Europe.

A refugee child's first meal in his new land.

Mrs. Chaim Weizmann and Eleanor Roosevelt are greeted with flowers during their visit to Ayanot on Child's Day.

An immigrant family enjoys dinner in their new house at Kfar Uriah.

Jewish girls from India.

migration one must examine the numbers of emigrants leaving Israel during the years 1948 to 1954. Seventy-one per cent of those who left Israel were the new immigrants who could not adjust themselves to the new life or who left for economic or family reasons. Very few of these came from Central Europe (Germany, Hungary, Czechoslovakia) and a large number went to Canada and the United States. Among the Jews from French North Africa hardly any went back to their original countries but some migrated to France. However most of the Turkish Jews who left Israel returned to Turkey. The largest percentage of returnees could be found among the Jews from Northern and Western Europe and the American continent.

THE GROWTH OF THE JEWISH POPULATION
IN ISRAEL

During the last 100 years, the population grew from 12,000 in the middle of the nineteenth century to 86,000 in 1922, to 650,000 in 1948. Since independence the growth has been tremendous, from 650,000 in the middle of 1948, to 1,591,000 at the end of 1955, and 2,062,000 at the end of May, 1959.

Because of the huge immigration, most Israel citizens are foreign-born. In the years 1916-18, 41.7 per cent of the population was foreign-born (excluding Jerusalem). In 1931, 48 per cent were foreign-born, in November, 1948, 64.6 per cent, and by the end of 1951, 75.5 per cent. Before World War I, most of the foreign-born were from Czarist Russia. Thus, by 1931, those from Eastern Europe, including Russia, amounted to 72.6 per cent, of which 35.4 per cent were from Poland. In 1948, the number from Eastern Europe went down to 58.6 per cent and by 1954 the Eastern Europeans were already a minority of 38.3 per cent; among them 22.1 per cent from Poland. Those from Central Europe amounted to 3.1 per cent in 1931, 18.5 per cent in 1948 and 10.6 per cent at the present time. On the other hand those from Asia and Africa which were 19.6 per cent in 1931, and 15.1 per cent in 1948, jumped to 36.7 per cent in 1951, and 39.2 per cent in 1954.

4 THE 59TH MEMBER OF THE UNITED NATIONS

The fight which Palestine Jewry waged against British attempts to suppress their national aspirations had, in the words of the British Foreign Secretary, compelled the British Government to place the problem in the hands of the United Nations.

Contemporary political analysts have seen in this British decision a device through which the English expected to gain a firmer hold on Palestine. Palestine Jewry, faced with the military forces of the combined Arab states, was expected to be frightened into submission. Their need for British protection would be made obvious and, in return for this protection, they had only to accept all legislative measures and dispose of the fighting underground forces which had been defying the anti-immigration laws. The British hoped that the Soviet-Bloc countries, together with the Arab states, the Dominions, and some of the Latin-American countries, would produce a stalemate in the discussions which would result in a decision to reinstate Great Britain as trustee of Palestine, in this way strengthening her position by prolonging her rule.

The British request for a special session of the United Nations General Assembly was made on April 2, 1947. The majority of the fifty-five member nations indicated approval, and the special session on Palestine was scheduled to begin on April 28.

The Jewish people were at a great disadvantage: at that time the Arabs had five member states in the United Nations (Egypt, Iraq, Syria, Lebanon, and Saudi Arabia) while the Jews had no representation of recognized standing. Even before the actual discussion took place, the right of the Jewish Agency to represent the Jewish Community of Palestine at the meeting was questioned although the Agency had been recognized by the League of Nations as an authorized legal body. In the final analysis, the Jewish Agency was allowed to present its representatives: Dr. Chaim Weizmann, David Ben Gurion, Dr. Abba Hillel Silver, and Moshe Shertok (Sharett). It was at this time that the Russian delegate, Andrei Gromyko, surprised the entire world with his statement of May 14 in which he said: "The aspirations of an important part of the Jewish people are bound up with the question of Palestine, and with the future structure of that country. This interest is comprehensible and completely justified." The basic argument of the British, that of the necessity of making concessions to the Arabs in order to prevent Russia from utilizing Arab opposition to Zionism for its own imperialistic aims, was completely destroyed. Gromyko proposed in this speech a bi-national Jewish-Arab State, without partition of the country, offering equal rights for both sides. It became apparent that the Jewish Community in Palestine had gained, in addition to the basic sympathy of the United States, the sympathy of another great power, Soviet Russia. This unofficial support gave much needed confidence to the Jewish Community. Of course, the fight had just begun.

On May 15, 1947, the General Assembly adopted, by a majority vote, a resolution which stated:

Whereas the General Assembly of the United Na-

David Ben Gurion addresses the Political and Security Committee at the special session of the United Nations General Assembly convened to establish the United Nations Special Committee on Palestine (May 12, 1947).

Ben Yehuda Street, in the heart of the New City of Jerusalem, after the Arab bombing of February, 1948.

tions has been called into special session for the purpose of constituting and instructing a special committee to prepare for the consideration at the next regular session of the Assembly a report on the question of Palestine, the General Assembly resolves that:

1. A special committee be created for the above mentioned purpose consisting of the representatives of Australia, Canada, Czechoslovakia, Guatemala, India, Iran, Netherlands, Peru, Sweden, Uruguay and Yugoslavia;

2. The special committee shall have the widest powers to ascertain and record facts, and to investigate all questions and issues relevant to the problem of Palestine. . . .

In four additional paragraphs, the resolution instructed the committee to submit its report to the United Nations Secretary General by September 1, 1947, so that it might be circulated to the members in time for consideration by the second regular General Assembly.

The United Nations Special Committee on Palestine investigated the entire problem for three months. The members visited Europe, Palestine,

Jews of Jerusalem receive their meager water ration. Man at right carries his belongings after being forced to evacuate his house because of Arab snipers (March, 1948).

One of the convoys that broke through Arab lines to provide the beleaguered Jewish population of Jerusalem with food, arms, and ammunition (April, 1948).

Princess Mary Avenue in Jerusalem is turned into "Barbed Wire Alley" during the last days of the British Mandatory Government. The wire was laid by the British to prevent Jews and Arabs from coming into contact. The building at right center is Police Headquarters, especially fortified to prevent attacks by Jewish underground fighters (May, 1948).

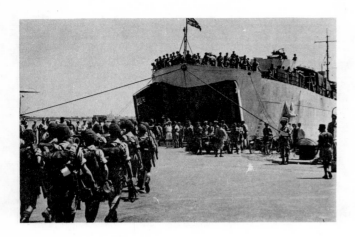

The last British troops board an LTC at Haifa after the termination of the British Palestine Mandate (June 30, 1948).

and the Arab states. In conclusion they arrived at the unanimous decision to adopt eleven recommendations, the most important of which emphasized that the Palestine Mandate had to be terminated at the earliest practicable date; the economic unity of Palestine as a whole had to be preserved; and the sacred character of the Holy Places had to be safeguarded.

However, a majority and a minority report were submitted on the problem of the political future of the country. A minority of three—India, Iran, and Yugoslavia—recommended the creation of an independent federal State of Palestine, with two federal legislative bodies, one elected on the basis of proportionate representation by all inhabitants of Palestine, the other giving equal representation to both Arabs and Jews. They recommended regulation of immigration, the number of immigrants in the first three years to be determined by a special United Nations Agency, and eventually by the Federal Government. The majority report, with the exclusion of one abstainer, Australia, recommended a partition of the land into three political units: a Jewish state, an Arab state, and an international region for Jerusalem and environs, with the two states organized into an economic unit.

When, on September 17, 1947, the General Assembly convened at Lake Success, New York, the hour of decision was imminent. Again arguments were presented for and against the partition proposal. Dr. Silver, on behalf of the Jewish Agency, announced that although it entailed a very heavy sacrifice on the part of the Jewish people, "the Jewish Agency was ready to accept the plan." When

the final vote was taken on November 29, 1947, thirty-three voted for the partition, thirteen against, and ten abstained. More than the required two-thirds majority, the United States and Soviet Russia among them, voted for the partition plan.

ATTEMPTS AT RETRACTION

The decision lacked one basic provision, a clear-cut procedure of implementation. On the day following the partition decision the Arabs started their military offensive, tolerated and perpetrated under the auspices of the British rule, which according to a statement of December 11, 1947, had to be terminated May 15, 1948. There had been no provisions made for insuring the implementation of the resolution. Bickering started. The five-nation Palestine committee appointed by the General Assembly to supervise the setting up of the Arab and Jewish states, composed of representatives of Panama, Bolivia, Czechoslavakia, the Philippines, and Denmark, could reach no decision.

The British Mandate Government refused to cooperate and busily disarmed the Jews while tolerating the invasion of the "Arab Liberation Army" from the North, large-scale Arab attacks over the entire country, the siege of Jerusalem by the Trans-Jordan Arab Legion under British command, and bombardment of Jerusalem, including the Holy Places. The British Commander of the Arab Legion, the incredible Glubb Pasha, carried on with great zeal. In his recent book he writes with obvious relish of the ground "dotted with the

After the British departure, Jewish stores in Jerusalem, closed by the Mandatory Government in retaliation for attacks of the underground fighters, are stripped of their protective cement coverings as owners prepare to open for business.

If you can't come to town, please telephone 4607

Lighting, Heating, Cooking, Refrigeration

CARL MARX
3 PRINCESS MARY AVE., JERUSALEM

JERUSALEM
SUNDAY, MAY 16, 1948

THE PALESTINE POST

PRICE: 25 MILS
VOL. XXIII. No. 6714

THE PALESTINE POST

THE SUBSCRIPTION DEPARTMENT
has returned to The Palestine Post
offices, Hassolel Street,
Jerusalem, Tel. 4233.

STATE OF ISRAEL IS BORN

The first independent Jewish State in 19 centuries was born in Tel Aviv as the British Mandate over Palestine came to an end at midnight on Friday, and it was immediately subjected to the test of fire. As "Medinat Yisrael" (State of Israel) was proclaimed, the battle for Jerusalem raged, with most of the city falling to the Jews. At the same time, President Truman announced that the United States would accord recognition to the new State. A few hours later, Palestine was invaded by Moslem armies from the south, east and north, and Tel Aviv was raided from the air. On Friday the United Nations Special Assembly adjourned after adopting a resolution to appoint a mediator but without taking any action on the Partition Resolution of November 29.

Yesterday the battle for the Jerusalem-Tel Aviv road was still under way, and two Arab villages were taken. In the north, Acre town was captured, and the Jewish Army consolidated its positions in Western Galilee.

Most Crowded Hours in Palestine's History

Between Thursday night and this morning Palestine went through what by all standards must be among the most crowded hours in its history.

For the Jewish population there was the anguish over the fate of the few hundred Haganah men and women in the Kfar Etzion bloc of settlements near Hebron. Their surrender to a fully equipped superior foreign force desperately in need of a victory was a foregone conclusion. What could not be known, with no communications since Thursday morning, was whether and to what extent the Red Cross and the Truce Consuls would secure civilized conditions for prisoners and wounded, and proper respect for the dead. Doubts on some of these anxious questions have now been resolved.

On Friday afternoon, from Tel Aviv, came the expected - announcement of the Jewish State, and its official naming at birth, "Medinat Yisrael"—State of Israel, with the swearing in of the first Council of Government. The proclamation of the State was made at midnight, coinciding with the sailing from Haifa of Britain's last High Commissioner. Within the hour, President Truman announced in Washington that the Government of the United States had decided to give de facto recognition to the Jewish State, with

der of Jewish settlements in North-Eastern Galilee.

The Security Council met yesterday in a special session to consider action on the invasion of Palestine by member states of the U.N.

In the afternoon, Jerusalem was subjected to shelling from the northwest.

Haganah forces throughout the country continued mopping up, and Jewish sources claimed most of Western Galilee safe against attack. Naharayim, near Jisr el Majamie, inside Trans-Jordan,

JEWS TAKE OVER SECURITY ZONES

The Battle for Jerusalem, which began when the British forces withdrew on Friday morning, continued all day Friday and yesterday. The crackle of small-arms fire and explosions of mortar shells were still being heard in the early hours of this morning as the battle entered its third day.

Repeated efforts on Friday evening and again on Saturday by the U.N. Truce Commission to bring about a "cease fire" were brought to nought when the Arab representatives failed to agree within the specified time limit.

On Friday morning, Jewish forces entered the Russian Compound and Zone C to reoccupy the buildings requisitioned from Jews last year. This operation was almost bloodless, but beyond the western edge of Zone C, Arabs engaged the Jews in Jaffa Road. The Arabs were forced back and the Barclays Bank area was taken.

In other parts of the city fighting flared up. Jews overran one area after another the areas evacuated by the British. By last night, the quarters and

Egyptian Air Force Spitfires Bomb Tel Aviv; One Shot Down

Kol Israel, the Tel Aviv broadcasting station, reported at 2 o'clock yesterday afternoon that Tel Aviv had been bombed three times in the previous evening and morning, and that one plane had been shot down and its Egyptian pilot taken prisoner.

In the first raid, four planes attacked from a height of 300 feet. Two dropped bombs, while the others strafed the city. Little damage was caused. In the second attack two hours later, the airport to the north of the city was bombed, and an Air France plane parked there was damaged. The third raid was launched shortly before midday, but the planes were driven off without causing any damage.

Two settlements in the Negev had also been attacked from the air, the radio reported

A country-wide blackout was ordered by Air Raid Precaution Headquarters in Tel Aviv.

Mr. David Ben Gurion, the Prime Minister, broadcast from Tel Aviv to the people of America yesterday morning. As he spoke, Egyptian planes were bombing the city.

In the north, the settlements of Ein Gev and Shaar Hagolan and Dan had been shelled, but no further details were available.

Kalandia airfield was taken by the Jewish army on Friday morning, shortly after the High Commissioner had left there by plane for Haifa. The field was evacuated, together with the neighbouring settlement of Ataroth, on Friday night. The settlement itself was burnt by Arabs yesterday.

2 Columns Cross Southern Border

By WALTER COLLINS
U.P. Correspondent
CAIRO, Saturday. — A com-

Etzion Settlers Taken P.O.W.

Fighting in the Kfar Etzion bloc continued throughout Friday, after Kfar Etzion it-

U.S. RECOGNIZES JEWISH STATE

WASHINGTON, Saturday. — Ten minutes after the termination of the British Mandate on Friday, the White House released a formal statement by President Truman that the U.S. Government as the de facto authority representing the Jewish State.

The U.S. is also considering lifting the arms embargo but it is not known whether to Palestine only or the entire Middle East, and the establishment of diplomatic relations with the Jewish Provisional Government.

The White House press secretary, Mr. Charles Ross, told correspondents today that reaction so far to the recognition had been overwhelmingly favourable. He said this step had been discussed with Mr. Marshall and Mr. Lovett before action was taken, and it had their complete support.

Mr. Ross said that the President had decided several days ago to grant American recogni-

Proclamation by Head Of Government

The creation of "Medinat Yisrael", the State of Israel, was proclaimed at midnight on Friday by Mr. David Ben Gurion, until then Chairman of the Jewish Agency Executive and now head of the State's Provisional Council of Government.

David Ben Gurion, Prime Minister

Special Assembly Adjourns

FLUSHING MEADOWS, Saturday. — The Special U.N. Assembly, called four weeks ago to discuss the U.S. propo-

The first act of the Council of Government, as announced by its head, was to abolish all legislation of the 1939 White Paper of the late Mandatory Power, particularly the Ordinances and Orders relating to immigration and land transfer.

In the declaration of independence, Mr. Ben Gurion called on the Arabs of Palestine to restore peace, assuring them full civic rights and full representation in all governmental organs of the State.

Mr. Ben Gurion prefaced the declaration with a review of the historic connection of the Jewish people with the Land of Israel and of their efforts to return, which never ceased throughout the generations of their dispersal, until the Nazi holocaust proved anew the urgency of the need for a Jewish State.

The Balfour Declaration of 1917, confirmed by the League of Nations, had given explicit international recognition to the right of the Jewish

A banner headline announces the birth of the new State. Although the State of Israel was proclaimed on Friday afternoon, May 14, 1948, the paper is dated Sunday, May 16, because no papers in Israel are printed on the Jewish Sabbath.

corpses of at least forty Jewish soldiers whose spread-eagled bodies paid adequate tribute to the power and accuracy of Arab Legion fire." It was only through the supreme effort of the Hagana, the Jewish volunteer force, joined by the smaller legion from Irgun Zvai Leumi and Lechi (the Fighters of Freedom), that they were able to resist this Arab onslaught and secure control of Tiberias, Haifa, Safed, Jaffa, Acre, and a large part of Jerusalem with the corridor connecting it with the coastal plain.

This fighting provided opportunity for attempts to change the United Nations decision, to postpone its implementation, to supplant it by a United Nations Trusteeship which, according to the United States proposal, would have to act until Jews and Arabs could agree on the future Government of Palestine, would provide for a legislature with a Jewish minority, and would make immigration and land purchases dependent upon Arab and

Jewish agreement. On April 10, 1948, the United Nations Palestine Commission reported to the General Assembly that:

The Jewish Agency for Palestine cooperated with the Commission in its task of implementing the Assembly's resolution. The governments of the Arab states and the Arab Higher Committee not only withheld their cooperation from the Commission but actively opposed the Assembly's resolution. Armed Arab bands from neighboring Arab states have infiltrated into the territory of Palestine together with local Arab forces defeating the purposes of the resolution by acts of violence.

When news of the United States proposal reached Israel a joint meeting of the Jewish Agency for Palestine and the Council of the People on March 23 produced the following resolution:

The Jewish Agency and the Council of the People declare:

The Jewish people and the *Yishuv* in Palestine will

61

The Tel Aviv bus station bombed by Egyptian planes a few days after the proclamation of the State. More than forty civilians lost their lives.

oppose any proposal designed to prevent or postpone the establishment of the Jewish State.

We categorically reject any plan to set up a trusteeship regime for Palestine even for a short period of time. A trusteeship would necessarily entail a denial of the Jewish right to national independence. It would leave Palestine under a foreign military regime. . . .

The Provisional Council of the People of the Jewish State should be recognized without delay by the United Nations Palestine Commission so that authority may be transferred to it as envisaged in the United Nations decisions. . . .

Upon termination of the mandatory administration and not later than May 16, a provisional Jewish Government will commence to function in cooperation with the representatives of the United Nations then in Palestine. In the meantime we shall do our utmost to minimize the chaos created by the present Government and we shall maintain, so far as is in our power, the public services neglected by it. . . .

The Jewish people extends the hand of peace to the Arab people and invites representatives of the Arab population of the Jewish State to take their rightful place in all organs of government. The Jewish State will be glad to cooperate with the neighboring Arab states and to enter into permanent treaty relations with them to strengthen world peace and to advance the development of all the countries of the Middle East.

Against this background the United States Ambassador to the United Nations, Warren R. Austin, requested United Nations Secretary General Trygve Lie to call a special session of the General Assembly "to consider further the question of the future Government of Palestine."

Mr. Austin's demand was promptly fulfilled. On April 16 the General Assembly convened in special session and deliberations on the future of Palestine

were reopened. The United Nations was again preparing to submit to Arab aggression, making its Charter no more than a meaningless pious declaration. Great Britain eagerly supported the Austin plan, seeing in it renewed hope for the retention of British rule in Palestine.

As the discussions in the General Assembly dragged on it became clear that only repressive force could prevent Israel from setting up an independent State as decided by the United Nations resolution of November 29, 1947. When the delegates to the second special session of the General Assembly on Palestine began to assemble on May 14 for their afternoon meeting which was scheduled to open at 5:00 P.M.—they had before them a report from Tel Aviv announcing that at 4:06 P.M. on Friday, May 14, 1948, the Jewish State, Israel, was proclaimed at a ceremony in the Museum of Tel Aviv. The excitement was intensified when, eleven minutes after the proclamation of the State of Israel, news came that the President of the United States, Harry S. Truman, extended *de facto* recognition to the new State. The discussion came to an end; a new nation came into being.

The announcement of the new State reached the United Nations together with the news that five Arab countries—Egypt, Syria, Lebanon, Iraq, and Trans-Jordan (named Jordan after the annexation of part of Palestine on the west bank of the Jordan)—had invaded Israel only a few hours after the proclamation of the State, in accordance with the decision of the Arab League on May 13, to invade Palestine on the day the British Mandate was terminated.

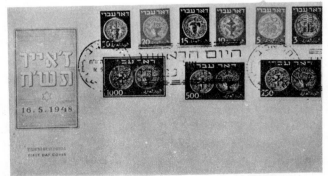

A first-day cover of the initial stamp issue of the Republic of Israel. Showing ancient Hebrew coins, the stamps bear the inscription "Hebrew Mail," for they were designed and printed before Israel was officially adopted as the name of the new State.

Mopping-up operations by an Israeli cavalry unit after the invasion by the Arab states.

Fighting started on all fronts simultaneously. The Egyptian Army struck from the South, the Syrians and Lebanese, from the North, and Iraq and Trans-Jordan from the East. Even attempts to attack from the sea were made as Tel Aviv was exposed to an unsuccessful bombardment from an Egyptian naval craft. The Egyptian Army advanced quickly over the thinly populated Negev, but was compelled to leave behind its lines heroic strongholds of small Jewish communities—*kibbutzim*—which withstood the onslaught. But this advance and those from the North and East were soon stopped at the gates of the more densely populated areas. The plan for a surprise attack was a failure.

The first week of fighting against the invading Arab armies proved sufficiently that the Jews would not be pushed "into the sea." When Swedish Count Folke Bernadotte accepted his office as United Nations Mediator on May 21, 1948, it was already apparent to military experts that Israel was going to withstand the onslaught. The Arabs alone did not make a valid appraisal of the situa-

tion. They still hoped to present the United Nations with a *fait accompli*. Of course, the term used by the United Nations—Mediator—implied compromise with Arab aggressors. This direct breach of the United Nations Charter and the Security Council provisions called not for "mediation," but for full-fledged implementation of the 1947 resolution. This blow to the resolution resulted, ultimately, in its complete dissolution, and the die was cast for war.

THE WAR OF LIBERATION

Israel did not look for this encounter. Hope for cooperation between the Jewish and Arab states, the goal of the United Nations Partition Plan, vanished the first day after the resolution had been adopted. The representatives of the Arab states at the United Nations debate announced their decision to withhold recognition of the resolution, and veto it through military force. Their attitude is reflected in a statement by the representative of the Arab Palestine Committee, Jamal El-Husseini: "The partition line proposed shall be nothing but a line of blood and fire." The "blood and fire" had come on the day following the adoption of the plan, November 30, when the first eight Jews fell victim to Arab violence in defiance of the United Nations decision.

For five months this blood-and-fire policy had been carried into every Jewish city and settlement, applied to every line of communication, and executed with utmost vehemence. Victims fell by the thousands. Jerusalem was attacked, and its population bombed and starved, until the official end

Egyptian prisoners of war are marched past one of the two tanks in the possession of the Israel Defense Forces after the first cease-fire ordered by the United Nations Security Council.

the well-armed forces of five Arab states. A population of less than 650,000 Israelis, with an untrained militia and no military equipment, managed to resist a population of thirty million—the entire Arab world."

This resistance shattered the Arab dream of an easy victory. The truce called for by the United Nations Security Council was blatantly ignored by the Arab states (Egypt, Jordan, Syria, Lebanon, Iraq), and their armies continued to invade Israel. Only the sweeping victories of the hastily gathered Jewish volunteers were able to compel the Arab states to agree to a four-week truce. The Arab armies were compelled to take the defensive; the Israeli forces were poised for a counterattack. Nevertheless, Israel was ready to accept the United Nations decision to have the truce extended. The Arab states rejected the order on July 8, 1948.

Hagana soldiers passing through an Arab village in the first days of fighting before Israel established its Army on May 26, 1948.

of British rule on May 15, 1948, cleared the path for what the Arab leaders anticipated as the final assault against the Jewish Community in Palestine. The 1947 Partition Plan was renounced by the Arabs from the very beginning. The failure of the United Nations to implement it delivered the final blow. The resolution was buried under the ruins left in the wake of Egyptian bombing raids. The Israelis had to fight almost barehanded against

Accompanied by Ralph Bunche, Count Folke Bernadotte, United Nations Mediator, holds a press conference in Haifa (1948).

A brief respite is taken by battle-weary Israeli soldiers near Latrun.

Hostilities were resumed and the horror of bombardment from the air filled the Holy City. The Israel Army developed a strong offensive and continued to expel the invaders. A second truce was arranged on July 18, but violations were frequent. Jerusalem was shelled again, pumping stations were blown up, Israeli positions in the Negev were attacked, Israeli convoys to Negev settlements were besieged, and an Arab "Liberation Army" attacked from the North, in Galilee. The Israelis made a valiant attempt to maintain the truce, but they were forced to repel the continuous Arab attacks. In the counterattack the Israeli Army reopened the roads in the Negev and drove the Arab forces from the Galilee.

After a short period of relative quiet, with occasional flare-ups and skirmishes, the United Nations

Somewhere in the Negev an Israeli machine-gun rakes enemy positions.

Security Council requested the parties to open negotiations for an armistice, but the Arabs were reluctant, and so, once again, attacks, bombardments, and shellings became daily routine. Only after the Israeli Army resumed fighting and, in a period of days, managed to sweep the whole Negev, driving the Egyptian Army back into the Sinai Peninsula, penetrate to El-Arish in pursuit of the fleeing Egyptians, and clear a path for a decisive march into the heart of Egyptian territory, did the Egyptian-Israeli cease-fire come into effect. Egypt agreed to enter negotiations on an armistice agreement. During this period, British

An Egyptian soldier captured behind Israeli lines is brought to an Army post for questioning.

planes had intervened on behalf of the Egyptians and the United States Ambassador to Israel, James McDonald, delivered an angry note to Prime Minister Ben Gurion in an attempt to rescue the completely beaten Egyptians.

The sole representative of the United Nations in the Middle East, Count Bernadotte, had in the meantime proposed a new partition plan. On September 18, 1948, Count Bernadotte's Progress

Israeli officers interrogating an Egyptian lieutenant taken prisoner in Beersheba (December, 1948).

Report reached the Secretary General of the United Nations.

Among the numerous recommendations there was a proposed radical change in the boundaries. He insisted that geographical homogeneity and integration should be the determining factors in setting the boundaries between the Jewish and Arab territories. With this in mind, he added that these frontiers should not be rigidly controlled by the decisions of the 1947 resolution and that, contrary to the resolution, the area known as Negev, south of the line running from the sea near Majdal, east-southeast of Faluja (both of which places would be in Arab territory), should be officially recognized as Arab territory. Thus the Negev, comprising almost 50 per cent of the territory of the Jewish State, had to be cut away. Ramle and Lydda, included in the Arab territory, and other areas not included in the boundaries of the Jewish State but left to the discretion of the Arab governments, should have been, in Count Bernadotte's opinion, included in the territory of Trans-Jordan. He included many such territorial provisions, apportioning the Galilee to Jewish territory, declaring Haifa a free port, and placing the Holy City of Jerusalem under the territorial rule of Trans-Jordan. These official recommendations were open declarations as to the inadequacy of the boundaries previously set. When the news of Count Bernadotte's assassination in Jerusalem on September 17, 1948, reached the United Nations Headquarters, his proposals had become a lasting testament to the inadequacy of the 1947 plan. The Arab war against Israel had put an end to the partition resolution. Dr. Ralph Bunche, a former

professor of political science at Howard University, took over as the United Nations Mediator.

While full acknowledgment was, and is, given to Dr. Bunche's outstanding gifts of mediation, there is no doubt that, had it not been for the victories of the Israeli Army, nothing would have induced the Arabs to enter negotiations and sign an Armistice Agreement with Israel.

Armistice talks with Egypt started on the Isle of Rhodes on January 13, 1949, and were followed by similar talks with Lebanon, Jordan, and Syria. The armistice agreements were signed only with the Arab states bordering Israel, but not with Iraq. According to these agreements, the territory of the State of Israel would extend over approximately 8,048 square miles, about 80 per cent of the area of Palestine under the British Mandate. Among the many stipulations of these agreements was one of particular importance: "The terms of Armistice Agreements and the boundaries fixed by them can be changed only by mutual consent, unless they are replaced by freely negotiated peace treaties."

VIOLATION OF THE ARMISTICE AGREEMENT

The bitter taste of defeat on the battlefield

Egyptian prisoners of war are released after the signing of the Israeli-Egyptian Armistice Agreement.

Jewish inhabitants of Jerusalem who had been captured by the Arab Legion return to their homes.

driving them on, the Arab states used the United Nations forum as a means by which they could keep the Palestine problem alive, simultaneously applying a more direct method, guerilla war on Israel's borders.

The United Nations was forced to concern itself with Arab-Israel relations at a time when its directive energies were needed for countless international problems. The Security Council was almost permanently occupied with Arab complaints, which had become well-conceived tactics to cover up the incessant aggression.

The United Nations had to deal with a peculiar problem. The Arab states tried to qualify their warlike acts against Israel with a theory of the existence of a "state of war." The "state of war" theory was used to justify the Suez Canal blockade. In spite of the fact that the Security Council ruled on September 1, 1951, that "since the Armistice regime is of permanent character, neither party can reasonably assert that it is actively belligerent," the Arab states continued to activate the little war for years. The United Nations Truce Supervision Organization, the Mixed Armistice Commissions, composed of representatives from Israel and Arab states, and headed by officers of the UNTSO, were able to act as a modifying factor but could not prevent the guerilla war which forced the Israeli's to armed self-defense.

The armistice agreements broke down completely. Competition for Arab favor was manifested in the United Nations by the Great Powers. It appeared that no provocation could justify Israel's defense actions in the opinion of the Security Council. Prior to the adoption of a resolution which condemned Israel's action, only mildly reprimanding the Arabs for their acts of aggression, United States Ambassador Henry Cabot Lodge, Jr., declared that "whatever the provocation might have been in this case, there was no justification for the Israeli military action in Gaza." The Arab provocation was only casually mentioned.

The preoccupation of the United Nations with the Arab-Israel conflict (which generated quite a few Soviet Russian vetoes in the Security Council as they sought opportunities to outdo the West in demonstrations of sympathy toward the Arabs) became intensely serious after the Egyptian-Russian arms deal. Even those who desired appeasement of the Arabs could see that the danger of large-scale hostilities was imminent. It was this, together with the disintegration of the armistice machinery, which prompted the United States Government to take the initiative and demand, on March 20, 1956, a meeting of the Security Council with the following proposed agenda: "The Palestine Question: Status of Compliance with the General Armistice Agreements." It was suggested that the United Nations Secretary General, Dag Hammarskjold, go on a fact-finding mission to the Middle East. Strangely enough, but indicative of the real state of affairs, the Arab states asked for a postponement of the decision on this proposal, which was granted, so that the resolution was not adopted until April 3, 1956.

Mr. Hammarskjold's report was encouraging. At a press conference he spoke about "a general will for peace in the Middle East." But the facts were less encouraging. The Arab guerila war continued and their military preparations were has-

Memorial for war heroes in Jerusalem.

A mother weeps at the grave of her son who fell
during the War of Liberation.

tened. The military pact of October, 1955, between Egypt, Syria, and Saudi Arabia, aimed openly against Israel, was followed in May, 1956, by a bilateral military pact between Egypt and Jordan. In October, 1956, this pact was integrated into the Egyptian-Syrian pact and a common command was established, headed by the Chief of Staff of the Egyptian armed forces. The Arab states boasted: "The iron ring around Israel is closed." When Israel attempted, on October 29, 1956, to break this "iron ring," to liquidate the strongholds of the Fadayin units and the commando units which perpetrated acts of sabotage and murder inside Israel on orders of the Arab military command, and to force the discontinuance of the Gulf of Aqaba blockade, the United Nations proved more effective than in the days of the Arab aggression against the newly formed State of Israel in 1948. A special session of the General Assembly was called, a cease-fire order was issued, and a united front of Soviet Russia and the United States helped the Arabs continue their belligerency against Israel. They would not accept the proposals to accompany the resolutions for the withdrawal of the Israeli forces "behind the Armistice lines" with an agreement to abolish the situation which was the cause of the Israeli defensive action. Even the simple demand of Israel, that the Arabs agree to renounce their belligerency, did not find sufficient support. Once again, the Arab states had been given, by implication, the "green light."

On March 1, 1957, Israel's Minister for Foreign Affairs, Mrs. Golda Meir, stated at the United Nations General Assembly that Israel would complete her withdrawal from the tip of the Sinai Peninsula, Sharem el-Sheikh, which overlooks the entrance to the Gulf of Aqaba (Gulf of Eilat), and from the Gaza strip, in accordance with the United Nations Assembly resolution of February 2, 1957. This would be done only under the assumption that there "will be continued freedom of navigation for international and Israeli shipping in the Gulf and the Straits" and that "if conditions are created in Gaza which indicate a return to the conditions of deterioration existing previously, Israel reserves its freedom to act in defense of its rights."

Many of these assumptions were later repudiated by Arab action. This was especially true in the Gaza strip where the Egyptian administration moved in immediately after the United Nations Emergency Force had taken over after the withdrawal of the Israeli forces. Only one important military factor remained: the United Nations Emergency Force guarding the entrance to the Gulf of Aqaba and the Egyptian-Israel frontier.

The creation of the Force, in which units of Brazil, Denmark, Finland, Canada, Norway, Sweden, India, Indonesia, Colombia, and Yugoslavia participated, was hailed as a step forward toward the preservation of world peace and the beginning of a new era in international relations. This Force, voted into being by the United Nations Assembly as the result of a suggestion by the Foreign Minister of Canada, Lester Pearson, was opposed, and is still opposed, by Russia and other East European countries, but has nevertheless survived to this day, playing a vital pacifying role on the Israel-Egyptian frontier.

The internal strife in the Arab world and the competition between the big powers kept the heated situation in the Middle East at the boiling point. The United Nations Security Council found itself, at the end of 1957 and the beginning of 1958, faced with complaints from Jordan, including the protest against Israel planting trees in the demilitarized zone in Jerusalem. Israel accused Jordan of not complying with the basic provisions of the Armistice Agreement, Article Eight, which provided for free access to the Jewish Holy Places in the Old City of Jerusalem (which is in Jordan's hands), free passage to Jerusalem on the old Latrun Road, and free access to the Hebrew University buildings and the Hadassah Hospital. Though the pattern had changed considerably after the Sinai campaign, and the hostile acts had been greatly reduced, it was apparent that, in not arranging for a long-range peace program, the United Nations had allowed the Arabs to retain the "belligerency theory" as justification for their policy toward Israel.

ISRAEL BECOMES A MEMBER OF THE UNITED NATIONS

United Nations relations with Israel had another chapter, a happier one, although not without its own problems. When, on the first anniversary of the United Nations vote for the establishment of the Jewish State, Foreign Minister Moshe Sharett presented Israel's application for membership in the United Nations, a new series of events began. The application stated that "since that date (No-

PALESTINE 1920 - 1948

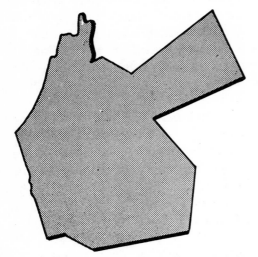

PALESTINE 1920-1922—45,000 Sq. Miles

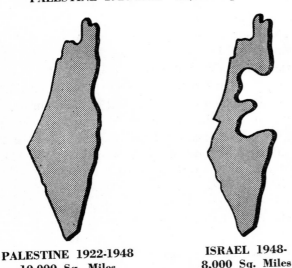

**PALESTINE 1922-1948
10,000 Sq. Miles**

**ISRAEL 1948-
8,000 Sq. Miles**

**The map at lower right shows the extent to which
Israel's frontiers shrank even after its victory over
the Arab invaders.**

vember 29, 1947) Israel has been consolidated, administratively, and defended itself successfully against aggression of neighboring states. It has also achieved recognition by nineteen powers."

The United States and Soviet Russia immediately expressed their support of Israel's application, but Great Britain could not abandon the game of opposition. The British representative declared that His Majesty's Government considered Israel's application "both premature and rather doubtful." The French representative proposed to defer the consideration of the application until the meeting of the General Assembly. In conformity with the rules of procedure, the application was turned over to the Membership Committee, which did not see fit to come to any decision. When the Security Council's vote on the application was taken, the United States, Soviet Russia, and the Ukraine voted in favor; Nationalist China, Canada, Great Britain, and Belgium abstained; and Syria voted in opposition.

This setback at the United Nations did no harm to Israel's international position. The number of countries extending recognition to the new State rose to forty-four and China (i.e., Nationalist China) presented itself as wholly in favor of admitting the new member.

The debate on Israel's application was reopened. Great Britain's representative took a "last ditch" stand but, in accordance with Britain's non-veto policy, abstained. In the discussion, in which the Egyptian representative (Egypt having replaced Syria in the Security Council) was the only opponent, an interesting point was made by the Russian representative in the face of the British and Egyptian references to the Arab refugee problem. He stated that, in the opinion of the Russian Government, Israel was not responsible for the plight of the Arab refugees. Again the United States representative in the Security Council introduced a resolution favoring Israel's application and, with Argentina, China, Canada, Cuba, France, Norway, the Ukraine, the United States, and Soviet Russia in favor of, Britain abstaining, and Egypt opposing the proposal, the President of the Council was forced to rule that the abstention of one of the permanent members did not invalidate the favorable vote.

A new procedural entanglement developed when, at the United Nations General Assembly which had to take the final vote, the Arab states attempted to delay the decision by questioning the legality of the ruling mentioned above. They initiated the introduction of resolutions requesting authoritative opinions on the Holy Places, Jerusalem, and the necessity for free access to them. Even an attempted filibuster was unsuccessful. The Australian representative in the *Ad Hoc* Political Committee introduced a resolution calling for the approval of the Israeli application. On May 11, 1949, almost a year after the proclamation of the State, the United Nations General Assembly adopted the Australian resolution thirty-seven to twelve, with nine abstentions. The resolution

First Independence Day Parade in Tel Aviv (July, 1949).

states: "The General Assembly decides that Israel is a peace-loving State, which accepts the obligations contained in the Charter and is able and willing to carry out these obligations."

JERUSALEM—AN INTEGRAL PART OF ISRAEL

At the discussions on Israel's admission to United Nations membership, the problem of Jerusalem's internationalization was repeatedly mentioned. In all discussions and proposals on this subject one basic fact was overlooked: Jerusalem is divided into two parts, one of them in Jordanian hands, the other under Israeli rule. The Old City of Jerusalem, which harbors most of the Holy Places, is under Jordanian rule. Nevertheless, the general impression emerging is that Israel has blocked the internationalization, though Jordan has repeatedly vowed that it will never relinquish its rule over the Old City of Jerusalem.

The internationalization plan of November 29, 1947, was rejected by the Arabs. And, as had been the case with the fated Partition Plan, no authority was provided for implementation. Ironically, the first major attack of the Arabs against the Jewish population started in Jerusalem—on the day following the internationalization resolution. The Jewish community had no choice but to defend itself. Arab artillery, Arab mortars, and Arab-flown British Spitfires shelled Jerusalem incessantly, turned the Holy City into a battlefield,

damaged and destroyed many of the Holy Places of Christianity and Judaism, and no power among those who fought for internationalization stood up to prevent this desecration which was perpetrated with the veiled assistance of Great Britain. Jewish Jerusalem came under Arab siege, its population starving and deprived of water, but still heroic in its self-defense. In April, 1948, a daring military operation, *Nakshon*, broke the siege as three great convoys provided the besieged city with food, arms, and ammunition. It became clear that this valiant city, which stood up to the greatest tradition of historic Jerusalem in times of Seleucidian and Roman sieges, had not paid with death, mutilation, destruction, and suffering in order to defend international territory.

Facts prove sufficiently that those who spoke in favor of the internationalization of the city spewed forth eloquent but meaningless phrases. The representative of Iraq stated, at the United Nations Trusteeship Council: "It is my duty to show that the plan for the city of Jerusalem is illegal. Neither the Iraqi Government nor the Arab states are prepared to enter the details or participate in the discussion of the plan." The Jewish Mayor of Jerusalem appealed to the United Nations Security Council to isolate Jerusalem from the conflict, to assert United Nations authority, but no action resulted. In addition, it was the United Nations Mediator Count Folke Bernadotte, who proposed integration of Jerusalem in the Arab State, completely disregarding the arguments for the internationalization of the Eternal City.

Israel's Government recognized the obligation the world had evaded. With no other effective course of action at hand, on July 26, 1948, Israel

The sign on the truck—"It is no legend any more" —set the spirit for the first Independence Day Parade in Jerusalem.

71

proclaimed Jerusalem Israeli territory, and appointed a military governor.

With this action, revived interest in Jerusalem's fate became evident. The Palestine Conciliation Commission again proposed internationalization. The United Nations General Assembly adopted the plan which the United States, Great Britain, and other countries with large Protestant populations, opposed. The intervention of the Vatican made formal headway, but this resolution was to be no more successful than its predecessors. Among the first to protest was Jordan, whose Foreign Minister, Rubi Abdul Hadi, cabled to the United Nations that Jordan "considers the internationalization of Jerusalem harmful to its vital interests" and that it would "not approve the execution of whatever is decided contrary to its rightful wishes."

The plan for the internationalization of Jerusalem remained in abeyance. On June 14, 1950, the United Nations Trusteeship Council formally admitted that it had failed to implement the statute of the internationalization of Jerusalem, and reported Israel's plan for international guardianship over the Holy Places. Robert Garreau, President of the Trusteeship Council, said, in submitting Israel's plan to the Assembly: "Israel has shown a spirit of conciliation and understanding and benevolent attitude toward the legitimate demands of all parties concerned."

In November, the General Assembly rejected a Belgian resolution reaffirming the principle of internationalization of Jerusalem, requesting a negotiating committee for this purpose. Two years later, in December, 1952, the General Assembly once again rejected reaffirmation. In this international situation the Israeli Government maintained its resolution of 1950, proclaiming Jerusalem as the capital of the State. The Knesset was the first of the governing bodies to be moved to Jerusalem; the Government Offices soon followed, and the Foreign Office was transferred in June, 1953.

The repercussions of this step reverberated around the world. There were protests; a few states refused to have their representatives, embassies, and legations transferred to Jerusalem. Some of them even refused to pay official visits to the Government Offices in Jerusalem. Nevertheless, Jerusalem was once more the capital of Israel.

RELATIONS WITH EAST AND WEST

The *de facto* recognition of the State of Israel by the United States Government, on May 14, 1948, and the *de jure* recognition by Soviet Russia on May 18, 1948, gave Israel international standing even before it became a member of the United Nations. In 1950, after Israel had proved its viability, the British Government negotiated and concluded an agreement with Israel on the terms of releasing the blocked sterling accounts that had accumulated in London in the years of World War II for the tremendous wartime services and goods deliveries to the British fighting forces in the Middle East.

The intensification of the "cold war" had inflamed Israel's desire to keep out of this contest between the big powers. When internal pressure demanded on one side Western orientation, on the other neutrality, and, from a negligible minority, Eastern orientation, Israel's spokesmen repeated that Israel was oriented toward the United Nations and the unity of the Jewish people everywhere. Israel put its faith in the United Nations though it had failed her so many times in the past.

This was not evasion of international respon-

Monument at Hulda to those who fell in the defense of the road to Jerusalem.

sibility on Israel's part. In terms of the world ideological struggle, Israel's leaders have made it clear that Israel is committed to the goal of individual freedom and true democracy, but the little nation refuses to be enmeshed in the web created by the struggles for world power.

The outbreak of the Korean War in 1950 made a decision imperative. The strength of the United Nations was in question, and Israel felt that the world organization should really be a guardian against aggression. As a State whose existence was continuously threatened by its neighbors, Israel recognized her support of United Nations intervention as imperative, as an act of international justice.

The Korean episode did not change the basic Israeli policy. Israel continued to avoid the growing friction between East and West. This attitude was dictated by national interest as well as the hope that the almost three million Jews in Soviet Russia, and the Jewish communities in the Peoples' Democracies in East Europe, would eventually be permitted to have contact with, and perhaps emigrate to, the State of Israel. Israel wished to prevent certain elements in Soviet Russia from placing on Russian Jewry the responsibility for Israel's foreign policy.

In fact, this was an extremely vital consideration. The Soviet Government did make up its mind in relation to Israel much earlier than was discernible. The tremendous reception, spontaneous and moving, which the Jews in Moscow rendered Israel's first Ambassador to the U.S.S.R., Golda Meir, placed the Russian Government on alert. The deep-seated love of Zion which broke open, despite thirty years of suppression, shocked Stalin and his advisers. We now know that this turnout of tens of thousands of Moscow Jews to see the Israeli Ambassador enter and leave the synagogue on the High Holidays, incited the series of acts directed against any vestiges of Jewish national life.

In October, 1948, the official daily, *Pravda*, published a sharp attack on Zionism and demanded the immediate cessation of Jewish immigration to Israel from all countries of the Russian orbit, closing the period of liberal emigration policy in Poland, Czechoslovakia, Hungary, Rumania, and Bulgaria.

Tension between Israel and the Soviet Union increased. On November 20, 1952, fourteen lead-

Monument in Tel Aviv to the Israeli airmen who died in the War of Liberation.

ing Czechoslovak Communists were brought to court and charges were made against the Israeli Government, its accredited diplomatic representatives in Eastern Europe, and Zionist organizations. During the court procedure anti-Semitic accusations were made in connection with the Jewish origin of some of the defendants. The retort of the Israeli Government came in the form of a sharp statement by Foreign Minister Sharett in the Knesset, who branded the trial and the accusations voiced at it as anti-Jewish incitement in the Nazi tradition.

Only two months later, in January, 1953, a new round of anti-Jewish attacks started in Russia. The so-called "physicians' plot" accused Russia's leading physicians, the majority of them of Jewish origin, of fomenting a plot to kill leading personalities of Russia's regime. The resentment in Israel led to an ill-advised attack on the Russian Embassy in Tel Aviv, on February 9, followed by a rupture of Israeli-Russian diplomatic relations, which were restored on July 20 of the same year.

73

The United Nations Security Council meeting in Lake Success, New York, at which Israel was recommended for admission to the United Nations (March 4, 1949).

This strain in Israeli-Russian relations was not relieved by Israel's repeated statements that Israel would, under no circumstances, join any bloc which would have aggressive tendencies in general and against Russia in particular. The big game for influence in the Middle East had already begun and Russia unreservedly assisted all moves of Arab policy. The United Nations became the most suitable forum for Russian demonstrations of pro-Arab policies. Whether enmity to Israel or a desire to befriend the Arabs dictated Russian policy is irrelevant. The end result is of importance, the notable change in Russia's attitude. While in 1951 Russia supported in the Security Council the resolution calling on Egypt to terminate her anti-Israel blockade, the same Russia supported the Egyptian aggressor when the problem of the blockade came up again before the Security Council. On another occasion, in January, 1954, the Russian veto defeated a Security Council resolution to permit Israel to continue with its hydroelectric project for the utilization of the Jordan and Yarmuck river waters.

The arms deal with Egypt was only a logical step forward in the direction of courting the Arabs and gaining their sympathy at the expense of the Israelis. Since then, before, during, and after the defense action in the Sinai, Russia became the prime mover of anti-Israel policies on the international scene. From Russia came the initiative to accuse Israel of being a "base for imperialist plottings in the Middle East." Open threats against Israel's very existence became a part of Russian propaganda.

But, in spite of these policies, for the first time in many years, Jews were allowed to leave for Israel. The numbers were very small, only the aged were permitted to leave, and from territories annexed after World War II, but still this signified a change in the rigid policy of closed doors.

In fact, this policy of freedom of emigration for Jews was renewed after Stalin's death in Poland and in Hungary, and limitations were relaxed in Rumania. In recent years, relations between Israel and the People's Democracies have improved, with some of them, Poland for instance, often bordering on real friendship, opening broad vistas of cooperation. This development put the Russian anti-Israel policy into perspective, as dictated by strict considerations of expansionism in the Middle East, with only little bearing on the problem of ideological differences.

The Western Powers have also done their best to appease the Arabs. A policy of direct and open discrimination against Israel was an integral part of Western policy in the Middle East. Great Britain still had her mutual security and defense agreements with some Arab countries and continued to supply them with arms. In April, 1954, the United States Government signed an agreement with Iraq granting military assistance, followed by actual arms shipments. Simultaneously, under United States pressure, Great Britain agreed to evacuate the Suez Canal Zone, without any provisions for the cessation of the anti-Israel blockade of the Suez.

These policies alarmed the Israeli Government. Israel warned that these arms have no value whatever for defense purposes against aggression from a non-Middle Eastern power, and they could be used only in one way—against Israel. On September 1, 1954, the Knesset adopted a resolution which expressed "deep concern with the policy of arming the Arab states pursued by the United States and Great Britain, while the Arab states threaten the existence and peace of Israel; and with the disregard of Israel's security and the needs of stability and peace in the Middle East entailed in the agreement on the evacuation of the Suez Canal Zone." The resolution concluded: "The Knesset proclaims that the State of Israel will not reconcile itself to this policy."

The Turkish-Iraqi Pact of February, 1955, for mutual cooperation in the defense of the Middle East, which was open to accession by other states with the exclusion of Israel, and later developed into the Baghdad Pact, implemented threats against Israel's security because it lacked any clause, customarily included in all mutual security treaties, stipulating that the signatories will refrain from use of force in their international relations. These implications of the Baghdad Pact provisions were never denied and the only Arab member of this pact, Iraq, did not miss an occasion to repeat its hostile statements against Israel.

In their quest for stability in the Middle East and in order to dispel Arab and Israeli fears, the three Western Powers, the United States, Britain, and France, issued, on May 25, 1950, a joint statement on arms supply to Arab states and Israel "for the purpose of assuring internal security and legitimate defense." This statement, which the three signatory powers proclaimed as being the guarantee of peace in the Middle East, continued: "The three governments, should they find any of these states preparing to violate the frontiers or Armistice Lines, would, consistent with their obligations as members of the United Nations, immediately take action both in and outside the United Nations to prevent such a violation."

Although this statement, which entered the arena of international policy under the name of the Tripartite Declaration, was considered as a

The Israeli flag is hoisted to fly among the flags of member nations at United Nations Headquarters, Lake Success. Abba Eban (to left of flagpole), **Moshe Sharett** (right), **and other members of the Israeli delegation celebrate the occasion (May 12, 1949).**

guarantee of the Armistice frontiers, subsequent political developments turned it into a worthless document. When a similar declaration was proposed by France at the North Atlantic Treaty Organization Council in December, 1957, neither the United States nor Great Britain supported this move.

It was France which became the most faithful, although not formal, ally of Israel. In times of Israel's dire position, when the Egyptian-Czechoslovakian arms deal had put Israel in danger of destruction, no power responded to Israel's plea for defensive arms except France. Canada's professed readiness to deliver jet planes was cancelled, and so France was the only power which remained true to its friendship for Israel. Great Britain remained true to its hostility toward Israel, its attitude demonstrated in a speech by Prime Minister Eden in Guildhall, London, on August 25, 1955, in which he advocated Israel's withdrawal from its frontiers and compromise between the frontiers of 1947 and the frontiers fixed in the Armistice Agreement. These divergent attitudes toward Israel reappeared again after the Israeli-Sinai campaign of which both France and Great Britain took advantage in their dispute with Egypt over the Suez Canal. While Great Britain returned to its policy of courting the Arabs at the expense of Israel, France strengthened its ties with Israel, and continued to assist the little country in its military and economic needs.

Meanwhile, Israel developed close relations with most of the Latin American states, the countries of Benelux, the Scandinavian countries, and most of the British Commonwealth nations. A series of trade agreements concluded and successively renewed, and an exchange of parliamentary delegations and official visitors, strengthened ties with these countries. Greece, however, refused recognition for fear of Arab reaction and the fate of the Greek population in Egypt. No diplomatic relations have been undertaken with Franco's Spain. Cordial relations developed with Italy, a great Mediterranean power with interests in the Middle East. Israel has developed international friendships with many countries which have found it beneficial for themselves and for world peace to cooperate and strengthen ties with the new nation.

The development of a relationship between Israel and the Western European Union, the process of consolidation of Western Europe with the beginnings of a parliamentary institution (the European Payment Union), and the plans for a common market are considered of great significance to Israel. Representatives of the Knesset and officials of the Foreign Ministry are already participating as observers in the meetings of the inter-European organizations.

The demand for $1,500,000,000 as a Recompense Payment by Germany for an estimated $6,000,000,000 of Jewish property confiscated and plundered by the Germans during the Nazi regime was presented by the Israeli Government on March 11, 1951, to the governments of the Big Four—the United States, the Soviet Union, the United Kingdom, and France. Shortly afterward, the Chancellor of West Germany, Konrad Adenauer, proposed to enter negotiations with Israel on the problem of reparations, a proposal which caused an unprecedented division of opinion in Israel. At the debate in the Knesset, Moshe Sharett stated that: The Israeli Government remains firm in its conviction that the responsibility for the destruction of the masses of Jews in Europe rests upon the German nation as a whole; that the Government sees no convincing signs that anti-Semitism

Dag Hammarskjold, Secretary General of the United Nations, greets an Israeli from Yemen during his visit to one of the settlements in the "Jerusalem Corridor" (February, 1956).

has been eradicated among the German people, whether East or West, even after the War; and that Israel does not regard the recompense as fully remedying the situation, since the claim presented is only the restoration of part of the property taken from Jews.

Negotiations were carried on in spite of popular opposition marked by mass demonstrations and, on September 10, 1952, an agreement was signed in Luxemburg between Moshe Sharett and Chancellor Konrad Adenauer. Under the pact, West Germany agreed to pay, in twelve or fourteen annual installments, $822,000,000 worth of goods. Of this amount, $715,000,000 was earmarked for Israel to resettle the uprooted and destitute Jewish refugees from Germany and the territories occupied by the Nazis, and $107,000,000 for the benefit of the Conference on Jewish Material Claims against Germany to be used for the relief and rehabilitation of Jewish survivors of Nazi persecution now living outside Israel.

This agreement became a basis for some political rapprochement between Israel and West Germany, especially in view of West Germany's resistance against Arab pressure to disown the agreement and stop payments. In the framework of Israel—West European contacts, West Germany became an important link.

The relations with the Latin-American countries have, from the very inception of the State of Israel, developed into a friendship which is much deeper than any relationship based on considerations of expediency, political or otherwise. Almost all Latin-American countries voted for the establishment of the State of Israel—and, since then, have never failed to remain faithful to their primary decision. It is, as political observers think, their deep sense of historical justice and sincere devotion to the ideals of freedom which made them staunch supporters of Israel.

The attitude of the Arab states often creates the impression that their anti-Israel crusade is an expression of the feelings of all the Asian and African nations, especially those which have only recently gained independence.

Nothing is farther from the truth. Among the first nations to recognize Israel were two Moslem states—Turkey and Iran. Later, Iran severed its official relations under Arab pressure, but Turkey continued close relations with Israel until the creation of the Baghdad Pact. Nevertheless, the

Dag Hammarskjold with Israel's Prime Minister David Ben Gurion and Major General Moshe Dayan, then Israel Army Chief of Staff, in the Prime Minister's office in Jerusalem (1956).

people of Turkey still maintained their friendship with Israel and the economic relations between the two countries continued to flourish.

Another example of Arab influence in Asia is reflected by the story of Israel-India relations. In spite of the fact that India extended recognition to Israel in September, 1950, no formal diplomatic relations between the two countries were installed. India's problems with Moslem Pakistan influenced her ties with the Arab countries—the easiest way to placate the Arabs was to refrain from diplomatic ties with Israel.

But, in spite of Arab influence and pressure, which kept Israel from the Bandung Conference of Asian-African countries and, in spite of the concentrated Arab-Russian effort to label Israel as an "outpost of the West," a "stooge of Western imperialism," Israel has made remarkable headway in many of the Asian and African countries. The Israel-Burma friendship became much more than a formal relationship between two states—it became a striking example of international cooperation and good will. The official Israel visit of Burma's Prime Minister U Nu, despite Arab protests, was an example to be emulated by many larger and stronger nations.

Burma is not the only Asian nation with which Israel has fruitful relations. Japan, the Philippines, Thailand, Laos, Ceylon, Malaya—all of these countries not only have formal relations with Israel, but have realized economic, cultural, and technical benefits as well.

Despite persistent Arab intimidations, one of the newest nations, Ghana, on the West Coast of

Africa, established a relationship with Israel far exceeding the bounds of international friendships. This Israel-Ghana relationship is an encouraging occurrence in view of the animosities that have divided the world. A small nation like Israel is sharing its experience and technical skill with an undeveloped country in the best interests of both partners, thus setting an example of international cooperation worthy of emulation.

Only a few years after Israel's establishment, the young State proved itself able to fulfill one of the noblest of world tasks. The program of technical assistance which Israel is extending to countries like Ghana and Burma has been entitled the "Israeli Point Four"; but, in fact, it implies much more than that—it proves that Israel's mission as a sovereign State in the midst of the awakening nations of Asia and Africa is not confined to spiritual values only, but carries within itself unlimited possibilities of becoming a center from which technical skill and experience will spread throughout the backward areas, assisting new nations in their development, technical progress, and raising their standard of living. On the basis of its geographic position Israel seems destined to become a physical bridge between three continents —Europe, Africa, and Asia—and an ambassador of good will and understanding between the peoples of the West and the East.

This great mission, which is firing the imagination of many Israelis, seems to be fully consistent with Israel's role as a Mediterranean nation, a nation which, together with Greece and Rome, gave birth to the main spiritual, moral, aesthetic, and organizational values of our contemporary world.

5 ISRAEL-UNITED STATES RELATIONS

"Israel will have no cause for regret having thus conformed to the strong sentiment of the world community," wrote President Dwight D. Eisenhower in a letter of March 3, 1957, to Israel's Prime Minister, David Ben Gurion.

More than four months had passed since Israel's Army forestalled the Russian-equipped Egyptian Army in its long-planned and openly declared attack on Israel. United States Israel relations reached their lowest ebb. The United States Government led the efforts to force Israel behind the 1949 armistice lines without any assurance against future recurrence of Arab incursions, attacks, blockades, and boycotts.

This was an impressive force; after serving as the chief factor in saving Egypt and Nasser from complete defeat, the United States Government applied pressure on Israel. Threats of complete isolation of Israel on the international scene and the decision to stop economic assistance were weapons to drive Israel into submission.

These were but overtures to what was to come: the threat to cut off Israel from its friends in the United States, to stop the flow of money contributed by American Jewry followed, and this was only a prelude to the final declaration of the forthcoming economic sanctions against Israel.

It was the United States which influenced the Israeli Government's decision. Not the threats, not the dangers involved in alienation of the United States, not the consequences of an eventual complete and permanent stoppage of all forms of American assistance, but the desire to keep United States friendship was the decisive factor in Israel's decision. Israel made no secret of this. The communications from Israel's Prime Minister to President Eisenhower frequently repeated this basic consideration. In statements before the Knesset, it was repeated time and again that it was the resolute will to preserve good relations with the leading power of the free world, the power which Israel learned to appreciate and hold in high esteem, which superseded to a certain extent important considerations of Israel's national inter-

ests. In spite of the fact that United States policy absolved Egypt from its responsibility for aggression and enabled Nasser to continue his aggressions with impunity, the Israeli Government decided to comply with American demands.

This period of strain in United States-Israel relations was overcome. United States aid to Israel has been renewed, the ban on American travel to Israel has been lifted, and a loan from the Export-Import bank was granted.

Recent relations between Israel and the United States developed toward a greater understanding and a retreat from the positions taken under the pressure of the Arab states and the anti-Israel forces in the United States representing oil interests, pro-Arab elements, and anti-Jewish feeling.

The first indication of America's vacillating policy toward Israel came with United States retreat on the Partition Plan. In his statement before the United Nations Security Council on February 24, 1948, Warren R. Austin reviewed the events in Palestine, and said: "The Charter of the United Nations does not empower the Security Council to enforce a political settlement, whether it is pursuant to a recommendation of the General Assembly or of the Security Council itself." After several weeks of debate, and a number of meetings of the five major powers, Ambassador Austin left no further doubt that the United States had reversed its policy. On March 19, 1948, he declared that the Council was not prepared to implement the Partition Plan in the existing situation. He submitted in the name of the United States the following three proposals:

1. The plan proposed by the General Assembly is an integral plan which cannot succeed unless each of its parts can be carried out. There seems to be general agreement that the plan cannot be implemented by peaceful means.

2. We believe that further steps must be taken immediately not only to maintain the peace but also to afford a further opportunity to reach an agreement between the interested parties regarding the future Government of Palestine. To this end we believe that a temporary trusteeship for Palestine should be estab-

Jewish war veterans march in New York City in protest against the United States proposal to reverse the United Nations resolution to establish the Jewish State (April 4, 1948).

lished under the Trusteeship Council of the United Nations. . . . This would require an immediate special session of the General Assembly, which the Security Council should request the Secretary General to convoke under Article 20 of the Charter.

3. Pending the meeting of the proposed special session of the General Assembly, we believe that the Security Council should instruct the Palestine Commission to suspend its efforts to implement the proposed Partition Plan.

The real meaning of this United States proposal was clear: it declared null and void the United Nations decision of November 29, 1947, to establish a Jewish State in part of Palestine. This was the opinion of the Jewish Agency for Palestine and the Vaad Leumi, the National Council of the Jews of Palestine. Both these institutions replied on March 23, so that no doubt could be left as to Jewish intentions. "The Jewish people and the *Yishuv* in Palestine will oppose any proposal designed to prevent or postpone the establishment of the Jewish State." After rejecting the proposal for a trusteeship regime for Palestine, the declaration stated further: "Upon the termination of the mandatory administration, and not later than May next, a provisional Jewish Government will commence to function."

This appraisal of the meaning of the United States proposal did not emanate from Jewish circles exclusively. Andrei Gromyko of Russia declared that "full responsibility for the killing of the decision on the partition of Palestine rests on the United States." He added that he could see no reason for calling a special session of the General Assembly.

In early May it became apparent that a trusteeship would mean the use of repressive force against the Jewish population in Palestine, which was determined to abide by the decision of the General Assembly of November 29, 1947, and to declare its national independence.

The second special session of the General Assembly on Palestine carried on deliberations of the United States proposal. The last plenary meeting was opened at five o'clock on May 14, and it heard a report which no amount of legislative sophistry could explain away. At 4:06 P.M. on Friday, the fifth day of the Jewish month *Iyar*, May 15, 1948, the sovereign Republic of Israel, the third Jewish Commonwealth in the history of the human race, came into being.

RECOGNITION AND STRAIN

The United States trusteeship proposal was dead. The deadly blow dealt by the determination of the Jews in Palestine was successfully assisted by the Zionist movement the world over and especially by the American Jewish community. In this rather unstable history of United States-Israel relations, there has nevertheless emerged proof of latent sympathy toward Israel. The historic decision of President Harry S. Truman to extend the *de facto* recognition of the existence

Speakers at a Zionist meeting in New York's Madison Square Garden. Left to right: Mrs. Rose Halprin, Senator Herbert H. Lehman, Mayor William O'Dwyer, Senator Robert A. Taft, Dr. Abba Hillel Silver, and Henry Morgenthau (May 16, 1948).

and Provisional Government of the State of Israel was followed by that of the governments of Soviet Russia and other nations. All this came in the wake of an organized United States attempt to revoke the official decision to establish a Jewish State in part of Palestine.

On the very eve of the declaration of Israel's independence, concerted efforts were made by the highest United States authorities to influence leaders of the Jewish Agency for Palestine to refrain from proclaiming the State. Secretary of State Marshall expressed his full approval of the trusteeship proposals and in one instance even mentioned the possibility of a United States blockade of Israeli shores to bring the defiant leaders of the *Yishuv* and the Agency into submission. Along with these threats another maneuver was designed by members of the United States delegation to the United Nations, then laboring at the temporary headquarters at Flushing Meadows. They sought to engage the Jewish Agency in a "truce" conference and in a new trusteeship agreement. Some members of the Jewish Agency were ready to yield. They spoke of threats and of reprisals of the United States if the Jewish Agency should refuse.

The situation was serious as the leaders of the *Yishuv* decided to proceed. The members of the Provisional State Council of the Government of Israel issued the Proclamation of Independence in clear defiance of United States advice, fully aware that this defiance would endanger the friendship between the two countries. There was not one person among those who decided not to yield who could guarantee that the threats would not be carried out on the very day of the declaration of Israel's independence.

John Foster Dulles and Harold Stassen, accompanied by Moshe Sharett, review Israeli honor guard at Lydda airport (May 13, 1953).

President Truman's recognition of the Provisional Government as the *de facto* authority of the new State of Israel surprised his advisers. It was a dramatic change in the general attitude of the United States administration which had not missed a chance to try to stop the victorious young State which proved morally equipped to fight back against the unified aggression of five Arab armies which invaded Israel on the day of the declaration of independence.

Attempts to suppress Israel's assertion of independence came in the wake of the Israeli Army's closing military accomplishments in the War of Liberation. The Israeli Army not only destroyed the invading forces on Israeli territory, but pursued the fleeing Egyptian units into their own territory with the hope of arriving at an honorable peace, without victors. Israeli-Arab peace was within reach when a new attempt was made to protect the Arabs—putting an end to the hope for peace in the Middle East. As British Spitfires appeared in the skies of the Negev to protect the "Egyptian ally of Britain" (five of them were shot down in an encounter with Israeli forces), the United States Ambassador to Israel, James McDonald, delivered a note to Prime Minister Ben Gurion, no less strong worded and threatening than the notes delivered during and after the Sinai campaign in the autumn of 1956 and early in 1957.

These fluctuations in United States-Israel relations, often seemingly effected without the full knowledge of the Chief Executive, have been many. While the United States professed that it supported the existence of Israel as an integral part of United States policy, it was apparent that

James McDonald, first United States Ambassador to Israel, at a reception in Tel Aviv.

in any clash of interests the Arabs could count on American assistance.

Between the two major United States interventions, in 1948 and 1956, there were also other innumerable political acts which give ample proof that the propaganda accusing the United States of favoritism toward Israel was no more than Arab humbug. The list of the attempts to appease the Arab states on Israel's account is a long one. After Secretary of State John Foster Dulles toured the Middle East, a new doctrine of "impartiality" was announced. This "impartiality" was supposed "to allay the deep resentment against the United States that has resulted from the creation of Israel."

The United States demonstrated friendship for the Arabs by its treatment of Israel in the Jerusalem controversy, showing that it would not,

under any circumstances, acquiesce to Jerusalem becoming the capital of the State. When, in October, 1953, Israel decided to defend herself against Arab tactics to sabotage the most peaceful enterprises (the exploitation of Jordan waters for land irrigation), the United States applied pressure by halting economic aid to the Jewish State for a short time.

In 1954, the year which can be marked as the start of the feverish arming of the Middle East, the United States disclosed that arms would be offered to Iraq and Saudi Arabia, while none would be sold to Israel. Israel was expected to sit like "a lame duck" and patiently take the stepped-up guerilla warfare of the Arab states. Whenever, after a round of raids, death, and mutilation, Israel struck back in self-defense, the United States repre-

President Harry S. Truman holds Torah presented to him by Chaim Weizmann eleven days after Truman extended *de facto* recognition to the new State of Israel (May 25, 1948).

Albert Einstein, in a rare public appearance, as he spoke at the first national conference of the American Committee to Support Higher Education in Israel (May, 1950).

sentatives quickly condemned the little nation in the United Nations forum.

This policy was accompanied by ideological skirmishing. Assistant Secretary of State Byroade, attacked the very character of the young State as a haven for all who need shelter, and did not refrain from using propaganda to stop the support of American Jewry. When the United States actively supported Egyptian demands for the evacuation of British troops from the Suez Canal Zone, Israel's fear for its security was dismissed, and all suggestions to restrain Egypt were brushed aside.

Early in 1955 Israel asked, in vain, to have some guarantee of its independence and territorial integrity. The Arab boycott against Israel, open economic warfare accompanied by military attacks, the Egyptian breach of the United Nations Security Council decision to lift the anti-Israel blockade in the Suez Canal, Jordan's non-compliance with the armistice agreement, were not met by the resolute United States actions taken against Israel.

In March, 1955, Deputy Assistant Secretary of State, Jernegan, publicly dismissed Israel's contention that the Arab countries were preparing for war. Though the press reported daily on Arab war preparations, on military pacts, and open threats to annihilate Israel, accompanied by "small war" acts, Jernegan stated: "There is no evidence of any intent on the part of its neighbors to attack Israel." But, at the same time, he argued that

Israel would not be included in the Middle Eastern defense arrangements due to tensions and "the absence of political cooperation between Israel and the Arab states."

Israel's repeated efforts toward a mutual defense treaty, toward any kind of guarantee, went unheeded, while shipments of United States arms to Arab countries, especially Iraq, continued. Secretary of State Dulles' speech of August 26, 1955, contained many positive suggestions, even readiness to guarantee the frontiers of Israel and of the Arab states, but under one condition which nullified the whole concept: that this guarantee be conditioned by the Arab-Israeli frontier agreement.

Even the Egyptian-Russian-Czechoslovakian arms deal of September 27, 1955, which greatly increased Egypt's armed might, and made the country Russia's gateway for penetration into the Middle East, did not change the attitude of the State Department. On October 11, 1955, Israel's Ambassador to the United States, Abba Eban, issued an urgent plea to Assistant Secretary of State Allen for a United States guarantee of Israel's borders and help in the maintenance of an arms-balance between Israel and the Arab states. There was no response. Two months later, the United States and Britain retreated from the Tripartite Declaration of May, 1950, committing them to the preservation of the *status quo* in the Middle East, clearly indicating by implication that the Arab states were free to change the *status quo,* at the expense of Israel.

But, in time, Arab behavior was to influence the United States attitude toward Israel. The growing cooperation between Egypt and Soviet Russia, despite all the help and favors the United States had bestowed on the Arabs, put an end to

United States Ambassador Edward Lawson addresses the audience at a ZOA House celebration. Behind him is a 120-member choir.

the theory that the sacrifice of Israel's political and security needs would bring the Arabs "into the fold." While continuing to refuse Israel arms (United States arms were being shipped to Iraq and Saudi Arabia), the State Department privately urged some NATO countries to deliver jet planes to Israel in order to avoid leaving this staunch ally of democracy easy prey for Arab aggression and Russian penetration into the Middle East.

At the beginning of 1957, when Israel acceded to the "Eisenhower Doctrine" which pledged United States assistance to every Middle East nation which sought help against Communist aggression, the State Department refused to declare whether this pledge would assure assistance to Israel in the event that nation was attacked by a Communist-dominated or -inspired Arab state.

ECONOMIC ASSISTANCE TO ISRAEL

This vacillating attitude toward Israel's political problems did not affect, with one brief exception, the flow of United States economic aid. And, with the exception of a small group of left-wingers, the overwhelming majority of the Israeli population seized upon even the slightest sign of United States friendship with gratitude and appreciation.

In 1951, Congress voted the sum of sixty-five million dollars as a Grant in Aid, largely earmarked for relief and resettlement of Jewish refugees. This decision was incorporated in the United States Mutual Security Act of 1951, a document expressing unprecedented international generosity. This decision was preceded by the

The ZOA (Zionist Organization of America) House in Tel Aviv.

adoption of a Point Four agreement for technical cooperation between the two countries. This act was not unanimously hailed in Israel. There were many who argued that Israel should not depend upon United States aid, but should struggle to strengthen its economic independence. On January 24, 1951, Israel's Foreign Minister, Moshe Sharett, saw the necessity of assuring the Knesset that there was no truth in the rumor that acceptance of United States aid involved "a political price."

Within the next year and a half, two other agreements cemented the economic ties between the two countries. On June 9, 1952, an agreement was signed to permit Israel to import American works of literature and periodicals under the Information Media Guarantee Program. The Treaty of Friendship, Commerce, and Navigation was initiated, and later ratified.

In order to allay Middle East tensions and simultaneously raise the standard of living of the peoples in the area by utilizing barren land, the United States inaugurated the plan to exploit Jordan River waters for irrigation purposes in the four neighboring countries—Israel, Jordan, Syria, and Lebanon. In 1953, Eric Johnston was sent on a special mission to explore the possibilities of implementing the plan. The United States was prepared to finance the project, but the Arab nations repeatedly refused to cooperate (Israel agreed immediately) so that at present there seems to be no chance that this great humanitarian project will be put into operation.

View of the Goodman Auditorium in the ZOA House. Portraits of United States Presidents appear above the entrances.

Eleanor Roosevelt at a meeting in the ZOA House during her visit to Israel in 1956.

There has been a gradual decline in American economic aid to Israel. A loan of one hundred thirty-five million dollars was given by the Export-Import Bank on a strict commercial basis (Israel has already paid forty million dollars in interest). The American Government has also authorized the sales of agricultural surpluses on special conditions equivalent to a thirty-year loan to be repaid in Israeli local currency.

American grants in aid have continued to assist the Israeli economy in its efforts to develop the country for the absorption of new immigrants. This aid, its volume once greatly exaggerated by Israel's adversaries, alleging that the country is economically inviable and its economy dependent upon United States aid, is, in fact, less than that given to many countries, none of which has had to absorb thousands of immigrants annually. Since the inception of the State, the over-all sum of United States grants in aid and agricultural surpluses amounted to $265,000,000 as of June 30, 1957. Of this sum, $226,800,000 are marked for economic and technical assistance, within the framework of mutual security, and $39,000,000 as aid in the form of agricultural commodities.

An interesting feature of United States-Israel economic cooperation is the system of administration of this economic aid. A special United States Operations Mission functions in Israel in full cooperation with the Israeli Government in the coordination of plans for the development of the country. There is almost no field of activity to which the members of this Mission have not added their experience and knowledge: road planning, port-improvements, mineral research, cattle breeding for the solution of the Israel meat problem. In every field these experts work hand in hand with the Israelis. As many observers have pointed out, Israel is an example of how United States aid can be used to benefit a country which is properly appreciative, and not suspicious or resentful.

THE FAITHFUL HINTERLAND

In its struggle, first for independence and later for security and economic viability, the Jewish Community in Palestine did not stand alone. It had, and has, allies—devoted, courageous, ready to sacrifice.

These allies are many: Jews the world over and non-Jews animated by the prophetic words of return to Zion. Since the first days of modern Zionism there has been wide support for the cause of Israel.

Among those who have extended the greatest assistance to the development of Israel, the Jews

David Ben Gurion with Dr. Louis Finkelstein, President of the Jewish Theological Seminary of America, before the ceremony at which an honorary degree was conferred upon the Prime Minister by the Seminary.

of America hold first place. As the United States attained leadership in world affairs, so, too, American Jewry, after World War II, reached the peak of its influence on Jewish destiny everywhere, and the peak of its activities on behalf of the young democracy in the Middle East.

From the very beginning of the Zionist movement in Europe, American Jewry has been a reliable companion. Louis D. Brandeis, to mention the most outstanding, was not alone. At the Versailles Peace Conference a delegation of American Jews assisted Zionist efforts to get international aid to reestablish the Jewish Commonwealth in Palestine. During the struggle against British attempts to renege, to block Jewish revival of Palestine, American Jewry served as a forceful arm on the political and economic fronts. When days of decision arrived, days of faltering and disintegrating British administration in Palestine, it was again American Jewry which succeeded in mobilizing itself and general public opinion for a decisive stand crowned with the United Nations decision for the establishment of a Jewish State in Palestine.

Times of crisis were abundant. Israel could always count on at least one ally—American Jewry. And this was not only political faithfulness. United States Jewry became the most important source of economic assistance. In this respect unparalleled results were achieved: a voluntary collection system produced over half a billion dollars (through the United Jewish Appeal) within the few years from 1948 to 1957. Together with the Jewish National Fund, Hadassah, Histadrut campaigns, and funds from other institutions, Israel received $656,000,000. The central agency for fund-raising, the United Jewish Appeal (United Israel Appeal, formerly United Palestine Appeal) grew through the years from ten million dollars a year to over a hundred million dollars.

The great and generous help given through the U.J.A. makes mass immigration to Israel possible, but it had to be supplemented by another source of foreign currency to aid in the economic absorption of the hundreds of thousands of new immigrants. For these purposes, the old Herzlian idea of a national loan, on a sound business basis, was renewed. A conference of fifty prominent United States Jewish leaders, Zionists and non-Zionists, held in September, 1950, in Jerusalem, was concluded with a resolution to call upon American Jewry to provide Israel with one billion dollars during the three-year period from 1952 to 1954, through: an enlarged and strengthened U.J.A., intensive efforts to secure private investments, purchase of State of Israel bonds should the Government decide to float such bonds in the United States, and efforts to secure grants in aid to Israel from the United States Government. This fourth point was added in 1950 when a large conference of delegates or observers from virtually every important Jewish organization in the United States met in Washington, and ratified the four-point program.

When the Israel Bond Drive was officially launched on May 10, 1951, with a mass meeting in Madison Square Garden in New York, Prime Minister Ben Gurion, who came especially for this occasion, was the chief speaker. American Jewry received a new instrument for its efforts on behalf of Israel, an instrument which supplied the financial means (about $330,000,000) to cover one-third of Israel's housing expenditure, make possible the implementation of great irrigation projects, help to drain the Huleh marshes, encourage the development of crops, help establish 478 new agricultural settlements, further the quest for natural resources, and hasten the march of Israel's economy toward independence from foreign assistance.

Of course there has been a voice of dissent. While influential non-Zionist bodies such as the American Jewish Committee and B'nai B'rith supported Israel's request for aid, the American Council for Judaism denounced the "lobbying" in favor of Israel, "Zionist control of philanthropy," and the "spectacle of American Jews being mobilized as salesmen for Israeli bonds."

In spite of this "lunatic fringe," there is almost universal agreement on the subject of American Jewish support for Israel and its consistency with the real interests of the United States. In this respect it is worthwhile to quote a great American, Justice Brandeis, who wrote: "Let no American imagine that Zionism is inconsistent with Patriotism. Multiple loyalties are objectionable only if they are inconsistent. A man is a better citizen of the United States for being also a loyal citizen of his state, and of his city; for being loyal to his family, his profession or trade; for being loyal to his college or his lodge. Every Irish American who contributed towards advancing 'home rule' was a better man and a better American for the sacrifice he made. Every American Jew who aids in the advancing of the Jewish settlement in Palestine, though he feels that neither he nor his descendants will ever live there, will likewise be a better Jew and a Better American doing so."

THE "NEW CANAAN"

This national attachment of American Jewry to the Land of Israel and their brethren who have rebuilt the Jewish Commonwealth is not a strange phenomenon even in terms of the non-Jewish population in the United States. From the days of the Pilgrims and the Founding Fathers, attachment to the Land of the Bible and sympathy for the People of the Bible has been one of the most remarkable features of American conscience, political thought,

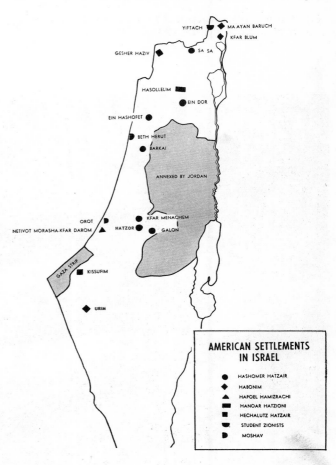

AMERICAN SETTLEMENTS
IN ISRAEL

● HASHOMER HATZAIR
◆ HABONIM
▲ HAPOEL HAMIZRACHI
◼ HANOAR HATZIONI
■ HECHALUTZ HATZAIR
▶ STUDENT ZIONISTS
◗ MOSHAV

and moral stature. As far back as John Adams, second President of the United States, American interest has extended to the rebirth of the Jewish Commonwealth. Three hundred and sixty-five communities in the United States bear Biblical names, for the most part names of places in the historical First and Second Jewish commonwealths in Palestine. The first leaders of this nation knew the Hebrew language, and when Harvard College was founded in 1636, Hebrew was one of the com-

The United Jewish Appeal holds a luncheon meeting in New York (June, 1957).

A sign at the entrance to an all-American *kibbutz* in the Galilee reads: "The path to the goal for American pioneers." The second line is a quotation from Ezekiel 34:14: "Upon the high mountains of Israel shall their fold be."

This propane storage tank is typical of the heavy industrial equipment shipped annually to Israel from the United States.

pulsory subjects, and no scholar could be admitted for a degree unless he was able to translate the Hebrew original of the Bible into Latin. Yale College took as an insignia on its shield the Hebrew words *Urim V'tummim,* still on its portals. Among the many proposals for an official language for the United States, the Hebrew language was not missing. The characteristics of Hebraic tradition, Hebraic law, and Hebraic moral standards have influenced the emerging American order.

The modern movement for the reestablishment of the Jewish Commonwealth therefore found a most natural ally and understanding supporter in the United States. Prior to the complexity of contemporary politics which obscure the picture, politics dictated by the oil interests in the Arab states and the Middle East, the efforts to rebuild a Jewish State had the fullest support of the American public and Government. The words of President John Adams to Major Mordecai Manuel Noah in 1818, "I really wish the Jews again in Judea, an independent nation," were only a beginning to America's concern with the problem of Jewish restoration in Palestine.

There were innumerable demonstrations of American faithfulness to the cause of Zionism. The statement of President Wilson in 1919; "I am persuaded that the Allied Nations, with the fullest concurrence of our Government and our people, are agreed that in Palestine should be laid the foundations of a Jewish Commonwealth," was only one of them, to be followed by a similar, unanimously accepted resolution of the Senate. Sponsored by Senator Henry Cabot Lodge, the resolution placed the United States in solid support of the obligations stemming from the Balfour Declaration and later the Palestine Mandate.

Quotations from statements of Presidents Harding, Coolidge, Hoover, Roosevelt, Truman and Eisenhower, could be extended by quotations from prominent statesmen, leaders in the field of religion, science, letters, labor, of both major political parties. There was never a crisis around Israel about which American public opinion did not speak up for the cause of right and justice. The pioneering spirit, the moral zest, the conquest of the desert, the respect for human dignity and for the freedom of the individual which characterized the young republic of the United States are so close to the central, basic values of the State of Israel, that there is a basic affinity, even if it is sometimes marred by intervals of political expediency. The basic approach of the American nation finds its most dramatic counterpart thousands of miles away, on the shores of the Mediterranean, in the little republic of Israel.

During his visit to the United States in March, 1960, Prime Minister David Ben Gurion met with President Dwight D. Eisenhower at the White House in Washington.

6 GOVERNMENT

On November 29, 1947, a Special General Assembly of the United Nations accepted the plan for partitioning Palestine into a Jewish State and an Arab State. Shortly after the decision, the executive members of the Jewish Agency for Palestine, together with members of the Vaad Leumi, (the National Council, elected by the *Yishuv*), combined to form an *Ad Hoc* body called the Vaadat Hamatzav (Emergency Committee), whose task was to prepare for the Jewish State. It soon became clear that this body was to take the place of the Mandatory Government, which was rapidly dissolving in chaos. The people endowed it with those legislative, executive, and judicial powers necessary to the fulfillment of its task, which came to include the preparation for the establishment of the State and the role of mediator between the State and the British rule.

The Vaadat Hamatzav divided itself into a number of committees to examine specific problems and prepare for their solution. It was soon found that while the Jews with their own traditions of administration, had experience in such matters as defense, political relations, financial and economic affairs, immigration, health, education, agriculture —in fact, all the matters in which the Jewish Agency for Palestine, or the Vaad Leumi, was active—they had limited practical experience in such matters as the routine aspects of national administration, including foreign affairs, the running of ports, airports, prisons, law courts, offices of registration and of district administration.

One of the most important of the sub-committees of the Vaadat Hamatzav was the Moetza Mishpatit (Legal Council). It had the tremendous task of examining the whole of Palestinian law in order to facilitate the transition from Mandate to Independence. This involved examining every function of the High Commissioner, in order to ascertain precisely the capacity in which he was acting— legislator, chief executive officer, representative of the King, or Head of State. The next question was to whom his powers should be transferred. The decision about the new functionaries was a politi-

cal matter and was thrashed out in those anxious days just before May 15. It found formal expression in the constitutional documents of the Provisional Government, namely, the Declaration of Independence of May 14, 1948, a Proclamation of the same date, and the Administration and Justice Law, enacted a few days later.

Declaration of the Establishment of the State of Israel

The Land of Israel was the birthplace of the Jewish people. Here their spiritual, religious and national identity was formed. Here they achieved independence and created a culture of national and universal significance. Here they wrote and gave the Bible to the world.

Exiled from Palestine, the Jewish people remained faithful to it in all the countries of their dispersion, never ceasing to pray and hope for their return and the restoration of their national freedom.

Impelled by this historic association, Jews strove throughout the centuries to go back to the land of their fathers and regain their statehood. In recent decades they returned in masses. They reclaimed the wilderness, revived their language, built cities and villages, and established a vigorous and evergrowing community, with its own economic and cultural life. They sought peace yet were ever prepared to defend themselves. They brought the blessings of progress to all inhabitants of the country.

David Ben Gurion presides at the ceremony announcing Israel's Declaration of Independence.

**Ben Gurion signs the Declaration of Independence
as Moshe Sharett *(right)* looks on (May 14, 1948).**

In the year 1897 the First Zionist Congress, inspired by Theodor Herzl's vision of the Jewish State, proclaimed the right of the Jewish people to national revival in their own country.

This right was acknowledged by the Balfour Declaration of November 2, 1917, and reaffirmed by the Mandate of the League of Nations, which gave explicit international recognition to the historic connection of the Jewish people with Palestine and their right to reconstitute their National Home.

The Nazi holocaust, which engulfed millions of Jews in Europe, proved anew the urgency of the re-establishment of the Jewish State, which would solve the problem of Jewish homelessness by opening the gates to all Jews and lifting the Jewish people to equality in the family of nations.

The survivors of the European catastrophe, as well as Jews from other lands, proclaiming their right to a life of dignity, freedom and labor, and undeterred by hazards, hardships and obstacles, have tried unceasingly to enter Palestine.

In the Second World War the Jewish people in Palestine made a full contribution in the struggle of the freedom-loving nations against the Nazi evil. The sacrifices of their soldiers and the efforts of their workers gained them title to rank with the peoples who founded the United Nations.

On November 29, 1947, the General Assembly of the United Nations adopted a Resolution for the establishment of an independent Jewish State in Palestine, and called upon the inhabitants of the country to take such steps as may be necessary on their part to put the plan into effect.

This recognition by the United Nations of the right of the Jewish people to establish their independent State may not be revoked. It is, moreover, the self-evident right of the Jewish people to be a nation, as all other nations, in its own sovereign State.

ACCORDINGLY WE, the members of the National Council, representing the Jewish people in Palestine and the Zionist movement of the world, met together in solemn assembly today, the day of termination of the British Mandate for Palestine, by virtue of the natural and historic right of the Jewish people and of the Resolution of the General Assembly of the United Nations.

WE HEREBY PROCLAIM the establishment of the Jewish State in Palestine, to be called Israel.

WE HEREBY DECLARE that as from the termination of the Mandate at midnight, this night of the 14th to 15th May, 1948, and until the setting up of the duly elected bodies of the State in accordance with a Constitution, to be drawn up by a Constituent Assembly not later than the first day of October, 1948, the present National Council shall act as the Provisional Administration, shall constitute the Provisional Government of the State of Israel.

THE STATE OF ISRAEL will be open to the immigration of Jews from all countries of their dispersion; will promote the development of the country for the benefit of all its inhabitants; will be based on the precepts of liberty, justice and peace taught by the Hebrew Prophets; will uphold the full social and

A seventy-two-year-old resident of Mea Shearim, Jerusalem, votes for the first time in a free Israel.

political equality of all its citizens, without distinction of race, creed or sex; will guarantee full freedom of conscience, worship, education and culture; will safeguard the sanctity and inviolability of the shrines and Holy Places of all religions; and will dedicate itself to the principles of the Charter of the United Nations.

THE STATE OF ISRAEL will be ready to cooperate with the organs and representatives of the United Nations in the implementation of the Resolution of the Assembly of November 29, 1947, and will take steps to bring about the Economic Union over the whole of Palestine.

We appeal to the United Nations to assist the Jewish people in the building of its State and to admit Israel into the family of nations.

In the midst of wanton aggression, we yet call upon the Arab inhabitants of the State of Israel to return to the ways of peace and play their part in the development of the State, with full and equal citizenship and due representation in all its bodies and institutions—provisional or permanent.

We offer peace and unity to all the neighboring states and their peoples, and invite them to cooperate with the independent Jewish nation for the common good of all.

Our call goes out to the Jewish people all over the world to rally to our side in the task of immigration

The Prime Minister casts his ballot in the first election.

**Citizens of the new State study election posters as
Israel prepared for its first general election (1949).**

and development and to stand by us in the great struggle for the fulfillment of the dream of generations—the redemption of Israel.

With trust in Almighty God, we set our hand to this Declaration, at this Session of the Provisional State Council, in the city of Tel Aviv, on this Sabbath eve, the fifth of *Iyar,* 5708, the fourteenth day of May, 1948.

THE DECLARATION OF THE ZIONIST GENERAL COUNCIL

In April, 1948, a meeting of the Zionist General Council was held in Tel Aviv.At this session, which was attended by representatives from Palestine and the Diaspora, it was decided, despite the wavering attitude of some of the countries which had supported the United Nations resolution, to establish the administrative institutions which would assume

official responsibility upon the termination of the British Mandate. The resolutions adopted by the Council on April 12, included the following strictures on England:

The days of British Mandatory rule are over. On May 15, the pledge entrusted to Britain by the League of Nations twenty eight years ago, and which that country has failed to carry out, will revert to the United Nations. During the past ten years the Mandatory Government's repudiation of its mission in Palestine has become the basis of its policy in the Middle East. Instead of facilitating Jewish immigration, it barred the gates to the down-trodden members of our people in the most tragic hour of the history of the Jews in exile. It enforced a blockade against immigrants who sought to gain entry into the country without certificates, and brought armed forces

93

The first meeting of the Israeli Cabinet (1948).

from afar to consign them to danger and destruction. It condemned the derelict areas of our country to eternal desolation, and chose as its allies our mortal enemies, the accomplices of the arch-persecutor of our people and the foe of all mankind. The hand that closed the gates of Palestine to our downtrodden brothers, for whose salvation the National Home was endorsed by the nations of the world, opened them to invaders whose purpose it was to prevent the implementation of the international decision and complete the work of the enemy of the human race. Before leaving the country of its trust the Mandatory Government proposes to break the foundations of our achievement and abandon to chaos all that we have built up by the assiduous work of generations. The country which holds out to us the hope of redemption is about to be transformed before our very eyes into a trap for the remnant of Israel.

We have therefore decided, on the authority of the World Zionist Movement and with the agreement of the entire Jewish people, that upon the termination of the Mandatory regime there shall be an end of foreign rule in Palestine. The nation will assume its birthright and establish its national independence in its Homeland.

THE GERM OF THE CONSTITUTION

The second part of the Proclamation of Independence is the most important of the entire document, and it follows directly from the Zionist General Council's declaration quoted above. In Sections 11 and 12 the National Council (composed of representatives of the *Yishuv* and the Zionist Movement, who issued the Proclamation) proclaimed the establishment of a Jewish State in Palestine under the name of Medinat Israel. This brought the State of Israel into legal existence.

For many weeks previously there had been wide discussion in the Hebrew press about the name of the future State. Numerous suggestions were put forward, but no one challenged the name of Israel, for it was generally agreed that it was right for the State to bear the name of its people.

These two sections are in effect the germ of the State's Constitution. The National Council, which was set up at the Zionist General Council's Meeting in 1948, was appointed to act as the Provisional State Council. This was to serve as a provisional Parliament pending a general election. The Parliament, or Constituent Assembly, was to be convened not later than October, 1948 (this date was set in accordance with the United Nations timetable, but for practical reasons the opening of the Constituent Assembly was deferred to February 14, 1949), and it would have the task of deciding upon the Constitution and form of administration. In the meantime, the National Administration, which was elected by the Zionist General Council in April, 1948, would act as a Provisional Government.

Thus, the two principal instruments of government were created; the Provisional State Council, which acted as a Legislature; and the Provisional Government, which acted as the supreme executive authority. The Provisional State Council consisted of thirty-seven members drawn from all parties, ranging from the Communists to the Revisionists and Agudat Israel, an organization opposed to Zionism. The thirteen members of the Provisional

Chaim Weizmann cuts the ribbon symbolizing the gateway to Jerusalem at his inauguration as the first President of Israel (1949). Mrs. Weizmann is on the President's right and Daniel Auster, Mayor of Jerusalem, is at his left.

Government were selected from among the members of the Provisional State Council.

During the succeeding months, a series of amendments and new laws was added to this first piece of legislation. An end was put to all enactments based upon the 1939 White Paper. In order, however, not to create a dangerous legal vacuum, it was decided to retain temporarily the existing laws of the country with such alterations as were rendered necessary by the establishment of the State and the abrogation of the White Paper. What may be termed the "Provisional Constitution" of the State was published on May 19, as a supplement to *Official Gazette No. 2*. It empowered the Provisional State Council to enact legislation, which were to be called Orders to distinguish them from Laws which were to be enacted by the permanent Parliament when it was duly elected. The Orders were to become binding upon publication in the *Official Gazette*. To insure smooth administrative functioning the State was divided into Districts and Sub-Districts.

By virtue of Section 9 of the "Provisional Constitution" the Provisional Government could authorize the Prime Minister, or any other cabinet minister, to make emergency regulations at his discretion for the defense of the State, safeguarding of public security, and the maintenance of essential supplies and services. At the same time all restrictions against immigrants enforced under the Mandatory regime were lifted, so that immigrants who had entered the country "illegally" were now given the same rights as "legal" immigrants.

The Mandate for Palestine was to terminate on Saturday, May 15, 1948; the Independent State of Israel was proclaimed on May 14, 1948.

THE ISRAELI GOVERNMENT

The proclamation of the establishment of the State of Israel on May 14, 1948, declared that the Provisional Council and the Provisional Government would function until the authorities could be chosen by an election. In accordance with a statute to be adopted by the elected Constituent Assembly not later than October 1, 1948, the Provisional Council began its consideration of legislation relative to the Constituent Assembly.

As the outcome of these deliberations, eleven ordinances were promulgated fixing the date of the elections, prescribing their procedure, voting an election budget, and providing assurance that the function of administration would continue until the Constituent Assembly could be inaugurated and convened. The ordinances in question were: Constituent Assembly Election Ordinance 1948 and five amendments; Constituent Assembly Election Ordinance (Elections in the Army) 1948; Constituent Assembly Elections Expenditure Ordinance 1948; Election Budget Ordinance 1948; Transition to the Constituent Assembly Ordinance 1948; Constituent Assembly Ordinance (Declaration of Representatives) 1948.

Elections for the Constituent Assembly were

President Weizmann and the first elected Cabinet of Israel.

An Arab representative addresses the Knesset.

Inside a Jerusalem police station.

Five members of the first Supreme Court of Israel, left to right: Dr. Israel Olshan, Professor Simcha Assaf, Dr. Moishe Smoira, Menachem Dunkle-bloom, and S. S. Chessin. The man in the suit is Dr. Felix Rosen, Minister of Justice.

Ceremony at the opening session of the Knesset in Jerusalem.

Political equality—Arab men and women at the polls.

held on January 25, 1949, in all areas under the jurisdiction of the State of Israel. They were country wide, general, and direct, with equal franchise, secret ballot, and proportional representation. The right of suffrage was granted to every person, man or woman, age eighteen and over, and right of candidature to every person age twenty-one and over. The number of representatives was fixed at one hundred and twenty.

Of the 782,000 inhabitants of the State (713,000 Jews and 69,000 others), registered in the population census of November 8, 1948, 506,567 were found eligible to vote. Of these 440,095 men and women (86.8 per cent of the eligible voters) went to the polls.

The Constituent Assembly as elected was drawn from the following Parties: the Workers Party of Israel (Mapai), 46 representatives; United Workers Party (Mapam), 19: United Religious Front, 16 (Poale Mizrachi 6, Mizrachi 4, Agudat Israel 3, Poale Agudat Israel 3); Freedom Movement (Herut), 14; General Zionists, 7; Progressive Party, 5; Sephardic Community, 4; Israel Communist Party, 4; Democratic List of Nazareth (Arab list), 4; Women's International Zionist Organization, 1; Yemenite Community, 1; the Fighters (Halohamim), 1.

On February 14, 1949, in Jerusalem, the Constituent Assembly was inaugurated in the Jewish Agency Building by the President of the Provisional State Council, Dr. Chaim Weizmann.

In the six sessions held in Jerusalem, the foundation was laid for the new State and its working Legislature. The representatives pledged their allegiance and appointed Steering, Minor Constitution, Transitional, and Credentials Committees. The Speaker of the Knesset (Joseph Sprinzak) and two Deputy Speakers (Nahum Nir Rafalkes and Joseph Burg) were elected.

The Assembly adopted the Minor Constitution Law of 1949, providing that the Legislature be called the Knesset, the Constituent Assembly the First Knesset, and a representative of the Constituent Assembly a Member of the Knesset.

On February 16, 1949, the First Knesset elected Dr. Chaim Weizmann to be President of the State. On the following day, after the inauguration of President Weizmann, the sessions in Jerusalem were adjourned.

On February 17, the Provisional Government submitted its resignation to the President. Following consultation with the representatives of the various Parties in the Knesset, the President charged David Ben Gurion, the leader of Mapai, the largest Party in the Knesset, with the task of forming a permanent Government.

In the seventh session, which opened in Tel Aviv

Inmates of a Government reformatory help masons mix cement as part of their rehabilitation program.

A Tel Aviv police officer writes a summons for a traffic violation.

on March 8, 1949, Ben Gurion submitted proposals for a permanent Government and its program. The composition of the Government was based on a coalition of four Parties, Mapai, the United Religious Front, the Progressive Party, and the Sephardim. Ministerial offices were assigned as follows: Ben Gurion, Prime Minister and Minister of Defense; Dr. Dov Joseph, Minister of Supply and Rationing; Rabbi Itzak Meir Levin, Minister of Social Welfare; Mrs. Golda Myerson, Minister of Labor and Social Insurance; Rabbi Yehuda Leib Hacohen Maimon, Minister for Religious Affairs; Eliezer Kaplan, Minister of Finance; Dr. Pinhas Rosen, Minister of Justice; David Remez, Minister of Communications; Zalman Shazar, Minister of Education and Culture; Behar Shalom Shitreet, Minister of Police; Moshe Shapiro, Minister of the Interior, Immigration and Health; Moshe Sharett, Minister for Foreign Affairs.

On March 10, 1949, the first permanent Government, thus constituted, was approved by the Knesset in a vote of confidence, 73 voting in favor and 45 against. This launched the State upon a course of ordered, parliamentary government.

The first session of the Knesset lasted from its inauguration in Jerusalem in February until the recess which began on September 12. During the second session, opened on November 7, 1949, and adjourned on March 29, 1950, the Prime Minister announced the Cabinet's decision to transfer the government offices from Tel Aviv to Jerusalem, the

capital of Israel. On December 26, 1949, the Knesset established its seat in the capital.

Ten years have passed since the first Government of Israel took in its hands the destiny of a country, performing in one decade the superhuman task of organizing immigration and resettlement, of integrating the people who came from the West with those who came from the Orient and Africa, of building up the strongest democratic force in the Middle East, and of establishing good relations on diplomatic and domestic fronts.

Israel had two major Government crises. The first occurred in October, 1950: the issue was ministerial reorganization intensified by the acute educational problem in the camps and *maabarot*. This crisis led to the dissolution of the first Knesset and new elections were held on July 30, 1951. The second crisis was initiated by the resignation of Rabbi Y. M. Levin, a representative of the Agudat Israel faction, in protest against inducting Orthodox women into the national service. At the same time there was bitter dissension about the economic policy of the Government. This crisis broke the United Religious Front, which Ben Gurion succeeded in putting together again by December, 1952. He formed a new coalition Government with a broader parliamentary basis including the General Zionists. As a result of his exhaustive work, Ben Gurion was forced to resign because of fatigue in December, 1953, and Moshe Sharett, who also held the portfolio of the foreign ministry, became Prime Minister of Israel. After a year-long vacation, Ben Gurion was able to return to the cabinet as Minister of Defense.

A religious court hears a dispute between a settler from Morocco and one from Iran.

The two highest religious authorities in Israel—Chief Rabbi Isaac Halevi Herzog of the Ashkenazic community *(right)* and Rabbi Nisim of the Sephardic and Oriental communities.

Israeli policewomen are trained as traffic officers.

Israel's post boxes are marked in Hebrew, Arabic, and French.

Headquarters of the National Institutions in Jerusalem—the Jewish Agency, Jewish National Fund, and the Keren Hayesod.

The installation ceremony for the Menorah presented to the Knesset by the British Parliament.

Later that same year friction between the two major coalition parties, the Labor Party and the General Zionist Party, became critical. They were divided on the question of the Government's attitude in relation to the case of Dr. Kastner, a Zionist leader from Hungary who was accused of collaboration with the Nazis during the Second World War. The coalition with the General Zionists remained until a few months before the election of the Third Knesset on July 26, 1955, when a new Government was formed from a coalition of all labor groups, the progressives, and the national religious blocs with Ben Gurion as Prime Minister. This Government was approved by the Knesset on September 2, 1955, with a vote of 73 to 32. There was some Cabinet reshuffling in 1956, and again in 1958, following a short-lived Government crisis. After the national elections of November, 1959, a new Cabinet was formed. Its members are as follows:

DAVID BEN GURION, Prime Minister and Minister of Defense

MOSHE DAYAN, Minister of Agriculture

PINHAS SAPIR, Minister of Commerce and Industry

YITZHAK BEN-AHARON, Minister of Communications

MORDECHAI BENTOV, Minister of Development

LEVI ESHKOL, Minister of Finance

GOLDA MEIR, Minister for Foreign Affairs

MOSHE SHAPIRA, Minister of the Interior

PINHAS ROSEN, Minister of Justice

ISRAEL BARZILAI, Minister of Health

GIORA JOSEPHTAL, Minister of Labor

BECHOR SHITREET, Minister of Police

YAACOV MOSHE TOLEDANO, Minister of Religious Affairs

JOSEPH BURG, Minister of Social Welfare

ABBA EBAN, Minister of Education

Constitutional Enactments. Israel has no comprehensive written Constitution. It has, however, a number of basic laws covering the same areas of Government, the most important of which are:

1. The Law and Administration Ordinance of 1948, and the Transition Law of 1949, organizing the Legislative and Executive authorities and demarcating their functions.

2. The Second Knesset Elections Law of 1951.

3. The State President (Tenure) Law of 1952, dealing with the election of the President and his office.

4. The Law of Return, 1950, conferring upon every Jew the right to immigrate into Israel.

5. The Nationality Law, 1952, which provides that Israel nationality may be acquired by virtue of "return" (in accordance with the Law of Return, 1950), by residence in Israel, by birth, or by naturalization.

6. The Law of Equal Rights for Women, 1951, establishing complete legal equality between men and women.

7. The Judges' Law of 1953, establishing an independent Judiciary.

The Legislature. The Israel Legislature, or Knesset, is a one-chamber parliament of one-hundred and twenty members, elected under a system of proportional representation for a four-year term by secret ballot and universal direct suffrage. The Third Knesset was elected on July 26, 1955.

Legislation is generally initiated by the Government, but sometimes by Knesset Committees or individual members of the Knesset. A Bill requires three readings before it becomes law; between the first and the second reading it passes, for discussion

Chief Rabbi Herzog greets President Weizmann on the first Independence Day as Foreign Minister Sharett looks on.

Mrs. Chaim Weizmann places a wreath on her husband's grave.

103

Yitzhak Ben Zvi, Israel's second President, examines a Biblical manuscript over six hundred years old.

and possible amendment, through one of the nine committees of the Knesset. All laws and secondary legislation are published in *Reshumot* (*Official Gazette*).

The following are the political parties represented in the Third Knesset, elected on July 26, 1955. The results for the First Knesset, elected on January 25, 1949, and the Second Knesset, elected on July 30 1951, are given for comparison.

The President. The President of the State is elected by the Knesset for a five-year term of office.

The powers and functions of the President, as laid down in the Transition Law of 1949, and in the State President (Tenure) Law of 1952, are to entrust the formation of the Government to a member of the Knesset; to receive the Government's resignation; to sign treaties with foreign states; to appoint diplomatic representatives; to receive diplomatic representatives from abroad; to confirm the appointment in Israel of consuls of foreign states; to grant amnesty to offenders and commute their sentences; and to appoint judges.

The first President was Dr. Chaim Weizmann, who held office until his death on November 9, 1952. Mr. Yitzhak Ben Zvi was elected President

of the State on December 8, 1952, and was reelected for the third term on October 30, 1957.

The Executive. The President, after consultation with the parties represented in the Knesset, appoints a member of the Knesset to form the Government. The Cabinet is made up of the Prime Minister and a number of Ministers who may or may not be members of the Knesset. Up to the present, only two members of the Cabinet have not been members of the Knesset.

The Government is constitutionally instituted upon obtaining a vote of confidence from the Knesset and holds office as long as it maintains the confidence of the Knesset.

The Judiciary. The judicial system comprises civil and religious courts.

The civil courts are:

(a) The Supreme Court composed of a President and eight Associate Justices. This court also sits as High Court of Justice.

(b) District courts, sitting in Jerusalem, Tel Aviv, and Haifa.

Mr. and Mrs. Ben Gurion return from Sdeh Boker, the settlement in the Negev where they lived as private citizens during Ben Gurion's temporary retirement from Government office (1954).

Golda Meir is enthusiastically welcomed by the Jews of Moscow as she leaves the synagogue on the High Holy Days in 1948. when she served as Israel's first Ambassador to the Soviet Union.

(c) Magistrates courts.

Religious courts of the Jewish, Moslem, Christian, and Druse communities exercise jurisdiction in certain personal matters such as marriage and divorce.

All Judges of the civil courts are appointed by the President of the State upon the recommendation of an Appointments Committee of nine members, three of whom are Justices of the Supreme Court, including its President, two members of the Cabinet, one of whom is Minister of Justice who serves as Chairman of the Committee, two members of the Knesset, and two practicing lawyers designated by the Bar.

The State Comptroller. The State Comptroller is appointed by the President of the State on the recommendation of the House Committee of the Knesset for a term of five years. The Comptroller is responsible only to the Knesset to which he submits his reports.

Administrative Divisions. The country is divided into six administrative districts. The Jerusalem, Tel Aviv, and Haifa districts are mainly urban;

the Northern, Central, and Southern districts are mainly rural. Each district is divided into subdistricts, and is headed by a District Commissioner.

Local Government. The local governments are administered by councils elected by the community residents. The heads of these councils are elected in turn by the council members. Each unit of local government establishes its bylaws and fixes its budget subject to the approval of the Minister of the Interior. Its activities are financed by local taxation and Government subsidy.

As of December 31, 1956, there were 941 centers of population in Israel.

The Government has initiated and encouraged local self-government in the Arab communities. For almost all of them this has been their first experience in democracy and self-government. There are now two Arab municipalities and twelve local Arab councils. (As of January, 1958, there· were about one thousand centers of population in Israel.)

Language. The official language of the State is Hebrew, although Arabic is extensively used for

President Ben Zvi with the Coalition Government (December 22, 1952).

the benefit of Arab citizens in official forms and publications and on coins and stamps. Knesset speeches are simultaneously translated into Arabic for the benefit of Arab members.

The Government and Religion. THE STATE OF ISRAEL . . . will be based on freedom, justice and peace as envisaged by the prophets of Israel; it will ensure complete equality of social and political rights to all its inhabitants irrespective of religion, conscience, language, education and culture; it will safeguard the Holy Places of all religions . . . (Declaration of Independence, May 14, 1948).

The Sabbath and the Jewish festivals, namely the two days of New Year, the Day of Atonement, the first day of the Feast of Tabernacles and the Eighth Day of Solemn Assembly, the first and seventh days of Passover and the Feast of Pentecost, shall be the prescribed days of rest in the State of Israel.

Non-Jews shall have the right to observe their own Sabbath and festivals as rest days (Days of Rest Ordinance, 5708–1948).

An employee's weekly rest shall be not less than thirty-six consecutive hours in the week.

The weekly rest shall include—

(1) In the case of a Jew, the Sabbath day;

(2) In the case of a person other than a Jew, the Sabbath day or Sunday or Friday, whichever is ordinarily observed by him as his weekly day of rest (Hours of Work and Rest Law, 5711–1951).

The Government of Israel, through the Ministry for Religious Affairs, assists the various religious communities in their activities. The Ministry has special departments for Jewish, Moslem, Christian, Druse, and Bahai communities which carry out their functions without Government intervention. The religious courts of the respective communities are autonomous, with jurisdiction in matters of marriage and divorce over members of their respective communities.

The rapidly increasing Jewish population and the establishment of about 450 new settlements necessitated the expansion of facilities for religious services and activities. The number of Rabbis and *Dayanim* (Judges in Rabbinical Courts) increased from 130 in 1948 to more than 400 in 1957. The number of synagogues rose from about 600 in 1948 to 2,853 in 1953. In 1954, 377 synagogues were established with the assistance of the Ministry for Religious Affairs.

The Chief Rabbinate is the highest Rabbinical authority in the country and serves as a Court of Appeal from the local Rabbinical Courts. There are two Chief Rabbis—one represents the Ashkenazic community, the other, Sephardic Jewry.

The Military Rabbinate appoints chaplains, supervises *Kashrut,* and provides religious services and rituals for soldiers in the Israel Defense Forces. The serving of non-kosher food is prohibited in all military as well as in other Government establishments.

The Religious Council, a representative body of the local religious community, appoints and pays the Rabbis, assists in the establishment and maintenance of synagogues, and supervises *Kashrut.* The number of Religious Councils increased from ten in 1948, to about two hundred in 1956. The bulk of their expenditures is covered by the Treasury of the Government.

The Civil Service. The Government appoints a Civil Service Commissioner who approves the establishments of Government Departments and

Labor leader Beryl Locker addresses the twenty-fourth Zionist Congress in Jerusalem (1956).

The Japanese Minister and his wife, on their way to congratulate President Ben Zvi on his re-election in 1957, pass an honor guard composed of women members of the Israeli Defense Forces.

institutions subordinated to them, within the limits of the approved budget, and the division of functions and powers between and within the administrative divisions. He must also establish, within the framework of Government decisions, arrangements for appointments, up-grading, etc. and approve appointments in all grades; propose to the Departments and to the Government methods of efficient Civil Service; organize and maintain institutions for training and education of Government employees; encourage the establishment of social services for Government employees and represent the Government in supervising them; foster good relations with the staff representatives in regard to working conditions, staff rights, etc.; coordinate working conditions with local authorities and public institutions; enforce administrative regulations in Government institutions; and deal with legislation in the field of Civil Service.

There is a Civil Service Commission, with advisory functions, consisting of the Civil Service Commissioner, the Directors General of the Ministries of Finance, Labor, Social Welfare, Justice, and Internal Affairs, the Postmaster General, and the Director of the Budget.

Government Employees. The total number of employees in the Civil Service on March 31, 1957 was 40,775, including 7,372 policemen, guards, and prison staff, 1,424 port employees, 2,473 railway employees, and 680 other communications employees.

These figures include permanent, temporary, and casual employees, but do not include teachers, soldiers in the regular army, civilian employees in the defense forces and military enterprises, and local personnel of embassies, legations, and consulates abroad.

Salaries. The basic salary scale is as follows:

Grade	Basic Salary
	I£*
2	430
3	345
4	270
5	210
7	155
8	135
9	100
10	92
11	85
12	78
13	72
14	68
15	63

*£—Israeli Pound—equivalent to 55 cents.

Basic salaries are supplemented by family and seniority allowances and by a variable cost-of-living allowance, which on June 1, 1957, ranged from about I£ .94 to I£ .140 according to salary.

There are special scales for doctors, engineers, lawyers, and other professional employees in the Government service.

Police. The Israel Police Force is controlled by National Police Headquarters, which is divided

The French Ambassador greets the President of Israel in the name of the Diplomatic Corps on Independence Day (1957).

A delegation from Ghana meets with the Prime
Minister to establish economic relations.

Prime Minister Ben Gurion, wearing a skullcap
(yarmulka), greets the fifth convention of Poale
Agudat Israel.

Leaders of the Ahdut Haavoda Party.

President Ben Zvi takes the oath of office in the Knesset.

Members of the new Cabinet with President Ben Zvi (1958).

into three Departments—Administration, Organization, and Investigation. The Force is divided territorially into Districts, Sub-Districts, Stations, and Posts.

The strength of the Israel Police Force is 5,991, including 341 officers, 282 policewomen, and 373 Arab and Druse policemen. The personnel are 17.5 per cent Israel-born 46 per cent born in European countries, 18.5 per cent in countries in Asia, and 18 per cent in North Africa.

Local Government Finances:

	I£
Total Budgets—1955 to 56	
Municipalities	81,622,400
Local Councils	17,738,400
Regional Councils	7,636,000
Total	106,996,800
Extraordinary Budgets—1955–56 (Capital Works):	
Construction of Sewers	1,810,200
Waterworks	1,434,300
Electricity	780,000
Roads and Pavements	1,403,000
Public Gardens	105,000
Markets, Abbatoirs, Garages	725,100
Street Lighting, Shelters	999,500
Sundry Public Works	474,200
Total I£	8,731,700

ZIONIST INSTITUTIONS

Before the establishment of the State of Israel in 1948, the World Zionist Organization and the Jewish Agency were responsible for the activities aimed at the establishment of a Jewish National Home in Palestine.

With the establishment of the State of Israel there was a division of tasks between the Government of Israel and the Jewish Agency, which was defined in the World Zionist Organization Status Law of 1952 and in a Covenant between the Jewish Agency and the Government signed by both parties in 1954.

The functions of the Jewish Agency include the organization of immigration abroad, the transfer of immigrants and their property to Israel, participation in the absorption of immigrants in Israel, youth immigration, agricultural settlement, land acquisition and amelioration through the Keren Kayemet le-Israel (Jewish National Fund), participation in development projects, the encouragement of private investments, aid for cultural projects and institutions of higher learning, the raising of funds to finance these activities, and the coordination of the activities in Israel of Jewish organizations functioning in these spheres with the aid of public funds, all in accordance with the laws of Israel.

The approved budget of the Jewish Agency for the Hebrew calendar year ending September, 1956, amounted to $89,069,444. The main item of expenditure was $38,611,111 for agricultural settlement. The other major items were immigration, absorption, and Youth Aliyah.

The Jewish Agency has been instrumental in bringing some seven hundred eighty thousand immigrants to Israel and is now engaged in the consolidation of some 440 agricultural settlements which have been established under its auspices,

Menachem Begin *(seated),* **leader of the Herut Party and former head of the Irgun, attends a political rally in 1948. The placard reads: "Freedom—Fatherland."**

Representatives of the Hapoel Hamizrachi Party celebrate their decision to join Ben Gurion's Coalition Government (1952).

most of which are new immigrants' villages.

Keren Kayemet le-Israel (Jewish National Fund), founded in 1901, is engaged primarily in land redemption, soil reclamation and reforestation. Jewish National Fund land cannot be sold, and is allotted to settlers on the basis of a forty-nine-year hereditary lease. By the end of 1955, the land held by the J.N.F. amounted to 855,750 acres; 584 agricultural settlements and 79,000 housing units have been established on J.N.F. land.

The J.N.F. has reclaimed 47,075 acres of land previously considered uncultivable and has planted 27,500 acres of forest land.

Keren Hayesod (United Israel Appeal, founded in 1920) is the central financial instrument of the Jewish Agency. The income of the Keren Hayesod is derived mainly from contributions by Jews both in Israel and abroad.

From the establishment of the State to September, 1955, the Jewish Agency and the Keren Heyesod have spent more than $230,000,000, mainly on immigration and settlement.

Youth Aliyah (founded in 1934 for the purpose of rescuing Jewish children from Nazi Germany) is engaged mainly in the rehabilitation and training of youth. Some fifteen thousand children and youths are being trained this year in agricultural work. Since its establishment, Youth Aliyah has brought to Israel, and cared for, about seventy-five thousand children from seventy different countries, who have established seventy-nine agricultural settlements.

A Joint Government-Jewish Agency Coordination Board, consisting of an equal number of representatives of both bodies, coordinates the ac-tivities of the Executive of the Jewish Agency and the Government of Israel in all spheres governed by the "Status Law" and the "Covenant."

ISRAEL BONDS

The State of Israel Bond Issue was approved by the Knesset and went into operation on May 1, 1951. The two issues—the Independence Issue, which terminated on May 1, 1954, and the Development Issue, which began on the same date—have resulted in the sale of close to three hundred fifty million dollars worth of bonds.

The revenue from Israel Bond sales enters the State's Development Budget. Since Bond sales began in 1951, Bond allocations represent 35 per cent of the total Development Budget outlay. As of the end of fiscal year 1955–56, almost two hundred million dollars had been injected into Israel's economy.

PRIME MINISTER BEN GURION'S NINE-POINT PROGRAM

A nine-point program for Israel's development and growth during the country's second ten years

Ezra Taft Benson, United States Secretary of Agriculture, visits Prime Minister Ben Gurion in Hadassah Hospital in Jerusalem. Ben Gurion was injured when a grenade, thrown by a psychotic, exploded in the Knesset (1957).

was outlined by the Prime Minister on November 1, 1957, in a statement read to one hundred American Jewish leaders (members of the United Jewish Appeal study mission which arrived from the United States for an eight-day survey on October 23, 1957):

As I see it, we must attain the following goals during the next ten years:

1. Welcome, absorb, and integrate additional hundreds of thousands of our brethren from distant lands who yearn to come to Israel, to walk in dignity and raise their children as free Jews. It is my hope that these will include our brethren from Eastern Europe.

2. Complete the integration of the multitudes who have already come.

3. Complete our long-range irrigation plan and the Jordan River project so that water from the abundant North can bring life to the arid South, as a primary move in the conquest of the Negev desert.

4. Cover the Negev with a rich network of agricultural settlements, cities, rail and road communication pipelines, industrial plants and mineral workings, and a large port at Eilat.

5. Establish peaceful relations with our Arab neighbors.

6. Prepare the country for the utilization of Atomic Energy for constructive development.

7. Maintain and strengthen the spirit of pioneering of our people.

8. Continue raising our standards of education with twin accents on the teaching of our ancient Hebrew Prophets and the knowledge of modern science.

9. Strengthen the bonds between Israel and World Jewry.

Ben Gurion pointed out that the efforts of Jewish communities abroad and of the people of Israel formed a "historic partnership," adding that "we all have a right to be comforted and inspired by our joint accomplishments in the last nine years, in the development of our land, and the refashioning of our people."

Following the Prime Minister's statement, the members of the Mission adopted a resolution which strongly recommended that, in 1958, American Jewish communities give the United Jewish Appeal a mandate to raise "special funds" to insure the complete absorption of the more than eighty thousand refugees who reached Israel in the last year and to advance the reception and integration of the seventy thousand who are expected this year.

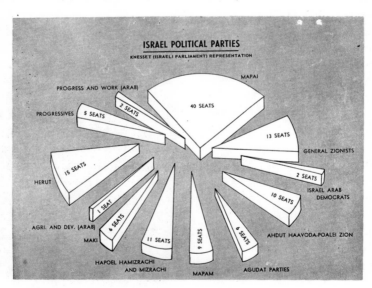

112

7 ARMY AND DEFENSE

The giant strides of progress made by the State of Israel have turned this tiny country into the most virile, healthy, and constructive democracy in the Middle East. Nowhere is this advance recorded in more spectacular and dramatic fashion than in the development of Israel's Defense Forces.

Israel's history of expansion and advance in all fields of endeavor is a history of birth amid chaos, followed by improvisation amid hardship, and planning in the teeth of intangibles. This is true of the development of the Israeli Army.

In May, 1948, in the midst of anarchy created by British departure and the simultaneous aggression of Israel's neighbors, the men and women of the Hagana, the nucleus of the national Army, served as the advance guard of the new State and flung themselves into the breaches. They were joined by every able-bodied man and woman in the country, quickly organized into a people's force to keep the enemy at bay and preserve the State from destruction. They were gloriously victorious.

With the end of this war came a breathing spell. The defense forces of the country had to be more rationally and effectively organized to safeguard the sovereignty of the new State. For the first time the Jews of Israel had to make the transition from an underground-defense force to an open and legal defense arm of the State. It had to be planned, organized, trained, and equipped. Before the creation of the State, Hagana had to defend Jewish life and property from local Arab attacks clandestinely, with all the limitation on arms, firepower, and organization imposed by its illegality. The defense force of the new State had to safeguard the country from possible attack by all the neighboring Arab states, keep the skies clear of enemy aircraft, and the coastline free of enemy vessels.

It had to be suited to the pattern of life in Israel and to the country's needs, resources, and purposes. The machinery of the State was dedicated to the ingathering and integration of immigrants. Government and Army leaders had to devise an eco-nomical and effective scheme of defense which would not drain the entire resources of the State. Immigrants had to be housed, clothed, and fed. The wilderness had to be cultivated, swamps drained, desert tracts reclaimed, roads built, ports extended, new airfields laid down, houses, schools, hospitals, and private dwellings constructed.

Israel's leaders realized that such projects could also serve for defense purposes. A well-settled population in a developed and built-up country is far more difficult to conquer than an open stretch of sterile desert. They succeeded in utilizing their limited physical and financial resources through skillful planning and efficient organization.

Israel has a long land frontier dividing it from its neighbors—these are hostile neighbors who waged an unsuccessful war of aggression against the new State and threaten another attack.

Soldiers of the Israel Army.

113

Immediately after the Declaration of Independence, leaders of the former Hagana meet to establish the Association of Hagana Members.

Israeli women—an integral part of the fighting force—learn to throw grenades.

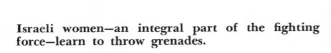

Israeli soldiers receive intensive training in the skills of modern warfare.

Members of the religious party, Poale Agudat Israel, receive military training.

Immigrant soldiers are taught Hebrew in an Israeli Army camp.

The Army of Israel not only fights, but also tills the soil. These youngsters are members of the Army's agricultural training program, Nahal.

Such are the special factors which have molded the distinctive features of Israel's system of defense. The land force has changed considerably since the time, in early 1948, when its heaviest weapon was a .20 mm. gun and the main weapon of the soldier was a Sten.

As with the land forces, the Air Force and Navy started from modest beginnings at the outbreak of the War of Liberation, achieved a noteworthy record during the fighting, and have since grown into highly developed services. The Navy had few facilities in May, 1948, but managed in October

The divisional emblem of the Infantry.

of that year to sink the Egyptian flagship off the coast of Gaza. The Air Force, which started the war with only a few Piper Cubs, succeeded in bringing down a number of enemy planes by the following December and January. Since then the Air Force has acquired a good deal more aircraft, including jets, and has opened training schools for pilots. Similarly, the parachute units now receive their entire training in Israel training camps.

ISRAEL'S DEFENSE FORCES

The General Staff. The three services—Army, Navy and Air Force—are integrated into a single

A unit of the Israeli Army marches through Jerusalem.

military structure known as the Israel Defense Forces. The Chief of Staff, who holds the rank of a Major General, and the General Staff are the top command of all three services. The General Staff consists of a Chief of Operations, the commanders of the Navy and the Air Force, the commanding officers of the Northern, Central, and Southern Ground Commands, the Adjutant General, the Quartermaster General, the Director of Training, and the Director of Intelligence. All these officers are Brigadiers.

Israel's defense system is based on four broad elements: the Regular Army, the National Conscript Services, the Reserves, and the Frontier Settlements. Behind these four elements stands the entire nation, ready at a moment's notice to commit its life and resources to the defense of the State.

The Regular Army. The Regular Army is the

The Camel Corps of the Army.

116

The Army displays its heavy tanks in Tel Aviv.

basic nucleus of the armed forces of the State of Israel. All members of the Regular Army are volunteers. Since the Army of Israel is a skilled, trained, and mobile force, it attracts the young Israeli of above average intelligence. It consists primarily of men who either possess or are capable of being trained at special skills. To keep abreast of the latest technical developments in military science, the Army, Air Force, and Navy require a high cultural standard.

The Regular Army came into being in 1950.

Since then it has made great strides with the number of volunteers exceeding the number capable of being absorbed. Regular Army officers can sign for two or five years of service. Longer terms of service are likely to be introduced in the near future.

The Regular Army maintains specialist schools, under the direction of the Training Command, which offer courses in all branches of the Army, Navy, and Air Force. In the spring of 1954, a staff officer's school was inaugurated for command and

A polling station in the field for soldiers on duty.

The Druse village of Yarka in Galilee sponsors a Druse unit of the Israeli Army.

The Women's Corps of Israel's Defense Force marches in Ramle on Independence Day.

Druse soldiers in an Independence Day parade.

top duties. Prior to this they had been sent abroad for military instruction. Other officers are attending the Hebrew University and the Israel Institute of Technology.

Rigid impartiality is the principle in the selection of officer personnel, both in the Conscript and Regular Army. Acceptance into commissioned ranks and promotion are based solely on merit. Neither length of citizenship, nor wealth, nor age affect the appointment of commissions or promotions. The Israel Regular Army has the largest number of young, high-ranking officers of any army in the world.

Conscript Service. The second major element in Israel's defense system is the National Conscript Service. This is the service which all young men and women perform on reaching the age of eighteen. Men of the age group eighteen to twenty-six now serve for two and a half years; unmarried women serve for two years. Women may be exempted from military service on religious grounds but, under the National Service Law of 1953, they are obligated to devote the same period of time to national service of a non-military character—in agricultural, health, educational, or social welfare services. The administration of this service is in the hands of the Ministry of Labor.

The nature of Israel's Conscript Service is unique. It is the only country in the world in which part of the service must be spent in agricultural training. This underlines the twin elements—military defense and pioneering—which form the principal design in the pattern of defense-service training, for Israel is a land with large stretches of arid wilderness that need to be settled and defended. It is a country which maintains a policy of mass immigration. The newcomers are a heterogeneous group of people with different case histories, social backgrounds, habits, and customs. The growth of the State is dependent upon their adjustment. They must become members of an integrated society, learn to speak the national language, Hebrew, and be trained in the democratic standards of Israel. The Conscript Service is designed to integrate the young newcomer quickly and effectively into his new life and, at the same time, provide defense for the unsettled territory.

A Navy unit.

The Israeli Air Force celebrates Independence Day.

Marines stand at attention during a Navy parade.

Military police with their trained dogs.

The destroyers *Eilat* and *Yaffo* at Haifa.

The destroyer *Miznak* in the Strait of Tiran.

The Israeli conscript may be drafted into a branch of the Army known as Nahal—mnemonic for "Noar Halutzi Lochem" (Fighting and Pioneering Youth). Wearing the Nahal badge of sword-blade and scythe, they undergo an intensive three-month course in military training. At the end of this period they are posted in groups in an agricultural settlement, usually on a frontier, and for the next nine months serve as agricultural apprentices. At the end of the year, the individual conscript has the choice of either joining a frontier settlement with his group or of spending the balance of his term in service solely on military duties.

The civilian and military advantages of such a system are numerous. Agricultural work develops physical well-being. Many new immigrants come from countries where both body and spirit have been undernourished. Moreover, contact with the land prompts tangible interest and knowledge of the soil which these conscripts may have to defend one day. Work on the land often initiates a lasting interest in agriculture, while contact with veteran settlers in the neighboring agricultural villages assists in the psychological integration of the new immigrant. Agricultural training within the scope of the Conscript Service helps to develop a "one hand on the plow and the other on the sword" outlook which is vital in a frontier community where constant vigilance is the sole condition of survival.

In the four years since its birth, Nahal has been responsible for the establishment of fifteen new frontier settlements, many in areas in which there had been no previous settlement, and has provided much-needed reserves for thirty-nine settlements throughout the country.

When Nahal was established, the outcome of the experiment was dubious, but both the idea and

121

A wounded Arab marauder receives first-aid from Israeli frontier policemen.

its execution have proved successful in stimulating pioneer settlement among young Israelis, in increasing the number of youngsters interested in agriculture, and in carrying out a vital education purpose among the new immigrants. The young immigrant who has served in Nahal emerges from the service as an integral part of the citizenry of Israel, familiar with the country and its language, its customs, its history, and its traditions.

The Reserves. The third major defense element is the Reserves. In terms of size it is by far the most important element in Israel's defense system. All men up to the age of forty-nine and women without children up to the age of thirty-four are eligible for Reserve service. Reservists up to the age of thirty-nine are liable to be called for one month every year for training with their Reserve unit; for those between the ages of thirty-nine to forty-nine the annual service is two weeks.

Members of the Poale Agudat Israel man a machine-gun in a practice drill at a *kibbutz* near the Jordanian border.

The Reserves is designed to facilitate Israel's need to direct all its energies toward absorbing mass immigration and settlement. But this function would be futile if the country could not be safeguarded against attack. With a considerable part of the population under arms, the country would be strong in defense but unproductive, yet, if all are engaged in production, the country would be developed, but would fall an easy prey to aggression. The system of Reserves in the Israel Army is designed so that the bulk of the population may be kept on productive jobs in field and factory almost up to the moment of attack. A mobilization method has been devised which enables the Israeli reservist to be called up, equipped, and posted to the front within a very short time.

On registration, the reservist is posted to a territorial unit and assigned a code word. In time of

A civilian stands guard on the outskirts of his settlement.

emergency the code words are announced by radio, poster, newspaper listing, letter, or telegram. The moment the reservist hears or sees his code word he knows exactly where he has to report so that the entire unit can be rushed off to any point in the country by land, sea, or air in a matter of hours.

FRONTIER SETTLEMENTS

During Israel's War of Liberation the settlements along Israel's frontiers performed valiant service. Military experts estimate that settlements like Negba, which stopped the Egyptians in the south, and Ein Gev, Dagania, and Gesher, which stopped the Syrians and Jordanians in the northeast and east, performed military tasks with a comparative handful of members that would otherwise

Prime Minister David Ben Gurion assists in fortifying a settlement.

Yemenite settlers prepare to start out on a defense patrol.

Non-Military Activities. No record of Israel's Defense Forces would be complete without mention of its extra-military activities. The Israel Army is probably the most significant adult education instrument in the State. The Army devotes a great deal of time, attention, and energy to general education. This is necessary because of the heterogeneous group of personnel. The teaching of Hebrew is mandatory and general educational subjects are requisites on the standard curriculum of all units. The Army also publishes a daily newspaper in voweled Hebrew for new immigrant soldiers and an illustrated weekly.

The Army is responsible for a good deal of social welfare work. Most notable was its "Operation *Maabarot*" in which the Army sent its engineers, doctors, nurses, teachers, and ordinary personnel to many of the *maabarot* to ease conditions during the heavy winter rains, maintaining the morale of the immigrants during the winters of 1950 and 1951. By 1952, conditions in the *maabarot* had sufficiently improved to make Army help unnecessary.

These extra-military activities underscore the theory that Army training involves guidance not only in the art of warfare, but also in the art of citizenship. Young men and women emerge from the Army as public-spirited members of society, capable of assuming responsible positions in the service of the nation in war and in peace.

THE SINAI CAMPAIGN

From the moment the State of Israel became a reality the Arab states began to prepare for and

have had to be undertaken by almost two battalions of regular troops.

It is axiomatic that in war people fighting on their own soil show a higher mettle than those fighting on an unfamiliar, distant battlefield. The pioneer settler who has created something out of nothing with his own hands is usually prepared to defend it to the very end. In no other terms can one explain the victory in the battle of the settlements where, in every case, they faced a vastly superior display of firepower and armor.

Chen. All women serving in the Army, at whatever post or duty, belong to the Chen, mnemonic for "Chail Nashim" (Women's Army—as a noun Chen means "charm"). Each woman soldier releases a man for combat duty, of utmost importance in view of Israeli's limited population. Women in the Defense Forces act as clerks, storekeepers, communication workers, telephonists, teleprinters, radio workers, nurses, sanitary workers, mechanics, and even non-combatant pilots. As such they are attached within their own special units to all three services and the ground command.

A first-aid station is set up in Jerusalem during a civil-defense drill.

124

Mother and child leave a trench shelter after the all-clear is sounded.

After his day's chores are completed, this civilian truckdriver does guard duty above the copper mines of Timna.

An armed guard at an agricultural training institute in southern Israel.

Heavy mortar units of the Israeli Army.

An Israeli gun crew springs into action on a motor torpedo boat during exercises in Haifa Bay.

A signal corps armed truck on maneuvers.

A jet fighter on a training flight.

Members of the Women's Corps train under simulated battle conditions.

promote armed conflict. Egypt, Syria, and Iraq enlarged their armies and organized armored formations, each with several hundred medium-heavy tanks. Their air forces acquired from the Western Powers (especially Great Britain) seven hundred fighters and fighter-bombers, one-third of them jets.

Israel was not lacking in diligence and ingenuity. The little country intended to be ready when the stockpiling of war and the tide of destructive propaganda could no longer be contained. As might be expected, events during 1955 and 1956 kindled the military campfires and accelerated the ratio of gloved diplomacy to iron-fisted war preparation. The Suez base, equipped with fifty thousand tons of ammunition, eleven ultra modern airfields with maximum radar and anti-aircraft

paraphernalia, 300,000 tons of engineering stores and mines, 80,000 tons of fuel, and 2,000 combat vehicles was transferred from British to Egyptian control.

The Baghdad Pact and the assistance supplied by the United States and Britain to Iraq, a country which was consistently hostile to Israel and had not even concluded an armistice agreement with it, comprised the second vital event, tripling the strength of Iraqi artillery by increasing its armored force ten-fold with one hundred thirty Centurion tanks, and its Air Force, which had control of eighty planes before the conclusion of the Pact, with one hundred eighty jet fighters and fighter bombers.

The last and most decisive step in the material preparations of the Arabs was the so-called arms deal between Egypt and Czechoslovakia, made public in September, 1955. On the strength of this deal the Eastern Bloc delivered to Egypt two hundred T-34 medium tanks, one hundred JS-3 heavy tanks, sixty SU-100 self-propelled guns, two hundred fifty Mig 15 and 17 jet fighters, sixty IL-28 jet bombers, two very modern destroyers, and a number of M.T.Bs., several hundred artillery pieces of all types, and a vast amount of small arms, transport, and communications equipment.

In view of the quantity and type of armaments purchased, there could be no doubt that Egypt was preparing for Blitzkrieg offensive warfare. Nor did Egyptian leaders leave room for doubt as to the proposed victim or limit their preparations to the accumulation of armaments only.

Pending an all-out assault, the Arab states made every effort to weaken and harass Israel by means of economic blockade, closing such important sea lanes as the Suez Canal and the Gulf of Eilat to its commerce and waging relentless guerilla warfare for nine years.

Until 1955, the main base for the Arab "small war" was Jordan. Raids were carried out by gangs of professional marauders, or by refugees who had been kept in squalid camps near the frontier and denied integration in the economic and social fabrics of the Arab countries in spite of the huge sums spent by the United Nations for their upkeep. From 1955 onward, the character of this guerilla campaign changed. Egypt, under the direction of its military *Junta*, took the lead. A special formation, the Fadayin, was created and trained within the framework of the Egyptian

A patrol car in the Negev.

Women of the Army relax in the field.

regular Army, in order to intensify the small war against Israel. The main body of that force was stationed in the Gaza Strip, but other units were organized by the Egyptian Military Attachés in Jordan, Syria, and Lebanon.

From the signing of the Armistice Agreement to the end of 1956, there occurred on Israel's borders 2,500 armed clashes, 200 incidents of mining and demolition, and 5,753 armed robberies. The casualties of Israel during the period amounted to 443 killed and 963 wounded.

But when the Fadayin started to operate, the small war grew in scope and in intensity. From January to October, 1956, the Israel casualty roll numbered 74 dead and 209 wounded. Israel was forced to combat the Arab guerillas with retaliation raids. These reprisals were effective for a limited time, as the Arab governments were afraid of a general conflagration. However, from 1955 on, reprisals brought no more than a temporary respite. Every time the Army destroyed one of the advance bases of the Arab guerillas, the activities of the latter were renewed after only a short period.

The situation became critically tense in the wake of a series of military alliances between Egypt and other Arab countries. In October, 1955, the so-called "military treaties" were signed between Syria and Saudi Arabia on the one hand and Egypt on the other, and a Joint Command headed by the Egyptian Minister of War was set up for the armed forces of the three states.

In October, 1956, Jordan joined the Egyptian military bloc. Nasser's Minister of War virtually became the supreme commander of the Arab Legion and the Jordan National Guard. From

Infantry attacking on the outskirts of the Gaza Strip.

Prisoners taken at an Egyptian stronghold.

An Israeli major presides at the first meeting of the Gaza Council after the city capitulated.

Infantry supported by tanks move forward in the Sinai Campaign.

130

Infantry making a beach landing.

then on the Fadayin could not only use bases in Jordan but Egyptian armored formations could be poised on Israel's waist line so as to split the country in a matter of hours.

September, 1955, found the Middle East still officially peaceful, but the Czech-Egyptian arms deal had placed Israel in a precarious position. Israel alerted the Western Powers to the danger but the response was discouraging. The United States supplied tanks and fighter bombers to Saudi Arabia; Great Britain agreed to sell two destroyers to Israel, but similarly re-enforced the Egyptian Navy. France gave Israel the opportunity to buy light tanks and a number of Mystère 4 planes. Canada promised Israel Sabre jet fighters.

Mid-1956 brought further alarming developments: Nasser defied the Western Powers in his Suez policy, Egypt increased its military operations, creating logistical bases and airfields for jets in the Sinai Peninsula, the MIG 15s were replaced by the more modern MIG 17 fighters—this as soon as Israel had received her Mystère 4's—and the Egyptian—Jordanian military alliance was consummated.

Faced with the inevitable attack by fully equipped, cooperating Arab forces under Egypt, and the lack of timely and effective assistance in preparing a strong defensive position to maintain the peaceful, tenuous balance, Israel made her momentous decision—to attack—though the odds against success were tremendous.

The Israeli counterstroke had to render ineffective the Egyptian preparations for an offensive by destroying the bases created for this purpose, eradicate the Fadayin springboards in the Gaza Strip and on the eastern border of Sinai, and open the Gulf of Eilat to the free movement of Israeli shipping by liquidating the Egyptian blocking positions in that region.

The Israeli strategic counterstroke met the Egyptian Army in a phase of transformation. It had not yet fully absorbed the huge quantities of Russian equipment delivered to it. The central routes for the invasion of Israel, the El Arish–Rafa–Gaza (coastal) Road, and the Ismailia–Abu Ageila–Nitzana Highway in northeast Sinai, were guarded by the Egyptian Sinai Army in some strength. The guard was made up of three full infantry brigades, each with a medium tank squadron, mobile heavy anti-tank guns, and several field artillery batteries; and they were stationed in the well-fortified triangle, Rafa–Abd Aegila–El Arish. The Eighth Division was stationed in the Gaza Strip.

Israel's mobilization was rapid and smooth. The standing Army was at its various posts, and the call-up plan was superlatively effective, for morale among the Israelis was high. The General Staff set about their task with the greatest efficiency. The Syrian and Jordanian frontiers were immediately covered and a strategic reserve set up, while a major concentration was deployed to the south-

The *Haifa,* a destroyer captured from the Egyptians and commissioned into the Israeli Navy.

Chief Chaplain Rabbi S. Goren conducts services in the field near Mount Sinai.

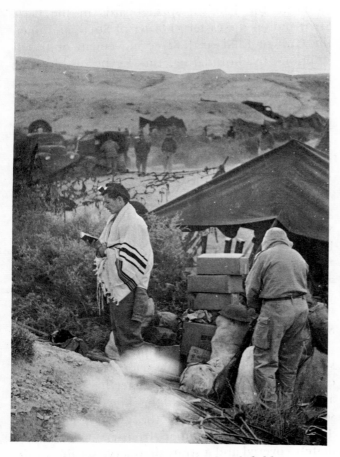

Morning prayers on the battlefield.

Airborne troops make a parachute landing at point of destination.

Israeli soldiers with equipment captured from the
Egyptians in the Sinai Peninsula.

**An Israeli soldier relaxes with an Egyptian maga-
zine in a position captured from the enemy.**

ern front. There, Israeli's force about equaled the
opposing Egyptians—infantry, artillery, engineers,
service units, and mobile armored and mechanized
companies were strengthened by paratroopers and
other airborne outfits. All the services were well
trained and conditioned for rapid maneuver warfare. The Air Force entered the Sinai campaign
with the greatest confidence in their excellently
trained and courageous pilots, skilled ground
staff, and the fast and efficient French Mystère 4.

The Israel forces on the southern front were
divided into six distinct bodies: two battle groups
composed of Armor, Infantry, and Artillery formations to carry out the main effort against the principal pillars of the Egyptian defense system, Abu-
Ageila and Rafa respectively; a composite force of
paratroopers and mechanized units to strike the
uncovered southern flank of the enemy main posi-

tion by driving a wedge into the central sector of
the peninsula in the direction of the Canal; a
mechanized column in cooperation with airborne
units, to liquidate the Egyptian garrison blocking
the Gulf of Eilat; an infantry formation supported
by artillery and armor, to mop up the Gaza Strip
after the fall of Rafa; and a reserve to reinforce
any of the operating bodies in the case of unfore-
seen contingencies.

Operation Kadesh developed in three distinct
phases. The first, the contact phase, lasted two
days from October 29 to the morning of October
31. During these 48 hours, Israel forces made full
use of the elements of surprise and initiative to
secure decisive advantages.

A paratroop unit assembled during the night of
October 29 at a point near the El-Nakhl-Suez
highway, within striking distance of the Canal.

Egyptian ground and air efforts to wipe out this advance unit were foiled by Israel fighter planes. On the evening of October 30 a mechanized column, brushing aside Egyptian resistance, proceeded despite topographical difficulties with great speed on the El-Nakhl road to join the airhead in the late hours of the evening. By this the Israel Army secured a threat against the Canal itself and another against the deep flank of the enemy main position in the northern sector of the peninsula.

In the northern sector the important road junction of Kusseima was taken on October 30; a success which afforded the Israel Army endless opportunities for maneuvers against the Egyptian fortified zone. A weak spot south of the Egyptian strongpoint of Abu-Ageila was discovered and occupied by an Israeli reconnaissance unit, setting the stage for the subsequent armor penetration. During the first forty-eight hours the Israel Air Force repeatedly clashed with Egyptian Mig 15s and 17s, Meteors, and Vampires and gained complete mastery of the sky over the peninsula. This decisively influenced developments in the next phase of the campaign.

On October 31, after heavy fighting, an Israel armored formation took the village and road junc-

Soldiers celebrate the cease-fire order at an Israeli position near Ismailia.

tion of Abu-Ageila, to the northwest of the Egyptian main positions, as well as the strongpoint of 'El-Rahoua to the southwest of it. Thus, they encircled a full Egyptian brigade which was at the same time subjected to heavy frontal pressure from the east.

On the same day, Israel armor fanned out and penetrated to a depth of 37.2 miles into enemy territory, occupying the supply posts and rear installations of Jebel-Libny, Bir-el-Hassaneh and Bir-el-Khama. In the night between October 31 and November 1, the second pillar of the Egyptian defense system, the brigade position of Rafa, was knocked out by concentrated Israel assault.

The Egyptians then made an effort to restore the situation by counter-attack. On October 31, an armored brigade, composed of Soviet tanks and self-propelled guns, advanced along the Ismailia Highway. At Bir-Gafgafa, it was intercepted and dispersed by the Israel Air Force, and Israel armor forced the remnants to withdraw. After this failure, and in view of the fact that complete encirclement and destruction threatened their forces in Sinai, the Egyptian High Command issued a general order of retreat on the evening of November 1.

It is evident from this timetable that the decision in the peninsula was reached before any large-scale action of the British-French forces in the Canal Zone had even begun. Subsequent descriptions of the campaign by Egyptian spokesmen, including Nasser, which asserted that the Egyptian

Writing home during a lull in the battle.

An Israeli soldier distributes cigarettes to Egyptian prisoners of war before their return to Egypt.

Sinai Army held all its positions intact and was only forced to withdraw by "the British-French stab in the back" are refuted by these facts.

Only a few coherent units of the Egyptian Army were able to withdraw in an orderly fashion. In the main it dissolved into a straggling mass and large numbers of soldiers and officers surrendered to Israel forces.

Accordingly, the third phase of the campaign started, the phase of mopping-up and pursuit. On November 2, El-Arish, with its huge supply depots was captured intact and the Israel forces advanced on a broad front westward, to positions ten miles from the Canal.

In the central sector the Israel forces had a sharp clash with Egyptian units stationed in the Mittla Pass during October 31 and November 1. After the enemy had been cleared out of these positions by heavy fighting, a portion of the Israel paratroopers were withdrawn to prepare for a new drop. This step initiated one of the most important operations during the exploitation phase—the drive against the Egyptian blocking positions on the Gulf of Eilat.

On November 2, paratroopers landed at Et-Tor, northwest of Sharem-el-Sheikh, in one arm of a pincers movement. The other arm was represented by a mechanized column issuing from Rasel-Nakeb and proceeding southward by a very difficult route. The Commander of the Egyptian garrison, misjudging Israel's intentions and movements, evacuated the strong fortress of Rass-Nassrani without a fight, and concentrated his forces in Sharem-el-Sheikh against the threat of the paratroopers who were advancing, reinforced by motorized units, to the oil wells of Rass-Sudr.

Between November 4 and 5, the pincers closed on Sharem-el-Sheikh. After heavy bombardment from the air, and short and sharp fighting on the ground, the Egyptian garrison surrendered. At the same time, mopping-up operations proceeded in the northern sector. Between November 2 and 3, the Eighth Division in the Gaza Strip, cut off by the fall of Rafa, disintegrated under an all-out assault of the Israelis. On November 6, the whole Sinai Peninsula was cleared of the Egyptians and fighting stopped.

During the seven-day campaign two Egyptian divisions were destroyed and more than five thousand prisoners were taken. A hundred tanks, a thousand transport vehicles, two hundred artillery pieces and anti-tank guns, a vast amount of small arms and signal equipment, as well as the store of the big El-Arish base, fell into Israeli hands.

The extent of Israel's success and the short time in which it was achieved astonished many foreign observers. The Sinai campaign, with its opposing

A unit of the United Nations Emergency Force on its way to take over the Sinai Peninsula and the Gaza Strip from the victorious Israeli Army.

armies differing in strategical, operational, and tactical theories, as well as opposing democratic and social philosophies, proved more than a mere feat of arms. There are those who would credit Israel's success merely to surprise, but, nevertheless, Egypt had in every way, but officially, declared war, she had been long preparing for the liquidation of Israel and her plan was anticipated and countermanded only through last minute rescheduling.

The Israel Government had exhausted every diplomatic means at its disposal in order to avert a military conflagration. But, when these efforts proved futile, the Israel counterstroke had to be timed so as to catch Egypt off guard. The advantages of surprise were not attained by chance. Success can be attributed to the speedy mobilization of the Reserves and the civilian vehicles which provided most of the transportation during this operation. The Israel soldier won because an integrated national war effort stood behind him. The Israel Air Force, in turn, achieved mastery of the sky, despite its inferior numbers, because of the high quality of the pilots and the unflinching devotion of the ground staff. Sound operational planning and high mobility and flexibility during the execution of the planned design, are additional reasons for Israel's success. These were the products of the Commanders, staffs, and fighting formations.

Major General E. L. M. Burns, Commander of the United Nations Emergency Force, visits an air station at El-Arish.

An Israeli soldier removes a road block on the outskirts of El-Arish minutes before evacuation of the city. On the road, in the background, the first vehicle of the United Nations Emergency Force column arrives to take over Israeli positions.

On the other hand, Egyptian soldiers, officers, and airmen were unable to put to full use the huge quantities of Russian equipment at their disposal. The High Command had not mastered the intricacies of mechanized warfare and, from the first day of the campaign, lost control over its units, which fought without plan, coordination, or determination. This fact is intimately connected with the social composition of the Egyptian armed forces. Despite continuous anti-Israel propaganda, the Egyptian soldier did not know what he was fighting for. Though priding themselves on being members of Nasser's "Liberation Movement," most of the officers were not ready and willing to risk their lives.

Now we can view the Sinai campaign with the wisdom and deliberate judgment of retrospect. The political-minded individual might have looked upon this as a mere military excursion to acquire territory or achieve a reputation for military strategy before the Arab states had completely mobilized and integrated, but now they must admit that the State of Israel had come of age, its morale motivated by the timeless future.

The immediate ending of the guerilla attacks, the moral effect upon the Egyptian soldier, his loss of face to his neighbors whose equipment was less modern than his, the lifting of blockades against Israel on world trade routes, the new sense of economic liberty—all these things were instantly and glaringly obvious, but there were greater objectives: freedom to Israel citizens within the State and when working on the remote borders and freedom of international action by the State as a unit. The internal pressures caused by the threats of the nations of the Middle East were soon dispelled, but it was more difficult to assure the State's freedom and respect abroad.

To guarantee the latter, Israel, having demonstrated through its armed forces its right to statehood, now demonstrated its desire for peace and justice through an "act of faith" by evacuating the Sinai Peninsula and the Gaza Strip—this step requires the continued support of the Great Powers and the revised policy of the Arab states.

"This is the way—there is no other. We faltered in our path—you must carry on." This inspiring quotation from his letter flanks the picture of a young Israeli who was killed in action during the War of Liberation.

8 LAND AND PEOPLE

From all corners of the world they came—a people to make a new nation. Separated by the divergent cultures of the countries of their origin, they came to one little spot on the shores of the Eastern Mediterranean to raise again from the ashes of history a tightly knit modern nation.

From the frozen plains and hills of Iceland, from the sun-parched deserts of Yemen, from the industrialized area of South Africa, and from the prehistoric woods on the Ganges, the people came, and are still coming, to the greatest rendezvous with destiny that history has ever recorded.

People without a common language, people from the most backward regions and those from the advanced areas of industrial civilization, people who had never seen a motor-driven vehicle, and people for whom the airplane has become a regular means of transportation merged in this tiny, Middle East country. Even the color of their skins differed: dark-skinned people from Yemen, the most ancient Hebrew tribe preserved in almost Biblical form, ebony-hued people from the *B'nai Israel* community in India, and blond "Nordic" types from northern Europe—all answered the call of redemption and returned to their homeland to help build it, develop it, and make of it a dream come true.

There was no time to waste, not much time for adjustment. Newcomers of today had to become hosts for the newcomers of tomorrow. They had to learn new trades and change lifelong traditions; they had to become defenders of the new State; they had to become part and parcel of a social revolution in which no blood was to be shed, no pain inflicted.

The nine hundred thousand immigrants who reached Israel during the ten years of the State's official existence did not overflow the country. Instead, there was an amazing integration prompted by the national and emotional ties established during the more than fifty years of periodic return to Palestine prior to the inception of the State. The dimensions of this achievement can be more readily perceived if one compares it to a similar situation taking place in the United States. It would be as if, within the short span of ten years, 220,000,000 immigrants had flowed into the country.

In Israel, people who had made a living as merchants and middlemen were turned into productive workers on the land and in the factories. Urbanites learned to till the soil, salesmen learned to handle a machinist's lathe. A great "experimental station," with almost one million people involved, was functioning with the utmost speed—with what was expected to be a detrimental element to progress: the free, voluntary choice of each individual.

Everything was in its beginning stages. The people had to learn Hebrew in order to communicate with one another; they had to acquire skills and learn to work productively; they had to be reeducated to regard themselves as members of equal standing in their old-new country. Many had to be taught to use a knife and fork and had their first introduction to that phenomenon of luxury—the bed. But the danger of diversity was always present. The numberless differences between immigrants and natives, the natural inclination of people to seek their own kind, could easily have created insurmountable problems. Yet, they did not, because of one all-embracing factor—the will to create a homogeneous nation based on the feeling of a common origin and of a shared historical past. And when inevitable conflicts arose, when misunderstanding marred the rose-tinted picture of the "ingathering of exiles," they were quickly smoothed over and a cohesive, national loyalty took preference even in the greatest of intergroup problems.

POPULATION DISTRIBUTION

Against this background of problems, the State of Israel had to undertake what could readily be described as "architecture in population distribution." The tens of thousands of people flocking into the country were quite naturally drawn into the neighborhood of great population centers, the

Aerial view of the Holy City.

If I forget thee, O Jerusalem, let my right hand forget her cunning. If I do not remember thee, let my tongue cleave to the roof of my mouth (Isaiah 137:5,6).

great cities. Tel Aviv, Haifa, Jerusalem, and the cities in the coastal areas were the most appealing centers. They could have easily swelled into tremendous "heads" on a meager body of the empty countryside. The problem of populating the countryside was twofold for in addition to the need for developing desolate areas and opening new stretches of land for agricultural cultivation and industrial growth, there was the urgent matter of national security. A country surrounded by enemies cannot afford the existence of barren, unpopulated areas. Economic needs and, to some extent, political considerations played an important role in the efforts to disperse the growing population as much as possible. The Negev had to be settled if its resources were to be utilized and the repeated demands for its amputation from the State of Israel stilled. Similarly, the northern part of the country, the Galilee and the hills of Judea, required cultivation and attention.

The people had to be directed to rural settlements, to border areas, and remote localities. This process demanded subtle persuasion, since no compulsion could be used and the desire to be close to urban centers was natural. Nevertheless, the process was successful. The statistical figures are convincing. In 1948, at the inception of the State, the population of the great urban centers, Tel Aviv, Haifa, and Jerusalem, amounted to 80 per cent of the Jewish population of the country, while in 1956 this number fell to 60 per cent. The Jewish population in the Negev rose from 3,000 in 1948 to 96,000 in 1957. The number of people in cooperative agricultural settlements (*moshav ovdim* and *moshav shitufi*) rose from 30,000 in 1948 to 100,000 in 1955, and in communal agricultural settlements (*kibbutzim*) from 54,000 to 78,000 over the same period, indicating the reluctance of the new immigrants to shoulder the responsibilities of communal life, which demand a high degree of idealism and a thorough ideological orientation.

The effort to direct people to rural areas did not stop. There have been years when the drive to convince people to go to the countryside took the form of an organized movement "from the city to the village," romanticizing the pastoral advantages with little success. Statistical data on the distribution of the population, as of the end of 1956, show 1,267,614 in towns with municipal status (small towns, suburban settlements, and urban villages), while the number of people living in rural settle-

An immigrant girl from the B'nei Israel community of Indian Jews.

ments (excluding Beduin tribes and new immigrants still in camps) was 496,545.

This planned experimental policy of population distribution was facilitated by the age composition of the Israelis. In this respect, Israel seems to suit her political status—the young State has one of the youngest populations in the world: 33.5 per cent are under fifteen years old, 43.5 per cent between the ages of fifteen and forty-four, 18.5 per cent between forty-four and sixty-four, and only 4.7 percent over the age of sixty-five. The mood of the country—the tempo of life, its spirit, its hopes and dreams—is not only a result of the character and condition of the State, its self-appointed tasks and goals, but also of this specific age distribution which makes youthfulness one of the most outstanding attributes which impress the foreign visitor.

In this "Eden of Youth," another distinctive feature is the fact that men outnumber women (1,031 men to 1,000 women), which, as many say, makes Israel a wonderful land for "husband safari," a sport which has become a national favorite.

141

Children in Jerusalem celebrate the Feast of Bik-kurim, the gathering of the first fruits.

Of course, the distribution of population and the age categories account for two other important facets of Israel's national life—the number of marriages and the rate of birth. The incidence of marriage, among every thousand people, is approximately ten, while the average divorce rate is 1.38 in every thousand. The absence of major obstacles to divorce in Jewish law does not seem to have had much effect on this percentage, nor has it marred family harmony, which was not destroyed by progress and new ideas. If progress has had any adverse effect, it is in the rate of birth

Remnants of the Holy Scrolls, partly destroyed by the Nazis, are kept as a permanent memorial on Mount Zion.

which has shown a downward trend, falling from 33.83 per cent in 1951 to 29.18 per cent in 1955. This trend is ascribed not only to local, social, and economic conditions, but also to the great influx in the early 1950's of immigrants from backward countries in Asia and Africa whose pattern of living produced a temporary increase in the birth rate which was bound to decline as the number of immigrants from those countries decreased.

FREEDOM OF WORSHIP

The Jews have always been acutely conscious of their heritage and the obligations it imposed. In

A Bukharian synagogue in Jerusalem.

Israel, the demand for "God's Kingdom on earth" was perhaps too severe in light of the many who would not submit their personal lives to the strict rules of the Mosaic faith. It was, and is still today, one of the most complicated and provoking problems faced by the people and leaders of Israel. Where clashes of principles occur, a compromise must be made. Compromise, by definition, is not wholly satisfactory to any of the factions involved.

In Israel there is no complete separation of religion and the State, for religious institutions in some vital areas of life, such as marriage and divorce, possess legal authority. While nobody is compelled to religious practice, the State budget assists various religious institutions, of all persuasions, which have their adherents within the boundaries of the State. This right to equality is an integral part of Israel's principal law. The Proclamation of Independence states clearly: "The

State of Israel will uphold the full social and political equality of all its citizens without distinction of race, creed or sex, and will guarantee full freedom of worship. It will safeguard the sanctity and inviolability of the Shrines and Holy Places of all religions."

Nothing is said about a "State religion." The only distinction made in Israeli legislation, that of the Days of Rest Ordinance, which mentions the Sabbath and Jewish festivals as the days of rest, while stating that "non-Jews shall have the right to observe their own Sabbath and festivals as rest days," is motivated by the fact that 90 per cent of the population can adhere to the former, and was not intended to subordinate any religious community.

Of course, in this respect, some special ordinances have to be mentioned. The Israeli Law recognizes the exclusive jurisdiction of rabbinical courts in all matters pertaining to marriage and divorce. As a result, this law, which is permanently contested by secular groups, causes, from time to time, considerable friction. However, the State manages to keep some kind of an equilibrium based not only on the voting strength of the religious and non-religious groups, but also on the growing awareness of the majority that tolerance has to be the commanding factor in Israel's life. In addition, it is only natural for a Jewish State to preserve the basic premises of Judaism, partially to maintain identification with the Jewish communities in the Diaspora, for whom the Jewish religion is often the only element of group identification, and as a factor in strengthening sympathy toward Israel.

Remnants of a Crusader church in the ancient town of Tsipori.

The "mayor" of a settlement of Yemenite Jews with his children.

This tolerance had to be proved in relations other than those between religious and secular groups. It is also on trial in a completely new and dramatic sphere, created by two Jewish sects which for thousands of years were separated from Judaism, yet have been drawn into this historic process of return to Zion. The Karaites (Kara'im), the Jewish sect which rejects the post-Biblical rabbinic tradition of the Talmud and claims to base its teaching on a literalistic interpretation of the Bible (Mikra), are at present concentrated to the extent of almost one-third of their total world population in Israel. Before the establishment of the State, only two Kara'im families lived in the whole country. Today their number reaches one thousand five hundred people, who have immigrated to the State built by their brethren from whom they estranged themselves some twelve centuries ago.

The second ancient sect involved is the Samari-

The High Priest of the Samaritans with the sacred scrolls of his sect.

Samaritans offer prayers on Mount Gerisim.

A gas station at Sodom, the lowest point of habitation in the world.

A *Hassid* and his wife return from Mount Zion.

The Y.M.C.A. building in Jerusalem.

View from Mandelbaum Gate which divides the Jordan- and Israeli-held sections of Jerusalem.

The Jewish quarter of Jerusalem.

King David Hotel, Jerusalem.

A procession winds its way up to Mount Zion to celebrate the ancient Hakhel ritual, when the land is allowed to lie fallow for an entire year.

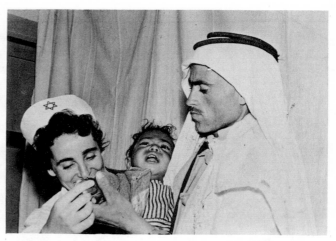

A Bedouin child of the Negev receives medical care. Infant mortality in this section is the lowest among all Arab groups in the Middle East.

The Bahai Temple in Haifa.

Father and son meet on the outskirts of a *moshava* (agricultural settlement).

A gazelle gratefully accepts a handful of sweet grass in the Jerusalem Biblical Zoo.

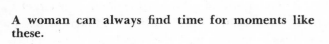

A woman can always find time for moments like these.

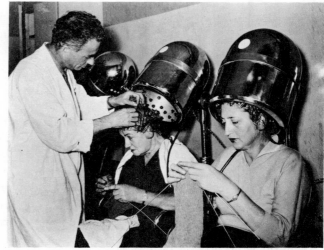

The tomb of Rabbi Shimon Bar Yohai, the founder of Cabalism, in the ancient town of Meron.

tan (*Shomronim*) mentioned in II Kings 17:24 who claim to be a remnant of the Kingdom of Israel that fell in 722 B.C.E. Recognizing only the Pentateuch (the Torah), they managed to stay in Palestine, without interruption, during all the years of exile as a living symbol of Jewish faithfulness to their country and to its past. They are few, a much smaller group than the Kara'im. Only one hundred Samaritans, about one-third of the whole sect, are at present living in Israel, but, like the Kara'im, they receive full assistance from the Treasury for their specific religious needs and are equal beneficiaries in all forms of assistance afforded new immigrants.

The fact that the Arabs in Israel although primarily Moslems, also include members of such Christian denominations as Greek Catholic, Greek

An outdoor market in Jerusalem.

Orthodox, Roman Catholic, Maronite, Armenian Gregorian, Anglican, Presbyterian, Lutheran, and Copt does not facilitate the efforts of the State authorities. Nevertheless, the State has done its best to preserve equality in treatment. The religious dignitaries of the Moslem faith, the Kadis of the Moslem religious courts (Sharia), as all other Moslem religious officials, are paid by the Government. There are about one hundred thirty members of the Moslem clergy, paid by the State. Regular services take place in almost a hundred mosques.

Moslem religious committees function in Jaffa,

Hassidim **dancing inside the tomb of Shimon Bar Yohai on Lag-Ba'omer.**

Haifa, and Acre. Their task is to advise the Ministry and to look after religious education and the needs of the orphans and aged. On their commendation allocations for destitute widows and orphans are made from Moslem charity funds (*Waqf*).

Arab clergymen from the neighboring Arab countries have been granted the privilege of crossing the border and of taking up residence in Israel. A newly established radio station regularly broadcasts Moslem prayers and readings from the Koran, as well as news commentaries in Arabic and Arabic music. The Ministry for Religious Affairs publishes an information bulletin dealing with the religious affairs of the Moslem community.

The members of the Christian communities are served by a thousand religious functionaries. Al-

150

A Tel Aviv fish market.

Although extensive efforts have been made to
establish a hygienic system of milk distribution,
this "motorized milkman" is still a welcome visitor
in many communities.

most every sect, every church in Christendom, has some foothold, however small, in the Holy Land. There are one hundred sixty churches and chapels, and six hundred monks and nuns belonging to some thirty monastic orders. The Ministry of Religious Affairs has special departments for all religious communities. It publishes a periodical, *Christian News from Israel,* in English, French, and Spanish, and cooperates with the Government Department of Antiquities in the restoration and preservation of ancient churches and in the preservation of the Christian Holy Places throughout the land.

Under Israeli law, a small minority within what was considered the Arab community finally achieved the status it had looked for: the Druses, a sect split away from Islam in the eleventh century, have achieved recognition in Israel as a separate cult. The British Mandatory Government did not recognize their community identity and considered them a part of the Moslem religious community. The religion of the Druses is believed to embody elements of Jewish, Christian, and

The ritual slaughter of poultry.

Professional porters, immigrants from Khurdistan, rest between jobs in Jerusalem.

The end of a long weekend at a seaside resort.

Moslem traditions. Their rites and dogmas are a close secret. They venerate Jethro (father-in-law of Moses) to whose tomb near Hittin, in lower Galilee, they undertake yearly pilgrimages. The Druses, of whom there are nineteen thousand in Israel, are considered among the most devoted citizens of the country. Their young men have served with the Israeli Army and their units have fought in the War of Liberation.

The picture of the religious communities in Israel would not be complete if one did not mention the Bahai religion. Although only a very few members of the world Bahai community live in the country, Israel is the world center of the Bahai faith. For this reason, a special department in the Ministry of Religious Affairs deals with the problems of Bahai, whose world spiritual leader resides in Haifa, where the founder of the faith, Mirza Ali Mohammed, was buried, and where the Bahai shrine, on the slopes of Mount Carmel, is a prominent landmark.

THE ARAB POPULATION

The unique experiment in human endeavor for which Israel was chosen is sprinkled not only with

A Bukharian Jew holds the traditional symbols of the Festival of Succot.

Eingev, a *kibbutz* on the eastern shore of the Sea of Galilee.

Sephardic women from Ramle bring their children to the Rabbi's home to receive his blessing.

problems of molding one nation out of immigrants from seventy-four countries, but also with the problem of the Arab population. There is no easy solution to the problem of spurring the process of their integration into the fabric of renewed Jewish statehood.

The two radical approaches toward a solution, isolation and assimilation, were out of the question. The Jewish State did not want to isolate the Arab community, because this would impede its efforts toward an over-all integration of all the inhabitants of Israel. Assimilation would be in opposition to the basic concepts of Jewish political thought, and would have provoked violent accusations that Israel is trying to annihilate the identity of the Arab nation through absorption. Instead, the Arab population has been afforded the opportunity to cultivate its specific national attributes and maintain itself as a community. It was an approach similar, though not identical, with that employed in the United States where integration of various groups does not necessitate the extinction of their national identity.

After a short period of adjustment, a great advance occurred in the progress of the Arab community. The best example is to be found in the percentage of Arab voters in Israel's three general elections, the first democratic process the Arabs of that country have ever participated in: the percentage of Arab voters rose from 79.3 per cent in 1949 to 85.5 per cent in 1951 and 91.2 per cent in 1955 (this last figure showing a higher percentage than was registered in the country as a whole).

The Arabs took full advantage of these democratic opportunities. Eight Arabs are members of the Third Knesset, five of them representing purely Arab lists, the others elected from lists representing the general population without national distinction.

The general progress of the country was of direct benefit to the Arabs. Local government allowed them to elect their representatives and freed them from an almost medieval, feudalistic form of organization. Development schemes brought into Arab villages (about one hundred fifty thousand Arabs are living in rural settlements) water, irrigation facilities, electricity, roads, and communication improvements. The Trade Union Movement gave the Arab worker professional protection to supplement the provisions of the State's labor and social legislation. The introduction of health services, social security, the protection of mothers, children, and working women is gradually producing a quiet revolution in the daily lives of the Arabs.

These continuously improving physical conditions have been accompanied by a growing economic wealth. The cultivation of 312,500 acres of their own lands and 125,000 acres of State land has brought a sixfold increase in Arab agricultural production in ten years, thus enabling them to meet the growing demand for food caused by the rapid growth of the population. There is no doubt that the standard of living of the Arabs in Israel is the highest among Arab-inhabited countries. The infant mortality rate alone is sufficient proof: while the mortality rate among the Moslems in Israel is at 62.37 per thousand, it is still at the

Beersheba.

156

A meeting in the Great Synagogue in Tel Aviv.

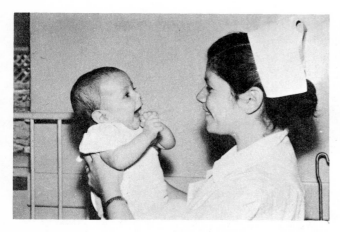

Gentle care is given this infant in the Hadassah Hospital of Beersheba.

rate of 280.4 per thousand in Egypt. This improved standard of living, the equality of rights permitting an Arab to address himself in Arabic to authorities, courts, the members of the Knesset, with the Government facilities for translating speeches for the Arabs from Hebrew, have resulted in a growing demand for cultural improvements, to which the Government gives special attention and assistance.

In this general picture, there is one flaw—the military regime set up by the Government in the areas populated chiefly by Arabs. This regime represents restriction, or rather control of movements, naturally creating bad feelings. But it is a necessity, according to Israeli authorities, which point out that the military regime is a necessity in areas bordering on Arab countries which profess their intention to annihilate Israel and have made clear that they consider themselves as being in a "state of war" with the new nation. Prevent-

The River Jordan.

ing sabotage, espionage, subversion, and "fifth-column" infiltration is necessary for self-defense. As Israeli officials have expressed it: "Did not the United States put special surveillance, for instance, on its Japanese citizens during World War II?" But, though putting this question, Israeli authorities are hoping to relax these security restrictions and, eventually, abolish them entirely.

PUBLIC WELFARE

This conglomerate mass of peoples, religions,

A shepherd cares for his sheep at Dorot.

and customs requires care. The State of Israel has assumed obligations of social care which many a more economically advanced country have not taken upon themselves. Some of the services are unavoidable. The great waves of immigration have brought thousands of sick, lame, and tubercular people, together with a considerable number of the aged. Israel is fully aware of the serious implications of assuming such a responsibility, but of greater importance is the obligation to give entrance to every Jew who seeks the State of Israel. As a result, the Ministry of Social Welfare became an important institution with branches devoted to General Relief Service, the prevention of Youth

The sabra cactus grows abundantly in the botanical gardens of Eilat.

159

The private beach of the Accadia Hotel in Herzlia.

Delinquency, Social Rehabilitation, Specialized Services, the Training of Social Welfare Personnel, and Legal Aid. In these missions of assisting the needy, the Government bodies are assisted by Malben, the American Joint Distribution Committee's program in Israel for the care of sick, aged, and handicapped immigrants, by the Hadassah Medical Organization, and by such women's organizations as Wizo, Women's Workers Council, Mizrachi Women's Organization, and the General Zionist Women's Organization. Along with them, important assistance is given by Ort for vocational training, and Ose for the care of infants.

Medical care is supervised by the Ministry of Health which is directly responsible for seventeen hospitals (general, tuberculosis, and mental) with four thousand five hundred beds, and the maintenance of two hundred infant welfare clinics, nursing schools, public health laboratories, etc. The Hadassah Medical Organization, the Mogen David Adom (the Israeli equivalent to The Red

Cross), and the Malben are supplemented by an organization which, though non-governmental, constitutes the backbone of Israel's health services —the Worker's Sick Fund (Kupat Cholim). This health insurance association of the General Federation of Labor (Histadrut), operates on a budget twice the size of the Ministry of Health budget, counting among its members two-thirds of the population, and employing about one-third of the country's physicians. There are also smaller voluntary health insurance associations such as the General Zionist Sick Fund, Kupat Cholim Leumit, and Kupat Cholim Amamit.

These arrangements for the health and welfare of the population led to the first National Insurance Law, which took effect in 1954. This law provides for Old Age Pensions (with men pensionable at the age of sixty-five and women at the age of sixty), for Survivor's Insurance, Industrial Accidents and Occupational Insurance, and Maternity Insurance. Over six hundred seventy-five thousand persons are registered with the National Insurance Institute, while dues collected amounted to thirty-six million dollars in the period from April 1, 1954, to March 31, 1956, and benefits paid exceeded ten million dollars.

Despite the facilities, arrangements for the welfare of the people, and progressive laws, problems and hardships are abundant. The entire life pattern of the majority of the people, immigrants from different countries, had to be changed. World Jewry, which helped in part to facilitate the absorption of the immigrants, knows little about the hardships the Israelis had to endure. Years of

The Great Synagogue in Tel Aviv.

austerity, rationing, with two thousand poorly balanced calories a day, and tremendous taxation were not always accepted cheerfully. Many political crises occurred. The Israelis contested the advisability or effectiveness of certain economic policies, but they remained united in their desire to receive as many new immigrants as possible. This desire was accompanied by the will to have all newcomers rapidly integrated into a homogeneous society. To achieve this goal, a struggle had to be waged against prejudice, against the natural longing of people for "togetherness" on the basis of past memories, or past allegiances. Organizations of immigrants from various countries or cities are still in existence, but they are losing importance as the elements which tied them together are dissolving. The urge for national self-preservation dictates that "integration of the *aliyot*," of the immigrants from all countries, be considered imperative. It is apparent that Ben Gurion's hope "that the day will come when a Jew from Yemen will forget his Yemenite origin as he (Ben Gurion) forgot his Polish background" will be realized in the not too distant future. Above all there is a feeling of common goals among the people who are wholeheartedly involved in the conquest of the desert which draws them closer, and bridges all superficial differences.

Dizengoff Square in the heart of Tel Aviv's residential area.

Seaside promenade in Tel Aviv.

Air-conditioned office buildings in Tel Aviv.

Cocktail hour at the Tadmor Hotel near Tel Aviv.

Allenby Road, the main thoroughfare of Tel Aviv.

163

A modern apartment building in Tel Aviv.

A new housing project in Tel Aviv.

THE MAN-MADE LAND

Among the many factors tying together this unique nation, is one which is perhaps the most extraordinary feature of Israeli life. It is the shared feeling that the country they now inhabit is really a land which men have made, which is still being created out of wilderness and desert.

The land is no longer "an exceedingly good land; a land which floweth with milk and honey" (Numbers 14: 6-8). Half of Israel's territory is desert—the Negev. Only half of the 8,048-square-mile area was inhabited before the inception of the State.

The configuration of the State's territory is somewhat peculiar. North of Tel Aviv the country is only twelve miles wide and, at its widest, south of Beersheba, it is seventy miles across. It is a long shaped, triangular country with boundaries along hostile states running into many hundreds of miles: with Lebanon, 49.5 miles; with Syria, 47.5 miles; with Jordan (and former Palestinian areas now under its control), 332 miles; with Egypt (and former Palestinian areas now under Egyptian control), 165 miles. And, in addition, there are 117.8 miles of Mediterranian Coast, 35 miles of Dead Sea Coast, and 6.2 miles of Eilat (Red Sea) Coast.

Within these disproportionately long borders grows a country no longer recognizable to anyone who saw it ten short years ago. Swamps have been irrigated, artificial lakes have been built, new villages and towns have been erected, and the desolate Negev now booms with life and activity.

An outdoor cafe in Tel Aviv.

The youngest son of this Bukharian family recites the "four questions" at a Passover *seder*.

**The Rabbi of the *S.S. Israel* conducting services in
the ship's synagogue.**

View of Nazareth.

Entrance to the tombs of the Sanhedrin in Jerusalem.

A first-generation "Sabra."

The Sea of Galilee, or Lake Kinneret.

A commuter studiously reads his daily newspaper.

CLIMATE

Climate is no problem to the Israelis. Asked what kind of a climate they have, the average Israeli would answer: "Any, to your liking." One can have 40° Fahrenheit in January in the Galilee, 50° to 60° on the coastal plain, and 70° in Eilat, at the Gulf of Aqaba. It takes only an hour's flight to change a cold winter climate, sprinkled with snow and frost, into cozy, warm weather where one can bathe and enjoy the sun. In August, this hottest of all hot months, one can still live in 65° to 85° in Jerusalem or on the mountains of Galilee, in 70° to 85° on the coastal plain with Tel Aviv as the center, or in 78° to 105° in the "deep south" of Eilat. Even in the hottest days of summer, the coastal plain enjoys a sea breeze which breaks the intensity of the hot summer sun. The relatively low humidity is a special blessing of this region. Eilat registers 28 per cent in the month of August and 35 per cent in January, the Galilee mountains register 51 per cent in August and 76 per cent in January, Jerusalem has 73.8 per cent in August and 47 per cent in January, and the coastal plain has a high of 80 per cent in August and 55 per cent in January.

Of course, there are many uncomfortable days. There are the easterly desert winds, at the beginning and end of summer, called *hamsin,* which, as their name indicates (*hamesh,* or Arabic *hamsah,* means five) should last no longer than five days; the torrential rainfalls and the occasional flood when the dry river beds, *vadis,* overflow in streams of yellow water dragging with them debris of every kind. To be in the desert on such a day is far from pleasant. Sand curls its strange air craters, and infiltrates into every hole, every niche; visibility is almost nil and one has to seek immediate shelter. In the towns the streets are deserted, many offices slacken the pace of work, and the people take it easy until the hot spell passes.

For the native-born Israeli, these *hamsins* cease to be a problem—they have discovered endless ways of overcoming the hardship. And the rains, even if they are often over-generous, fill hearts with joy. At the end of the High Holidays season, Sukkoth (the Feast of the Tabernacles), the Israelis voice their appeal to the Almighty that He bless the coming year with rain and dew.

The months of unbroken sunshine, from April to October, the mild winter which lasts only four

Motor scooters—an increasingly popular means of transportation.

Israeli girls practice rhythmic exercises in preparation for Israel's Tenth Anniversary celebrations.

Leisure time in a kindergarten with its promise of barefooted fun.

After work, the mothers of a communal settlement take their infants from the nursery to play on the lawn.

An immigrant from Iran who endowed his new country with a family of eight children.

A group of hikers stop to dance a *hora* in the shade of the mountains by the Dead Sea.

King Solomon's Mines, a short distance from the Red Sea port of Eilat.

On Israel Arbor Day a child plants a young fir.

A bugler heralds the arrival of the Sabbath in Tel Aviv.

Moslems at prayers in a mosque.

The Mea Shearim section of Jerusalem, inhabited by extremely Orthodox Jews who follow their own rigid social and religious code as exemplified in the tri-lingual sign stretched over the narrow street.

Druse pilgrimage to Hittin, burial place of their prophet, Jethro.

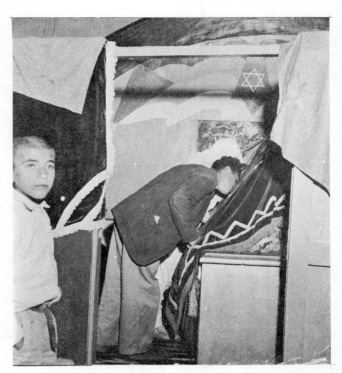

A Druse worshipper kisses the cloth that covers the sacred tomb of Jethro.

months, the rainy season, from November to April, play an important role in the agricultural economy of the country and in preserving the beauty of the landscape. From times immemorial the Israelis have displayed an artist's touch in the beauties of their landscapes. The Psalmist praised his dwellings as "beautiful for situation, the joy of the whole earth," and the Song of Songs sang in honor of the "Rose of Sharon and the Lily of the Valleys"; "the cluster of camphor in the vineyards of En-Gedi," and the gardens where the "plants are an orchard of pomegranates, with pleasant fruits, spikenard and saffron, calamus and cinnamon, with all trees of frankincense, myrrh, and aloes."

Of course, the modern meteorologist is not satisfied with the aromatic perfumes of spring blossoms in the orange groves. He looks for figures, for measurements of rainfall which show God's gift to the thirsty land: 42.2 inches in the wettest area, Upper Galilee; 22 to 24 inches in Jerusalem; 20 to 22 inches in Tel Aviv; 26 to 30 inches in Haifa, and only 0.8 inches in Eilat.

TOPOGRAPHICAL FEATURES

As amazing as the varied climates is the diversity of altitudes. Israel contains the lowest point in the world, the Dead Sea, 1,286 feet below sea level, yet there are mountains spreading proudly all over the country; the highest peak, the Atzmon (Meron) in Upper Galilee reaches the regal height of 3,962 feet.

The Church of Tabgha where, according to the New Testament, Jesus was said to have performed the miracle of the loaves and the fishes.

This woman from Habaniyah follows the Oriental
custom of smoking the *narghila*.

Religious leaders of various Christian denominations at an Independence Day parade.

The Hospice of the Mount of the Beatitudes overlooking the Sea of Galilee, where, according to Christian tradition, Jesus pronounced the Sermon on the Mount.

Arab workers march in the May Day parade of the Haifa Histadrut.

Kingsway, the main street of downtown Haifa.

An abandoned pillbox on the outskirts of Tel Aviv transformed into a cold-drink stand.

Chefzi Ba ("All that I desire"), a department store in Haifa.

Grain elevators at Haifa.

The haunting blast of the *shofar* sounds on Yom Kippur Eve.

Ramat Gan, the Garden City of Israel.

A scene at the artists' colony of Ein Hod near Haifa.

Bedouins in their tents in the Negev.

But nature was not generous with her flowing waters. The Jordan River flows through only 73 miles of Israel's territory. This river, the mighty Jordan of ancient lore, is no more than a stream, meager in waters and wide in its bed, often crossed without watercraft or bridge, lying idle until winter brings it to life. Its tributary, the Yarmuk, flows through 10 miles of Israel's territory, the Yarkon, at Tel Aviv, 16.1 miles, and the Kishon at Haifa, 8.1 miles. The entire water area, which includes some minor streams and lakes, covers 177 square miles. The Dead Sea is the principal body of inland water covering 108 square miles inside Israel territory (the total area of the Dead Sea is 262.5 square miles); the lake of Kinneret (Sea of Galilee, Lake Tiberias, Lake Gennesaret) stretches over 63.7 square miles, and the lake of Huleh once covered 5.4 square miles but has recently been turned into one of the most fertile parts of the country, providing work for thousands of new immigrants.

Between the latitudes 33°15′ and 29°30′ and longitudes 34°17′ and 3.5°41′, the terrain of Israel represents much of the world's landscape in miniature. Divided 'into three longitudinal strips, the coastal plain extends along the Mediterranean shore for 117 miles; the long range of hills which form the broad central column of the country, and the deep Jordan Rift, plunge into the Plain of the Arava and run south of the Dead Sea toward Eilat on the Red Sea.

Israel can be a paradise for tourists offering abundant opportunities for outings amidst the loveliest scenery. Steep, challenging mountain slopes ablaze with fantastic colors are scooped out by vast mile-wide craters. High ranges can be

The famous Mosque of Jazzar Pasha looms over an Acre street.

Swimmers form a *hora* circle at the Ber Ora pool in the Negev.

Ramat Aviv, a modern hotel outside of Tel Aviv.

A street market in Nazareth.

The new wing of Beilinson Hospital near Petach Tikvah.

The Dolphin House near Haifa.

A two-family house in one of Israel's many new housing projects.

Zichron Yaakov, famous for its wine cellars, celebrates its seventieth anniversary.

Dagania, the oldest communal settlement.

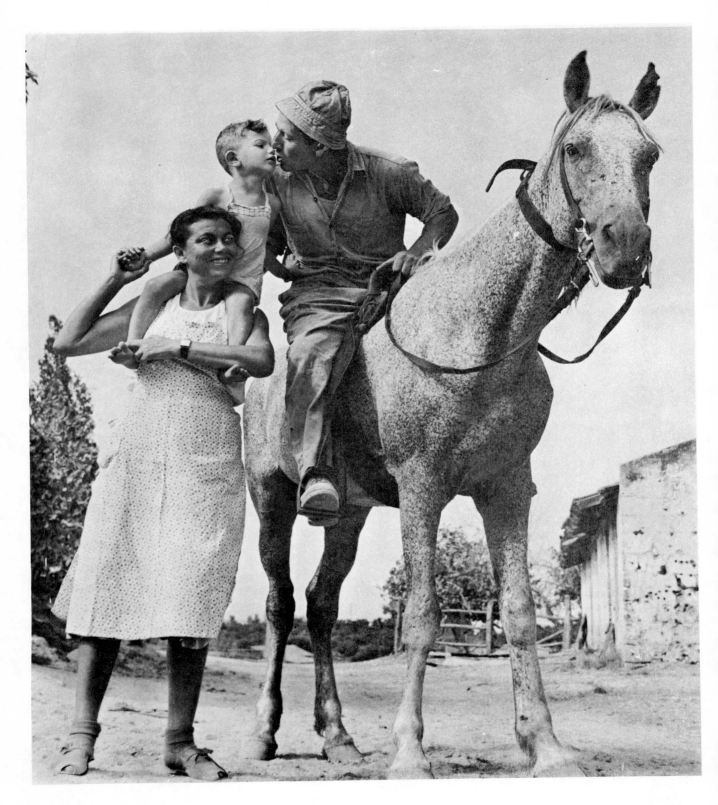

A farmer says goodbye before leaving to inspect his crops.

easily exchanged for the mild, relaxing atmosphere of the Valley of Yezreel (Esdraelon), bordering the Valley of Eiron, proudly marking the major routes of antiquity. At its northern entrance lies the famous fortress of Megiddo (Armageddon), the battlefield where good and evil struggled, as recorded in Revelation 16:16. Thirty miles long and twelve miles broad at its widest point, the Valley of Yezreel, changed from a malaria breeding swamp into life-giving grain fields, is representative of man's victory over the desolate lands of Israel. Beyond the valleys rise the gentle slopes of the hills, inland but close to the coast. These are the stone-ribbed, rain-eroded hills of Samaria, Ephraim, and Judea.

So it goes—up and down—from high mountain peaks to the lowest point on earth, the "other half of Israel," the Negev, which has miles of coastal plain, hills and mountains, cliffs and crags, craters and stony stretches, and where on a summer day the stories about the *Fata Morgana* (mirage) come true.

King David's Tomb on Mount Zion in Jerusalem.

"A LAND OF MILK AND HONEY"

This generally hilly land, barren for so many years, has been brought back to life again through the toil and labor of people whose will, winged by the dream of regenerating a nation, is once again making of Israel a "land of milk and honey." To the traditional "wheat and barley, vines and fig trees, pomegranates, olive oil, and honey" has been added date palms, bananas, citrus fruits, avocados, guavas, mangoes, tobacco, flax, cotton, peanuts, and beets. Israeli flora includes tamarick, carob, eucalyptus, pines, and acacia trees. An abundance of flowers turns the whole countryside into a blossoming garden of colors in late winter and spring. The cactus (*sabra*), a plant bearing a sweet, but prickly fruit, which was introduced into the country some eighty years ago, has become the symbol of the native-born Israeli, the "Sabra," who like to think of themselves as good hearted in spite of their rough exterior.

Countless animals, birds, and reptiles inhabit this land. Many species have disappeared. The Asian elephant, the Mesopotamian Hippopotamus, lions, and silvery Syrian bears are now extinct in this region. One can assume from the name of one of the rivers on the coastal plain, Nahal Hataninim

Signposts in English and Hebrew have been set up at three hundred Biblical and historical sites throughout Israel.

The Tower of King David in Jerusalem.

The walls of Jerusalem.

The beach at Bat Yam, south of Tel Aviv.

The war-damaged Jewish quarter in the Old City of Jerusalem.

Arabs of Nazareth gather around Mary's Well.

Mount Zion.

Massada, the last stronghold of the Jewish revolt against Rome. Recent excavations have uncovered remnants of Herod's Palace.

The ancient port of Jaffa, now part of the municipality of Tel Aviv.

Ruins of the synagogue of Capernaum in the Galilee.

The medieval practice of writing Torah scrolls is a rare art still practiced in twentieth-century Israel.

(Tanin—crocodile) that these reptiles once inhabited the waters of this part of Asia.

There are hyenas, jackals, wolves, wild cats, lynxes, otters, mongooses, and spotted weasels. Gazelles are appearing in large numbers again, porcupines and hedgehogs are plentiful; and the shrew, the smallest mammal in the world, is well represented. Four hundred species of birds are reproducing prolifically as the desert recedes to make room for the cultivated land. The Huleh swamps have been guarded against man's march of civilization to provide a reservation for herons, ducks, and wild geese. The poisonous snake, the chameleon, the house gecko, the multi-colored fish in the gulf of Eilat, and the fish bred artificially and naturally in lakes and rivers complete the array of animal life thriving with the expansion of cultivated land through irrigation.

FROM DAN TO EILAT

"From Dan to Eilat, ours is the land," the people sing. The 260-mile strip from the most north-

A mobile "post office," complete with letter box and stamp window, serves remote settlements.

Coenaculum (Hall of the Last Supper), the Tombs of the Sanhedrin, and Herod's Cave.

All roads radiate from this center. They pass a narrow strip, the Jerusalem corridor, with Ein Kerem, the birthplace of John the Baptist, Kiryat Yearin where the Holy Ark rested for twenty years, Tzora and Eashtaol, where Samson was born, and Modiin, the birthplace of the Maccabees. The Jerusalem corridor, only a few miles wide, flanked by Jordan's territory, leads to the coastal plain with its booming economic, social, and cultural center, Tel Aviv. As one American expressed it: "Jerusalem and Tel Aviv are like Washington and New York."

Tel Aviv-Jaffa, present population four hundred thousand, is the largest city in the country and more than fifty years old (established 1909). Tel Aviv was originally a suburb of Jaffa which did not become a municipality until 1921. This center of commercial and industrial life, the home of Israel's most renowned cultural institutions and publications, site of the Declaration of Independence, was "the first all-Jewish city in the world."

Haifa, the main port of the country, is highly industrialized, boasting oil refineries, foundries,

ern outpost, Dan, to the most southern, Eilat, provides convincing proof of the validity of the Bible and the new right of the children of Israel to their homeland. One needs no *Baedecker,* no guide—the Bible is sufficient.

An amazing return to the spirit of antiquity is taking place. A growing passion for archaeology as a hobby brings the young and old, shovel in hand, to look for a remnant of pottery or brick. These are strange "treasure hunters," fully aware of the ancient secrets of the past harbored by the soil they trod.

Jerusalem, the heart of the nation, its symbol, its ancient and new capital, its spiritual inspiration, now has a population of over one hundred sixty thousand. Inhabited since the dawn of history, it was made the capital by King David in about 1000 B.C.E. The Old City contains the most Holy relic of Judaism, the Wailing Wall, the last remnant of the Second Temple, now in Jordanian hands. To the west of the Old City is the New City of Jerusalem, splendidly set in majesty on the hills. The Jerusalem of the twentieth century stands as a monument to ancient and contemporary Judaism. It houses the seat of the President, the Knesset, (parliament), the Government, the Supreme Court, the Jewish Agency Headquarters, the grave of Theodor Herzl, the Military Cemetery, the Hebrew University, the Bezalel National Museum, the reputed Tomb of King David, the

A candelabrum sculptured in stone inside the Catacombs of Bet Shearim.

The Menorah, symbol of freedom, fascinates these immigrant children.

Druse chieftains.

Services at the Abyssinian Church in Jerusalem.

Entrance to the Garden Tomb, Jerusalem.

Tiberias, renowned as a winter resort and for the curative qualities of its hot springs which were once owned by Cleopatra and patronized by Herod.

production plants, and a population of close to two hundred thousand. This lovely city climbs from the seashore to the slopes of Mount Carmel, mountain and sea gently meeting, creating a panoramic view of incomparable beauty. The past is everywhere: in Elijah's Cave on Mount Carmel; the Zebulun Valley, reminiscent of the sea-faring tribe whose name it bears; and nearby Acre, the little city which existed during the Crusades and stoutly withstood a sixty-one day siege by Napoleon in 1799.

New and old, modern and ancient, are harmoniously intermingled in this traveler's paradise. For whether driven by pious or secular interests, Israel is a land commanding attention. It is as old as conceivable time, and as modern as the present boundaries of man's progress. In the north lies the Mount of Beatitudes where, according to Christian tradition, Jesus delivered the Sermon on the Mount; Kfar Nahum, the famous synagogue, associated with the New Testament; Safed, the ancient town of Galilee which was the center of medieval mysticism and grave of the great Karo; Meron, scene of pilgrimages to the tomb of Rabbi Simon Ben Yohai, founder of Cabalism; Tiberias, built in honor of the Roman Emperor by Herod Antipas, the center of a short-lived Jewish State in the sixteenth century and the location of the

Yaar Kdoshim (the forest of the martyrs), a memorial to the six million Jews who died at the hands of the Nazis.

tombs of Rabbi Meir Baal Haness and Maimonides. There is Tabgha, site of the New Testament miracle of the loaves and fish, with its exquisite mosaics; Hittin, scene of the battle between the Crusaders and Saracens; Cana, where Jesus performed his first miracle by changing water into wine; Nazareth, city of Jesus' childhood. Mount Tabor, where Debora defeated Sisera's hosts, is the site of a Franciscan and a Greek church, both built over the Cave of Melchizedek, King of Salem who blessed Abraham. Then there are Bet Shearim, once the seat of the Sanhedrin, and Mount Gilboa, where King Saul and Jonathan met their tragic end. In Atlit, built by the Crusaders around 1200 C.E., one can still see the remnants of a Crusader's castle, the ruins of Round Church, and what remains of the first experimental agricultural station in modern Palestine. Bet Shean (Beisan) has carried with it for posterity the scars of its past as a vital center of Hellenistic cultural life.

Antique sites and new achievements mark the entire length of the coastal plain: Caesarea, the Roman Capital of Palestine; Natanya, a beautiful seaside resort founded in 1929 and named after an American, Nathan Strauss; Ramat Gan, the enchanting garden city; Lod (Lydda), the traditional site of the Tomb of Saint George and now the home of the intercontinental airport; Rishon-le-Zion, founded in 1882, renowned for its fine wine cellars.

A Roman statue excavated at Caesarea.

At the southern end lies Rehovot (population thirty thousand), the center of the southern citrus belt; the Weizmann Institute of Science; Givat Brenner, one of the greatest collective settlements; Yavneh, the center of Jewish learning during the Roman conquest; Rabban Gamaliel's Tomb; Ashkelon, the birthplace of Herod, and now a seaside resort built chiefly by immigrants from South Africa within short distance of Hellenistic and Roman ruins; Beersheba, where Abraham dug his well, which grew from a town of three thousand inhabitants in 1948 to a prominent city with a population of fifty thousand. Massada, the last stronghold in the longest recorded siege of history during the Jewish revolt against Roman rule; King Solomon's Mines; Eilat, the Red Sea port of King Solomon, Israel's gate for commerce with Asia and East Africa, where skin diving and fishing are year-round sports.

This is the land and this is the people of Israel. They have combined to make up an experiment on a massive scale; they are the integral part of an incomparable drama in which daily routine is often imbued with heroism and heroism often becomes daily routine.

192

Passover is a happy holiday for this young immigrant girl from Morocco who carries *matzos* to her family in a *maabara*.

9 ECONOMY

If the word "planned" is to have meaning any place in the world—it is in Israel, the classical example of an economy growing in pace and form, while fulfilling its primary purpose: the building of a State, the creating of a nation, the furthering of immigration.

One of the leaders of Israel's economy defined its method as one in which the theory of "comparative suffering" determines the economic factors; i.e., it is the suffering of Jews which determines one of the basic elements of economic life —the rate of immigration. The degree of suffering inflicted in the countries of their origin, as opposed to that inflicted in building the new homeland in Israel, determines this important factor in the national economy, not the absorptive capacities of the country, nor the extent of its reserve capital, nor its already exploited natural resources.

AGRICULTURE

In this quest for a sound economy the Israelis turned to agricultural settlement for their solution. This was not only in line with tradition, ideology, and economic necessity, but settlement of the land after thousands of years of desolation, is also an integral part of Israel's political theory. The young State not only wants to execute sovereignty over the land, but also wants its citizens to share in its possession.

This unique approach to the land ownership problem, initiated in the early days of Jewish return to Eretz Israel, has been preserved. The Jewish National Fund continued to be the trustee of the nation's land, leased on a forty-nine-year basis, founded on the custom of the Biblical Jubilee. One of the main problems familiar to many of the underdeveloped countries of the world, that of big-land ownership and small tenants in an agrarian economy, is not a problem in Israel.

But Israel was not, and is not, able to cultivate all of its land. Great stretches of arid wasteland remain, and only superhuman efforts in land preservation and irrigation have made it possible to

cultivate many now productive areas.

A land utilization survey provided encouraging results: out of about 2,378,587 acres of examined land (excluding the southern Negev), 2,073,347 acres have been found suitable for agricultural uses. This survey, of rather recent date, was to a great extent a "postscript," performed after Israel had already proved that what used to be desert or deadly malaria-breeding areas could be turned into fertile land. The following statistics bear witness to this development:

THE GROWTH OF ISRAEL'S CULTIVATED AREA

Year	Total Cultivated Area (in *dunams*) *	Irrigated Area (in *dunams*)
1948-49	1,650,000	300,000
1949-50	2,480,000	375,000
1950-51	3,350,000	470,000
1951-52	3,475,000	540,000
1952-53	3,550,000	650,000
1953-54	3,560,000	760,000
1954-55	3,600,000	890,000
1955-56	3,680,000	1,000,000
1958-59	4,040,000	1,290,000

* 4 dunams equal one acre.

This expansion of the cultivated area has resulted in the increase of agricultural production. The ratio of productivity in these years was often proportionately higher than the expansion of cultivated land. While the area of cultivated land was more than doubled during the seven years from 1948 to 1955 (with irrigated areas increasing more than threefold), total agricultural production rose four times. Within the ten years, the value of agricultural production rose from seventy-five million dollars to three hundred million dollars, and more than two-thirds of the country's food consumption is now grown locally.

The rising agricultural production was not only a result of expansion but also of the introduction of new methods and mechanization. The number of caterpillar tractors rose from 400 in 1948 to 1,663 in 1955; wheel tractors increased from 280 to 2,005; combines from 260 to 1,216; balers from

Tending tomato plants near Migdal, Upper Galilee.

170 to 630. The growing supply of water also contributed greatly to the increase of production, so that, for the first time, Israel has encountered the problem of the developed countries—surpluses, especially of vegetables.

In this tremendous upsurge of agricultural growth, two special factors cannot be overlooked —the continuous effort to free Israel, as far as possible, from imports of agricultural products, especially grains, and the introduction of industrial crops. Groundnuts, sugar beets, and cotton, three crops unknown in Palestine's history before the inception of the State of Israel, have laid the foundation for a country self-sufficient in edible oils, sugar, and cotton.

Israel's method of striving to achieve its economic independence was as unique as the entire

effort to plan an agricultural system which would parallel the creation of a nation. Cultivation of the land was not enough; the immigrants, most of them used to urban living, had to be "cultivated" into farmers.

The hundreds of agricultural settlements which have been founded since 1948 did not completely fit into the pattern of agricultural colonization formed in the years preceding the State. Many of the new immigrants were quite reluctant to take upon themselves what could be considered a social and moral mission. The most cherished form of rural settlement in pre-State times, the *kibbutz*, the communal collective settlement, where all property is collectively owned and work is organized on a group basis, was not attractive to the new immigrants. They, at least an overwhelming major-

195

Plowing newly drained land in the Huleh Valley.

ity of them, were not ready to become members of a community where, in return for their labor, they would receive housing, food, clothing, education, and cultural and social services. They were not enthusiastic about a central dining room and kitchen, communal kindergarten and children's quarters, communal social and cultural centers, and central stores.

The newcomers were individualists. They preferred *moshvay ovdim,* where workers cooperate in small-holder settlements, based on the principle of mutual aid and equality of opportunity, where each individual farm is worked by the members of the family, but the produce is sold through a central cooperative and purchases are made cooperatively.

For many of these settlers even this was too communal in character. They desired the older type of agricultural settlement, the *moshava,* an ordinary village, based on private land ownership and private enterprise. The *moshava* resembles the *moshav ovdim* in many ways, but without the same basic ideology, and hired labor is permitted.

Strict adherence to any of the forms of settlement is not obligatory; there is even a special "mixed" form of colonization, the *moshav shitufi,* a settlement based on collective ownership, but with each family responsible for its own house and domestic services (cooking, laundry, and care of the children). Work and pay are adjusted to individual family circumstances.

This picture of Israel's agriculture, with stress

Bedouins reap their first harvest in the Negev with modern farm machinery supplied by the Israeli Government.

The Negev desert is brought to life once again as settlers plow land that has not been cultivated for thousands of years.

Old plowing methods have not been entirely abandoned—for the ox continues to serve man.

put on the expansion of the cultivated areas south-ward, deep into the Negev, remains incomplete in two of its major dimensions—the citrus plantations and forestry efforts.

Both are of mixed character. Many people do not consider citrus growing an agricultural profession, but rather a kind of industry. But, conceding this point, citrus (along with grape culture) is the oldest agricultural product of Israel and the most important source of revenue to the country. The 32,500 acres of fruit-bearing plantations in 1948 have been increased to 69,800 acres yielding annually over fifty million dollars in ex-

A new well gushes forth near Eilat.

Laying an irrigation pipeline to carry water to the barren Negev from the Yarkon River.

And the parched land shall become a pool, and the thirsty land springs of water: in the habitation of dragons shall be grass with reeds and rushes (Isaiah 35:7).

ports, especially of the world-renowned "Jaffa oranges."

The second agricultural effort, the large-scale afforestation program carried out jointly by the Government and the Jewish National Fund, has contributed to a great change in Israel's landscape within the last ten years. But of 48,750 acres of forested area in Israel, 35,500 acres have been planted since the State was officially established, and trees have been planted along 438 miles of roadside. This emphasis on reforestation, together with about 200,000 acres of natural forests and

forest reservations, has been of great importance for soil preservation and climate regulation, as well as providing a valuable source of lumber.

INDUSTRY

Although the stress on the importance of agriculture still exists, the Israelis realize that agriculture alone, even with the most modern equipment and the exploitation of all the cultivable land available, cannot support a rapidly growing population.

The pastoral dream of Israel, tailored when it was a country of farmers and shepherds, was no longer adequate. Isreal must depend largely upon industrialization for strength in both its economic and defense structure.

In the early phases of Israel's existence, when

A piper cub sprays thousands of acres with insecticide to combat a plague of locusts.

198

Conquest of the desert—farming irrigated land in the Negev.

Sheep roam a quiet valley.

A young girl from Turkey in the chicken-run of Tel-Schachar, a settlement named after Henry Morgenthau (*tel-schachar* and Morgenthau mean "morning dew").

These Israeli cowboys were trained in their work by a Wyoming cattleman.

Mares and stallions romp in the pasture of a stud farm and experimental station near Acre.

A citrus packing plant in the Sharon Valley.

The wine cellars of Zichron Yaakov.

Sorting the potato crop.

The first harvest of cabbages in a new settlement.

the country was almost completely besieged and cut off from foreign supply sources, the nucleus of Israeli industry filled the void. Products of the small metal industry equipped, though insufficiently, the improvised army, the textile industry supplied clothing material, and the food industry the necessary foodstuffs.

In 1949, not more than eighty thousand people were employed in industry, and the annual value of industrial production was $125,555,555. The number of employed persons was almost doubled within ten years and the value of industrial production grew to about $700,000,000. Since 1948, over $305,555,555 has been invested in industrial development, 70 per cent coming from foreign sources.

The rapid growth of the country was reflected in the industries singled out for expansion. A population which grew from 785,000 in 1948 to about 2,000,000 within ten years was primarily in need of consumer goods. The newcomers had to be dressed, fed, and, in fact, provided with everything. As a result, expansion took place mainly in the textile, shoe, and clothing industries, in which $63,888,888 have been invested. $55,550,000 have recently been invested in metallurgy and electrical products, and about $48,840,000 in the chemical industry.

The output of industry, measured in uniform prices, is estimated to have almost doubled between 1948 and 1952, to have increased 6 per cent

in 1953, 16 per cent in 1954, and 14 per cent in 1955. In 1956, a decrease in this percentage occurred, attributed to the critical international situation which preceded the Sinai campaign. During the last four years the annual growth of industry has been about 10 per cent and output has tripled. The national income grew from about $150,000,000 in 1950 to about $1,500,000,000 in 1959.

As in all countries, the consumption of power (in this case electric power, the only source of power in Israel) indicates the pace of economic growth—electric power sales to commercial establishments, workshops, factories, and irrigation networks multiplied five times since 1948, from almost 128,000,000 kilowatt hours. to 600,000,000 kilowatt hours.

The list of industries utilizing this power is a long one—food processing, 23.62 per cent; metals and ceramics, 12.60 per cent; textiles, 12.04 per cent; stone and cement, 9.63 per cent; wood, 6.60 per cent; chemicals, 6.42 per cent; clothing and footwear, 6.18 per cent; printing and paper, 3.83 per cent; minerals, 3.82 per cent; electrical appliances, 3.09 per cent; automobile assembly, 2.61 per

Date palms near Eilat.

Fishermen haul in their catch at Eilat on the Red
Sea.

cent; machinery, 2.16 per cent; diamond cutting and polishing, 1.97 per cent; rubber products, 1.70 per cent.

NATURAL RESOURCES

The industries based on Israel's own mineral resources do not loom large in the preceding list. They are only a fraction of the total industrial picture, but they hold great potentialities for Israel's economic future.

Installations have been started to enable Israel to produce, by 1961, one hundred thousand tons of vital metals in such forms as bullets, alloyed steel castings, and pig iron. At that time almost half of Israel's metal needs will be supplied from local sources, from locally mined iron ore, pyrites, and steel scrap.

The discovery of iron ore is not the only one made within the past ten years. As has been the case so often, the field of natural resources has responded "to the will of the man and his drive for achievements." And, as implausible as it may seem, the Bible served as the motivating force behind the search for the treasures concealed by this bare and arid land. The Bible speaks of Israel as a land in which the hills are of iron and the valleys of copper. The stories of King Solomon's copper mines were a spiritual guide to economic fulfillment.

The Talpiot Market in Haifa.

This search, which could well be called "the search for the legendary treasures," has produced daily results. Copper and manganese deposits have been discovered in the Timna region, about 18 miles north of Eilat near the site of King Solomon's copper mines. Copper ore reserves total 7,000,000 tons, with an average copper content of 70,000 tons, or 1.4 per cent. A copper plant with an annual capacity of 7,000 tons of copper is in the final stages of construction. Phosphate rock is mined at Oron, to the east of the Great Crater in the Negev. Production totaled 85,000 tons in 1955-56, 209,891 tons in 1958-59, with a phosphorus $(P_2 O_2)$ content of 25.8 per cent. All local needs are filled from this source and there is still over a third left for export.

The Dead Sea minerals represent an almost unlimited source. It is estimated that the Dead Sea contains millions of tons of magnesium chloride, common salt, and magnesium bromide, enough to supply an entire chemical industry. The Potash Works Company has exploited close to one hun-

A milk-bottling machine in a modern dairy plant.

A printing press in a modern newspaper plant.

An electric power station in Tel Aviv.

A Yemenite weaver in the Ata Mill near Haifa, the largest textile mill in Israel.

A fertilizer and chemical plant at Haifa Bay.

An auto body nears completion at the Kaiser-Frazer factory near Haifa.

dred thousand tons of potash annually and there is still promise of a greater yield.

The Negev proved to be even more generous with its offers of feldspar, mica, glass sand, ball clay, bituminous rock, gypsum, fluorite, chrome, sulphur, and kaolin. But the most vital of natural resources, oil, has not been found in great quantities. However, in September, 1955, oil was discovered in Heletz in quantities sufficient for commercial use. Israel's entire economy is dependent upon a flow of liquid fuel, the source of all man-made power. The country's fuel bill runs into over forty million dollars annually, representing almost 12 per cent of all imports and 7.5 per cent of the nation's total budget. Each of the sixteen wells of the Heletz oil field produces 120 barrels a day, which provides for only 5 per cent of Israel's oil requirements. A new gusher at Bror Hayil, discovered in June, 1957, produces 180 barrels a day and there is a well-founded hope that, even without new strikes of oil, the existing wells will produce up to 200,000 tons annually, which would

Workers at a paper mill sort flax fibers before baling.

amount to 15 per cent of Israel's yearly oil needs. A 16-inch pipeline to be completed late summer 1960 will carry oil from the port of Eilat to the heart of the country. The extension of the pipeline to Haifa with its oil refineries creates new possibilities of oil routes from the East to European countries with all the political and economic implications of such a development.

The Petroleum Law, passed by the Knesset in 1952, is intended to prevent any single company from gaining control of Israel's oil and to assure reasonably scaled royalties for the nation. On the basis of this law, nine oil companies are engaged in prospecting for oil in an area, granted by the Government, of 625,000 acres.

Among the basic industries, Fertilizers and Chemicals, Limited, deserves special attention. This enterprise controls a number of chemical plants in Haifa, which produce superphosphate fertilizers, sulphuric acid, hydrochloric acid, dicalcium phosphate, potassium sulphate, and ammonia. The output in 1956-57 earned $9,500,000 saving the country almost $4,500,000 in imports.

FOREIGN INVESTMENT

American investment plays a major role in this industrial development. The Kaiser-Fraser Assembly Plant, the American-Israel Paper Mills, and the tire-producing plants, are only a few of the enter-

A diamond polisher in Tel Aviv. Israel exports twenty million dollars' worth of gems annually to the United States.

A worker releases the hard-board press at the Sefen wallboard factory in Afiqim.

prises which private foreign capital, mainly American, has helped to establish.

This flow of foreign capital investment is of deep concern to Israel. This concern would be more readily understood if one would recall that, until 1914, even the United States depended upon foreign capital in a number of its industries. Special steps have been taken to increase capital investments. The Law for the Encouragement of Foreign Investments passed by the Knesset on August 6, 1959 extends the facilities and privileges provided to both foreign and local investors in the original Law of 1950 and amendments of 1955. These include relief from property tax in the first five years after an enterprise has been established (in some cases up to ten years), an increased allowance

A new hotel under construction near Herzlia.

for depreciation, and considerable reductions in the rates of income tax both for companies and individuals. The law also provides that a non-resident foreign investor may transfer his profits, in the same currency in which his investment was originally made without any limitations. The investor is also entitled to import free of duty building material, machinery, raw materials for start of production. A special amendment to the law provides for the inclusion of foreign-currency loans as a privilege of capital investment.

United States investments in Israel were greatly stimulated by the United States-Israel agreement of August 8, 1952. According to this agreement, American investors, upon receiving approval of their investments from the Israeli Government,

Assembly-line packaging of edible oils.

may apply to the United States Government for guarantees, under the Economic Cooperation Act of 1948, to insure themselves against confiscation and against the possibility of not being able to transfer their profits or assets into dollars.

A special investment center, established under the provisions of the Law for Encouragement of Capital Investment, with branches in the United States and other countries with potential investors, furnishes information on problems of capital investment in Israel, decides whether any proposed enterprise is "approved" under the Law and, therefore, entitled to all special benefits provided by it. During its first seven years, the Investment Center approved 790 enterprises involving investments totaling $232,933,555. Nearly half of this private foreign capital has come from the United States and Canada. These figures do not include some of

The Nesher cement works near Haifa.

the new, big projects such as a rayon factory with an investment of fourteen million dollars and the twelve-million-dollar expansion project of the American-Israel Paper Mill.

With an influx of population of more than double that at the inception of the State, in addition to the natural increase, the building industry is of primary importance. Housing is one of the heaviest, but unavoidable, burdens of the national economy. From 1949 to December, 1955, approximately 160,000 housing units, comprising nearly 350,000 rooms on an area of about 5,400,000 square feet, were completed. By 1957, over 180,000 housing units were constructed by the Government and Jewish Agency, and 50,000 through private enterprise. Close to $278,000,000 has thus far been expended. (These figures include housing and building for industrial and commercial purposes.) The building industry alone employs 40,000 people.

THE BUDGET

The special character of Israel's economy, undeveloped yet compelled to sustain the needs of a population that has more than doubled in ten years, requires a special budget system. The budget had to be built on two levels—a regular budget financed from taxes levied locally, covering the normal expenditures of Government departments; and a Development Budget, financed from the counterpart funds of foreign grants and loans, as well as by local loans.

The regular budget for the year 1957-58 clarifies these basic principles. The principle of a balanced budget is carefully preserved and there have been years when the regular budget was not only balanced, but showed a surplus of considerable amounts. The 1959-60 budget provides for an expenditure of $817,600,000. Of the local taxes, the

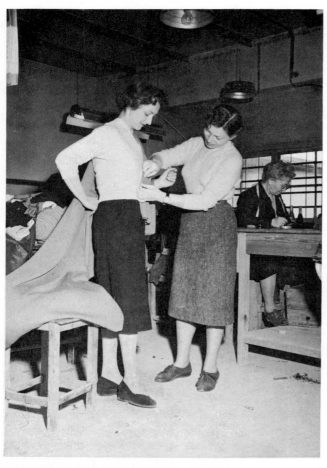

Fashioning a new design out of fabric woven in Israel.

by the Jewish Agency, Jewish National Fund, United Jewish Appeal, and Israel Bond sales. (From the inception of the State until the end of 1957, the following amounts of foreign currency have come into the Israel economy: $667,517,000 raised by the United Jewish Appeal and transferred to the Jewish Agency; $320,824,000 in the sale of Israel Bonds; reparations from Germany, $337,400,000; United States grants-in-aid and various other forms of American economic assistance, $328,000,000.)

The most natural source of foreign currency is that earned through exports. In this respect, growth has been remarkable. At the end of 1956, exports were 263 per cent higher than in 1949. During the period from January to July, 1957, the rise, compared with the same period in 1956, was 29 per cent, and has amounted to $83,000,000 in these six months (diamond exports played an important role). But this upsurge in export volume did not make up for the balance of trade. The deficit remains large and there is little consolation in the fact that a great percentage of the imports' value, $230,000,000 in the six months, are spent for the import of capital goods which are to in-

most important is the income tax levied progressively up to a maximum of 53.75 per cent. The Income Tax Law provides for personal deductions, deductions for dependents, life-insurance payments, trade union dues, and donations to charity. Wage-earners, persons over sixty, and students receive special deductions.

The Development Budget provides funds for selected projects required to open up the country for its rapidly growing population and to create new sources of income in order to improve the balance of trade. As was mentioned before, this budget is financed from the counterpart funds of foreign grants and loans, as well as by local loans. These include the counterpart funds for United States grants in aid, United States agricultural surplus, and loans of the Export-Import Bank.

The Foreign Currency Budget constitutes a special feature in Israel's budget structure. Important amounts of foreign currency are collected

A fashion show to stimulate the export of Israeli women's wear.

Drilling in the Negev to explore the oil and water resources of the area.

Potash works at the Dead Sea.

crease Israel's production capacity and thus help to increase exports and to curb imports as much as possible.

Inflation is a permanent component in this form of economy. In the constant struggle against inflation, the pressure of which is unavoidable in a country where the growth of the number of consumers outpaces the increase in production, the banking system plays an important role, especially the Bank of Israel, which issues currency.

Although Israel did not renew the pre-dispersion name of its currency and kept the pound as the monetary unit, the smaller currency units have been given the old, historic name "pruta." The Israeli Pound is divided into one thousand prutot and the official rate of exchange was fixed as follows: 1 Israeli pound equals 55.5 United States cents or 4 British shillings. The Bank of Israel balance statement of 1956 showed 360,597,436 Israeli pounds. Twenty-six commercial banks and ninety-one cooperative credit societies are serving the financial market of the country. 239,800,000 Israeli pounds in circulation at the end of 1955 were covered as follows:

Gold in International Monetary Fund	2.1 million
Foreign Currency Balance	87.4 million
Government Land Bonds	77.3 million
Treasury Bills	73.0 million
	238.8 million

A miner drilling for copper north of Eilat.
A land whose stones are iron and out of whose hills thou mayest dig brass (Deuteronomy 8:9).

211

Construction of a copper refining plant at Timna.

TRAVEL

Israelis like to travel. According to some sociologists, because most Israelis come from large countries, they try, by traveling, to overcome the fact that the country is very small and has comparatively little space for moving about. Others attribute the love of travel to a growing attachment for the country, a desire to know, to see, to learn about it through personal exploration.

Of course, it would be fallacious to imply that the Israelis travel mainly for pleasure. The rapid development of the country has made the United States phenomenon of suburban living and commuting to work a necessity in Israel. But, unlike Americans, only a few Israelis use private cars— not because of road jams, but because very few own cars. The Israelis have to use public transpor-

tation for pleasure trips, although, in ten years, the number of privately owned cars has tripled and now totals 116,600.

People who can afford the expense travel by taxi, Sherut, which provides service not only within urban localities, but also between cities. For a few more cents, the Israeli can get the feeling of traveling by car, though he is one of six or seven passengers crowded into one automobile. In 1957, almost two million Israelis traveled by Sherut, while the inter-urban bus Company, Eshed, carried about eight million passengers. (There are two other bus companies: the Dan in Tel Aviv and its neighborhood, and Hamekasher in Jerusalem).

To the many highways crossing the country, a new one of special importance and significance was opened at the beginning of 1958—the highway

Mining iron ore in the mountains of Naphtali.

Oil refineries, Haifa.

Drillers enjoy a shower of crude oil as they bring
in a new well.

Construction of a new highway that stretches **across the Negev to Eilat.**

from Beersheba to Eilat, which Prime Minister Ben Gurion called "the overland Suez Canal."

The bus has become the national means of travel. Legend and luxury are words associated with bus drivers. Legends abound about their daring excursions into terrorism-infested areas in pre-State times, when only the courage of the driver and his skill with a gun saved the lives of many of his passengers—luxury, because the bus-cooperatives have a virtual monopoly on inter-urban bus routes and the salaries far exceed the wages paid to those in other industries. No wonder, then, when an Israeli child is asked what he would like to be "when he grows up," his answer is almost invariably "a bus-driver."

This bus monopoly is being impaired to a growing extent by the Israeli State-owned Railway System. In addition to 2,221.2 miles of surfaced roads for automobile transportation, the railway system totaled at the beginning of 1957, 263.5 miles of main railroad lines as compared with 74.4 miles in 1949 and 161.2 miles at the beginning of 1950. Improvement in service, renewal of the rolling stock, and faster trains are factors which have motivated a growing number of Israelis to travel by railway.

Travel is not limited to the confines of Israel. A population which has had deeply rooted interests abroad is naturally eager to visit the countries of their origin—as tourists. In addition to this personal interest, there is another much more important factor which prompted the development of Israel's overseas transportation, Strange as it may sound, there are only two routes of transportation from Israel to foreign countries, sea and air. Sealed in by the ring of Arab hostility, Israel has never enjoyed overland transportation. A country put into such a precarious position, dependent upon imports, had to develop its shipping lanes and air routes in the most efficient manner.

Some two months after the inception of the State, the Israel merchant marine comprised ten vessels displacing some 14,000 tons. In June, 1956, thirty-four merchant ships with a total gross tonnage of 138,000 tons were registered in Israel. Other ships which were delivered till the end of

The Tel Aviv Central Bus Terminal.

The Tel Aviv Central Railroad Station.

1958 increased the Israeli merchant marine to 250,000 gross tonnage, at the cost of an investment of about 63 million dollars.

The Israel Airline Company, bearing the symbolic name El-Al, "Upward and Onward," has undertaken a great burden. El-Al has acquired four of the fastest commercial airliners in use in the Western world, turbojet Brittanias, and has entered into the most competitive overseas air service. For years there were only two or three "Constellations," which had to cover vast air routes, flying over the Atlantic, making flights to Rome, Paris, London, Istanbul, Vienna, and even to Johannesburg in South Africa. El-Al planes carried 42,868 passengers in 1956 and covered 88,247.08 miles.

Arkia, the inland airline which flies between Lod and Eilat, provides tourist accommodations and transports some freight.

Promotion of tourism has become one of the most important considerations in Israel. It is not only the desire to find additional sources of foreign currency which prompts this encouragement of foreign visitors, but it is also the desire to show the world what the young nation has created while maintaining contact with foreign countries and, especially, the Jews of the world. These efforts are bearing fruit: the number of tourists who visit Israel is growing annually. In 1955, 42,212 tourists brought $7,220,000 in trade. The unceasing political tension in the Middle East brought a marked drop in 1956 and 1957, but the years 1958 and 1959 have seen an increased flow of tourists with the promise of over 100,000 visitors in 1960.

Railroad station, Haifa.

Unloading cargo at the port of Haifa.

LABOR AND UNIONS

The labor unions in Israel have carried a considerable part of the burden in the struggle for national liberation. In spite of the growing professional character of the trade union, the General Federation of Labor, Histadrut, with almost half a million members out of a population of almost two million, differs from other labor movements the world over in two ways—by its direct political involvement in the life of the country and because it owns a considerable part of Israel's economic enterprises.

The General Federation of Labor is not only

Tel Aviv's port, established in 1936 when Arab riots cut off ready access to the port of Jaffa.

the legitimate defender of the interests of the wage-earner, but is also the most important single employer in the country.

The list of Histadrut enterprises illustrates the dimensions of its economic achievement—in 1955 there were 725 separate enterprises, employing 146,000 workers (40 per cent of all wage-earners organized in the federation and 25 per cent of the whole labor force of the country). The principal among these are: Tnuva, the agricultural marketing cooperative, handling over 70 per cent of Israel's farm products; Hamashbir Hamerkazi, the Cooperative Wholesale Society, which acts as buyer for the consumer's cooperatives, collective farms, and other federation enterprises; Solel Boneh, a contracting and construction company which, apart from its building and contracting

After lifting of the Egyptian blockade, the port of Eilat once more resumes its vital duties.

activities, runs some of the most important industrial plants in the country.

The entire range of the workers' needs are supplied by the many Histadrut-controlled institutions—pension funds, unemployment fund, vocational schools, publishing houses, daily and weekly newspapers, a theater and sport organization. This multiplicity of activities has led to the saying that one can be born, live, and die within the Histadrut organizational framework without any needs beyond the organization.

There are many other unions in Israel. The Hapoel Hamizrachi is an organization of religious workers with 55,000 members and 75 agricultural settlements. It operates central institutions for the settlement, education, and absorption of new immigrants.

216

The fishing harbor at *kibbutz* Genossar on Lake Kinneret.

A dam on the Kishon River.

The National Labor Organization, founded in 1934 by the Revisionist Party, with 54,000 members, maintains institutions for housing (*Sela*), cares for fifteen agricultural settlements, has the second largest Sick Fund in the country (the National Workers Sick Fund with 138,000 members), and maintains social services and mutual-aid institutions.

Agudat Israel Worker's Organization, made up of Orthodox workers, has a membership of over 19,000. Like the Hapoel Hamizrachi, this organization has its members insured in the Histadrut Sick Fund, and is represented in the General Federation of Labor Trade Union Department.

The legislation covering the working conditions of this labor force (about 600,000 gainfully employed workers) is most progressive when compared to generally prevailing European standards —a forty-seven-hour work week, a maximum work day of eight hours, a compulsory weekly rest period of thirty-six continuous hours, and overtime work only with the permission of the Ministry of Labor. The Paid Annual Holidays Law grants all Israeli workers fourteen days of annual vacation, of which twelve days must be with pay. The Youth Labor Law regulates conditions of workers under eighteen. The Female Labor Law grants women twelve weeks maternity leave and several additional months of leave without pay, and prohibits night work except by permission of the Ministry of Labor.

The productivity of the workers is not just a theoretical problem for Israel. The labor force has absorbed immigrants from backward countries, some still in medieval or even stone-age stages of civilization, placing the fate of Israel's production into unskilled hands. Government, industry, and labor are therefore united in the effort to increase productivity, for higher productivity means more goods and more goods mean smaller imports, growing exports, greater economic independence, and a higher standard of living.

THE VISION OF DEVELOPMENT

To sum up ten years of Israel's economic strides without due concern to future development would misrepresent the real character of Israel's economy —its dynamism, revolutionary changes, and its relentless effort to march forward. Man's belief in his capacity to conquer the elements, to discover the secrets of nature in order to utilize them, is the backbone of Israel's economic plans.

It is not only man's eternal thirst for knowledge that drives Israel's scientists, planners, economists, and statesmen. The unavoidable compulsion to make room for incoming brethren motivates this search for new and improved methods of developing the country's resources and the desire to create new sources of power, to extend the stretches of land which can be cultivated and extracted from the clutches of the desert.

As a result, the Yarkon-Negev irrigation project was developed. The sixty-five-mile Yarkon-Negev pipeline, diverting the waters of the Yarkon River north of Tel Aviv to the parched land of the Negev, was opened in July, 1955. The pipeline will eventually supply this desert region with 2,700,000 cubic feet of water annually, increase the area of land which can be irrigated by 25 per cent, and make possible the development of thirty new villages with some eight thousand agricultural units and thirty-five thousand people.

The *S.S. Zion,* a 10,000-ton, steam-turbine passenger-cargo ship, built in Germany in 1956 under the German reparations plan.

An El Al Constellation prepares to take off from Lydda airport on a flight to Rome, Paris, and New York.

But even these projects are only a part of the great visionary strides made toward Israel's self-sustenance. In light of the prophecy of Isaiah "and the parched land became a pool, and the thirsty ground springs of water"—Israel has taken practical measures. Not only the waters of the Yarkon, but also the waters of the Jordan will aid in transforming the Negev desert, comprising almost half of Israel's territory, back into the fruit-bearing region it was in ancient times. The Jordan Valley Authority, similar to the Tennessee Valley Authority, is slowly materializing. More than ten billion cubic feet of water from the Jordan will be carried annually over a distance of 116 miles to the Negev through a succession of open canals, reservoirs, giant pipe conduits, and tunnels. The conduits will be made of locally produced pre-stressed concrete pipes, 108 inches in diameter. The length of the three tunnels is 4.8 miles.

The full implementation of the project, which is already under way, will start a new era in Israel's agricultural methods. Over 250,000 acres of land will be added to Israel's agricultural area, and new sources of energy will come into being. A canal from the coast to the Dead Sea will make use of the difference of levels (the Dead Sea is 1,286 feet below sea level) and will supply cheap electric power in an amount that will almost double the present rate of electricity-generating capacity.

"Deeds of Genesis" are being accomplished in the little country. The end of 1957 has seen the drainage of the Huleh swamps and lake which added thousands of acres to Israel's most fertile lands and has wiped out a pestilential malaria-breeding area.

Israel is concentrating on experimentation for turning salt sea water into a source of fresh water for irrigation. Research institutes. such as the Weizmann Institute of Science in Rehovot, are working with considerable success to harness atomic energy for peaceful uses. New possibilities will open for the development of mineral resources that will prove there was no truth in the old argument that Israel is a barren country with no min-

219

eral wealth and no possibilities for economic self-support for its fast-growing population.

The Israeli authorities and the Israeli people fully understand the implications and possibilities of the coming era. For this reason, research is emphasized and compares favorably, in certain instances, with that being conducted in the most advanced countries. Israel seriously heeds the words of Sir Ben Lockspeiser, the chairman of Israel's Technological Advisory Board, a famed British scientist who now serves as President of the European Atomic Research Council: "Research is the goose that lays the golden egg."

Judging from past achievements, the "golden egg" of Israel's peaceful development seems to be within sight.

Stamps depicting the history of Israeli ships, from ancient sailing vessels to the modern S.S. *Zion*.

10 EDUCATION AND SCIENCE

The new State has continually concentrated on its educational and cultural activities. How else could it weld the diverse elements of its population—the native born, the old settlers, and the hundreds of thousands of immigrants from over seventy countries—with their varying cultural backgrounds and their veritable Babel of languages?

The Government of Israel inherited from the established Jewish community a series of autonomous school systems which had been developing over a period of some sixty years. Until the outbreak of World War I, there was no unified Hebrew educational system in Palestine. The pupils received their education in traditional religious institutions, *Talmud Torah,* where Yiddish was the language of instruction and the subjects of study were the Bible and the Talmud.

The first school with a modern European curriculum was the Lemel School, founded in 1856 in Jerusalem. Some years later the Àlliance Israelite Universelle, organized in France for the purpose of spreading culture among Jews, extended its activities to Palestine. In 1901, another organization for assistance to Jews abroad was organized in Germany, the Hilfsverein der Deutchen Juden. Both these organizations founded a few schools with French, German, or English as the language of instruction.

Hebrew subjects had their appropriate place, but these were not Hebrew schools. The first elementary Hebrew School was founded by the BILU movement. In 1902, the first institution of secondary education in Hebrew, the Herzlia High School, was founded in Jaffa.

Some years later, a Hebrew High School was established in Jerusalem and, in 1913, a teacher's seminary was opened in Jaffa.

The years prior to World War I saw continuous development in this field. The Hilfsverein der Deutchen Juden organized a high school of science and laid the foundation for the Israel Institute of Technology, the Technion. At this time, the first and decisive battle for the Hebrew language was fought—the Hilfsverein wanted to have the German language as the basis of study in these schools, but the Zionist members of the board revolted and, supported by the student body, finally succeeded in bringing the schools under the supervision of the Zionist organization, which took over the financial burden of the school. The foundations for a national Hebrew educational system had been laid.

The new school system gave impetus to the revival of the Hebrew language as a living instrument for expression, acting as both the workshop and the disseminating agent of the language.

Under the Department of Education of the National Council (Vaad Leumi), the school system was divided into three parts: general, Mizrachi and labor. The Mizrachi, represented a distinctly religious approach, while the labor schools attempted to channel their students toward a pioneering and cooperative society. The general schools placed emphasis on general education. When the Compulsory Education Law was passed in September, 1949, it recognized these divisions and added a fourth, the Orthodox Agudat Israel. Parents had the choice of sending their children to any of these schools.

In time it became more evident that these schools had outgrown their usefulness and had influenced each other to such a degree that the dividing lines were almost obliterated. Whatever remained to distinguish them only confused the immigrant parents who had difficulty in making an intelligent choice for their youngsters. The acute shortage of teachers, which resulted from the rapid growth of school attendance, made the maintenance of several schools in small communities an unnecessary extravagance.

The State Education Law, which was enacted by the Knesset in August, 1953, abolished the "trend system" and set up a unified system of kindergarten and elementary schools under the administration of the Ministry of Education and Culture. It also provided for State religious education and aid for private schools if their curricula,

Calisthenics at the Lemmel Elementary School in Jerusalem. Founded in 1856, this school was the first to introduce a modern European curriculum.

teaching standards, and facilities filled the requirements of the Ministry. Many of the Agudat Israel have taken advantage of this provision to set up their own school system. "The State educational system aims to establish primary education in the State on the values of the heritage of Israel and the achievements of science, on love for the homeland and loyalty to the State of Israel and the Jewish people, on training in agriculture and manual labor, on pioneering and on striving for the creation of a society built on freedom, mutual help, and love of humanity."

TEACHER TRAINING

The shortage of teachers is one of the main problems of Israel's school system. The source of supply for teachers during the pre-State period was limited and the number of trained teachers among the new immigrants was rather small. Another problem was the fact that most of the prospective

The first Hebrew secondary school, Herzlia, was founded in 1906.

teachers arriving in Israel had to master Hebrew first.

This critical situation has been partially alleviated through the institution of intensive training courses (four to six months) for suitable candidates, and the opening of new teachers' colleges.

The regular teachers' colleges offer a two-year course of study in educational theory and practice. They are the main source of supply for kindergartens and elementary schools. High-school teachers must have a university degree. Teachers lacking these qualifications were employed under emergency measures and may qualify for teacher diplomas by attending special courses and taking supplementary examinations. Hundreds of teachers are taking advantage of these opportunities.

Eight Pedagogic Centers in all parts of the country, are constantly working toward the improve-

Students and faculty of the first school in Tel Aviv, Neve Zedek, which is now a girl's school. Moshe Sharett was among the first pupils.

ment of teaching standards, providing the teachers with professional libraries and guidance in acquiring and applying teaching aids and school equipment.

ADMINISTRATION AND FINANCING

The Ministry of Education and Culture supervises the entire educational system. Its executive and supervisory functions are supplemented through six district offices. The State Education Act of 1953 created two councils, the State Education Council and the Council for State Religious Education. The Minister of Education consults the councils on all problems and draft regulations concerning his duties. The members of the councils are appointed by the Minister for a period of four years and are selected from leading educators, representatives of universities, the teachers' union, and local governments.

The financial responsibility for the nine years of primary education rests mainly with the Government. Local governments contribute their share in accordance with their financial resources. The Government bears all the costs in low-income localities, especially in new immigrant settlements.

The percentage spent on education rose from 5.6 per cent of the total Government budget in 1949—50, to 13.5 per cent of the budget in 1955—56. The Government appropriation for education, however, covers only about 40 per cent of the total expenditure for the education of the country. The other 60 per cent is derived from local governments, voluntary organizations, and tuition fees.

Kindergarten scene in Tel Aviv.

Israel's educational system provides for approximately half a million pupils and students. Thirty eight thousand of these are non-Jews. The State Education Act covers all children of school age. In the course of the 1957—58 financial year, a total of about thirty-five million dollars was spent on education alone.

ELEMENTARY SCHOOL EDUCATION

The Israel school system provides a continuous education from kindergarten to university. Compulsory and free education from the ages of five to thirteen takes the child through the last year of kindergarten and eight years of elementary school. Youths between the ages of fourteen and seventeen who have not completed an eight-year elementary-school education must attend special classes until

Kindergarten pupils rest after lunch.

they either complete the required curriculum or reach the age of seventeen.

A unique feature of Israel's education is the prevalence of kindergartens covering the ages from three to six. Attendance has been promoted by the inclusion of the fifth-year age group in the compulsory education provision. It is estimated that from 90 to 93 per cent of the five-year-olds attend Government kindergartens, and the remainder private ones. During the past ten years there has been a more than fourfold increase in the number of pupils attending kindergartens. In the school year 1948-49, 24,494 children attended kindergarten and in 1959 the enrollment was 78,500. The kindergarten plays a significant role in Israel's society. It is of primary importance in the cultural integration of immigrant children

Children in a settlement near Rehovot attend school while their parents are at work.

In this outdoor kindergarten at Maoz Zurim, an agricultural colony for the resettlement of Yemenite Jews, children who speak only Arabic, learn the rudiments of Hebrew.

Recess at an elementary school in Herzlia.

Most of the modern elementary schools have their own libraries.

Workshop in a Jaffa elementary school.

An informal classroom in an elementary school.

Playground of an elementary school in Tel Aviv where Jewish children from East and West play together.

The curriculum is divided into two parts—one to meet the needs of the State schools and the other to meet the needs of the State religious schools. The difference between them lies in the greater emphasis on religion in the State religious schools. A similar curriculum for Arab schools is in the final stages of preparation. The curriculum is based on the method of study units, training in independent work, and the measurement of actual knowledge required by the student.

In subject matter and pedagogy the elementary school follows the pattern of primary education developed in Europe and the United States, adapted to the ideals and particular needs of the renascent nation. The study of the Bible is at the heart of the educational system. The study of literature from the Talmudic, medieval, and modern periods, and a thorough survey of Jewish history, imbue the pupils with the sense of historical continuity and unity of the Jewish people—the mainsprings of the return to Zion.

The schools, mainly co-educational, aim at preparing the pupil for life as an individual and as a good citizen, and at shaping him into the image of a pioneer—selfless, courageous, and constructive. Farming, manual labor, and home economics are emphasized and most of the village and city schools have land for farming and shops for woodwork and metal work. Many are equipped with kitchens in which the pupils, boys and girls, prepare lunches for the entire school. Farm clubs and such are encouraged as extracurricular activities.

In 1955, twelve hours a week of practical work were added to the regular curriculum of the last grade. The project was designed for those students

and, in a country where many women work outside their homes, the kindergarten allows the mother to attend to her other duties.

Many schools are experimenting with kindergartens as an integral part of the primary school system. This has proved valuable among the Arab families who are not familiar with the principle of a kindergarten education.

The elementary school provides an eight-year education. Attendance of Jewish children from six to thirteen is almost 100 per cent. Arab school attendance increased from 48 per cent of the total Arab school-age population before the State to about 85 per cent in 1957. Many Arab girls are still prevented from attending school by their parents. In 1959-60, 90 per cent of all Arab boys and 50 per cent of Arab girls were studying in the Israel school system.

In 1954, the Ministry of Education and Culture introduced a comprehensive and detailed curriculum for the elementary schools, subject to review and evaluation after a trial period of a few years.

Nursery school children celebrate Shevuoth, the Festival of First Fruits.

226

An Arabian elementary school in Nazareth.   A Christian elementary school in Nazareth.

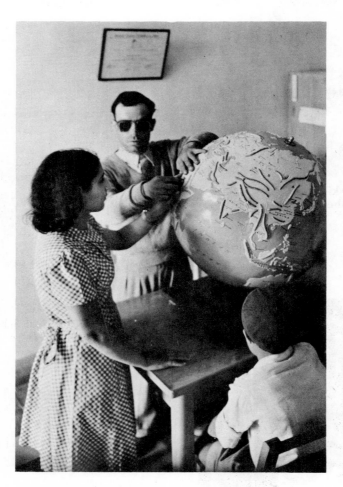

A blind girl in Chinuch Ivrim School of Jerusalem
studies geography.

A new secondary school in Tel Aviv.

Dormitory recreation room at Kfar Silver, the ZOA Agricultural Training Institute.

New immigrants acquire skills in the secondary schools that will enable them to be productive and self-supporting.

The Haifa Nautical School, where young boys are trained for a career in the merchant marine.

The pupils of the Weizmann Agricultural School learn how to milk cows.

Students of the Hebrew University help to build their new campus.

who were not expected to continue their formal education beyond the elementary school.

EDUCATION FOR RETARDED CHILDREN

Special arrangements are being made for the education of children who are unable to attend regular classes. Retarded and handicapped children are cared for in special classes or special institutions designed to fit their needs. In 1957 there were 296 special classes and 105 classes within the regular school system, caring for a total of 7,236 children with special needs.

SECONDARY EDUCATION

The high schools offer a four-year course of studies (some vocational high schools have a three-year course), provided by either private schools deriving their income from tuition or schools sponsored by local governments and civic organizations. The Government subsidizes many schools and offers scholarships to capable students who require financial aid. The Jewish Agency grants scholarships to students from Oriental countries to encourage these young people to continue their education. In 1956-57 more than one-third of the high-school student body was subsidized; nevertheless, many prospective students are still unable to attend because of tuition fees.

High-school students account for only one-third of the youth between the ages of fourteen and

The chemistry and physics laboratory building of the Hebrew University in Givat Ram.

eighteen. This is a cause of great concern, since it deters the cultural and economic development of the country. Efforts are being made toward increasing public support of secondary education until the Government is able to extend compulsory and free education beyond the elementary school level.

1956 marked the fiftieth anniversary of the first Hebrew high school, Herzlia, which was founded in 1907 in Jaffa. The curriculum of this school developed along lines similar to the European gymnasium or lyceum and the American high school. A considerable portion of the program is devoted to Judaic subjects—the Bible, ·the Talmud, medieval and modern Hebrew literature, and Jewish history. In most of the schools English is a required course. Many offer Arabic and French as an elective.

In the last two years of high school the student is free to select a particular field of studies—the humanities, sociology, pedagogy, science (mathematics, physics, chemistry), biology, agriculture, or Oriental studies.

Independent group study and general cultural activities, including dramatics, music, folk dancing, etc., supplement the curriculum. An intensive program of training in citizenship constitutes an integral part of high-school education. It encompasses aiding the cultural and social integration of new immigrants, the pioneering effort, the agricultural development of the country by working periodically on the farms, and defense through para-military training under the supervision of the Ministry of Education and Culture, within the framework of Gadna (abbreviation for Gdudei Noar, Youth Brigades).

Final examinations, primarily in written form, are given in six subjects at the end of the fourth year of studies. Students who have been unable to attend regular courses may nevertheless take these examinations if they meet certain preliminary requirements. The examinations are given by the Ministry of Education and Culture with the cooperation of the Hebrew University and the Israel Institute of Technology, the Technion. Bible, Hebrew, literature, mathematics, and a foreign language, usually English, are required subjects. The other two subjects are elective.

Recipients of a high-school diploma are admitted to the Hebrew University in Jerusalem, the Technion in Haifa, and other universities of high standing abroad without additional examinations. Many American colleges evaluate the Israeli diploma as the equivalent of twenty to thirty credits.

VOCATIONAL TRAINING

The expansion of vocational training is necessary for the economic development of the country. The technical and agricultural schools are mostly on a high-school level. They offer a three-year course of study in a particular trade, together with a general education. Working youth may acquire their vocational training in evening technical schools.

Research in the physics laboratory of the Hebrew University.

230

Hebrew University students conduct research in photochemistry.

HIGHER EDUCATION

The State of Israel is guided by the Biblical prophecy "Learning shall again come forth out of Zion." Jews were always considered the people of the Book and throughout the ages they have produced world-renowned scholars despite the fact that for hundreds of years the doors of the great European universities were closed to them. By the end of the nineteenth century, however, when Jewish students who had been hungry for modern, progressive education finally were allowed admission to most of the Western schools of higher learning, they were quick to prove their mark in many fields.

No wonder that with the return to Zion came the need for a Jewish university which would meet the scientific and cultural aspirations of Palestine Jewry and, at the same time, provide a center from which the Jewish people could make its own contribution to universal knowledge. The first person to activate this idea was Dr. Herman Shapiro, Professor of Mathematics at the University of Heidelberg, who wrote a series of essays published between 1882 and 1884. The idea steadily gained ground with the spread of anti-Semitism in many parts of the world. Subsequently the matter was vigorously taken up by a group of young intellectuals under the leadership of Dr. Chaim Weizmann, to whom a Hebrew university in Jerusalem was an integral part of Jewish national revival. At the eleventh Zionist Congress held in Vienna in 1913, Weizmann secured the adoption of a resolution proposing a Hebrew university in Palestine.

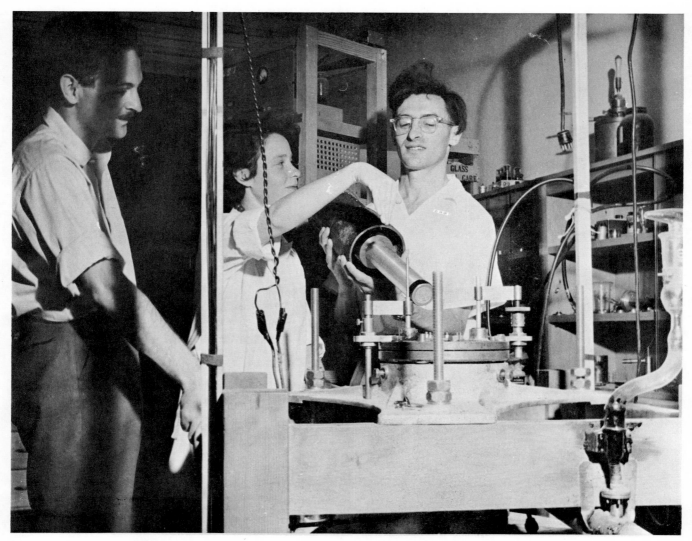

Working out a problem in physics at the Hebrew University.

He was also entrusted with the preparatory work. On July 24, 1918, the future first President of the reborn state of Israel laid the foundation stone for the Hebrew University on Mount Scopus; the formal opening of the University took place on April 1, 1925.

Two months earlier, on February 6, 1925, the Haifa Institute of Technology, the Technion, was officially opened on the slopes of Mount Carmel, overlooking the Mediterranean Sea.

Since the rebirth of Israel in 1948, three major institutions have been added: the Weizmann Institute of Science at Rehovot, inaugurated in 1949, on the occasion of the seventy-fifth birthday of the great scientist and President of the State; the Bar-Ilan University at Ramat Gan, founded in 1955; and the Tel Aviv University, integrated in 1956.

The aims of the Israel institutions of higher learning may be defined as follows:

a. To provide a focus for the free development of the Jewish spirit and humanism.

b. To extend the boundaries of knowledge and contribute to the moral, spiritual, and cultural values of humanity.

c. To promote the creative continuity of the Jewish cultural heritage.

d. To recreate and redefine Hebrew culture on the basis of a synthesis between the spiritual heritage of the Jewish people and the intellectual movements and aspirations of our age.

e. To provide for the intellectual, political, and socio-economic leadership of the nation (special emphasis is being put on closing the

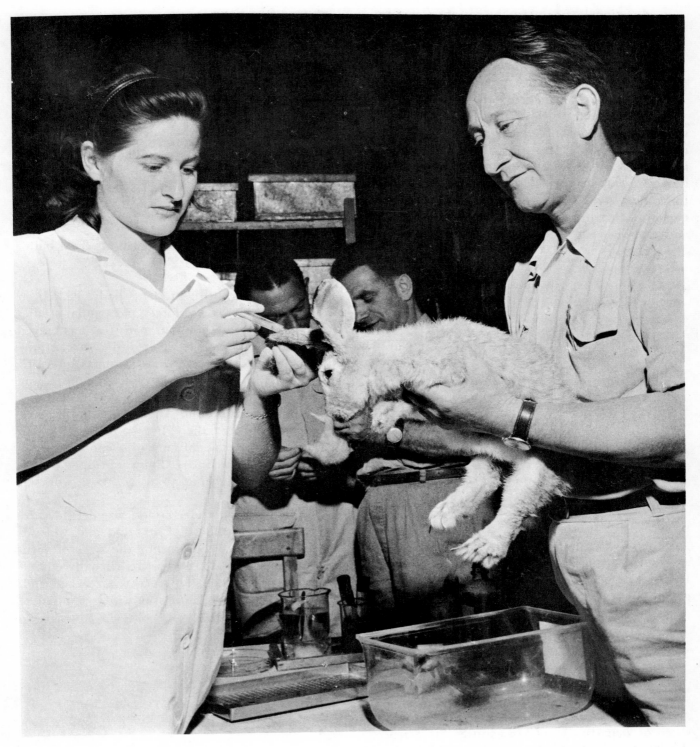

Cancer research at the Hebrew University.

educational gap among the various communities and integrating the new immigrants into that leadership).

f. To train professional manpower for the overall economic and cultural advancement of the country and people.

In pursuing these objectives, Israel's universities generally follow the pattern of similar schools in Western Europe and the United States. These institutions are privately operated, deriving their income from tuition, endowments, and contributions, both local and foreign. In recent years the Government, through the Ministry of Education and Culture, has aided expansion and building

Architect's model of the new medical school built by Hadassah and the Hebrew University.

Professor Martin Buber conducts a class in social philosophy at the Hebrew University.

projects with substantial grants. The schools are governed by their respective boards of trustees and academic councils. Many Jewish community leaders and scholars from abroad serve on these governing bodies.

THE HEBREW UNIVERSITY

The Hebrew University of Jerusalem started originally as a research center. The University soon developed into a full-fledged undergraduate and graduate school. By 1947, the University consisted of Departments of Humanities and Science, the Institute of Jewish Studies, and the Schools of Oriental Studies, Education, and Agriculture.

The Arab attacks on the Jewish community in Jerusalem following the United Nations Partition Resolution of November, 1947, cut Mount Scopus off from the rest of the city and made the campus and the Hadassah Medical Center inaccessible.

Practically the entire student body had been drafted into the defense forces and regular studies were out of the question, but many teachers braved the hazards of the journey in order to continue their research work on Mount Scopus. On April 13, 1948, an exceptionally large convoy on its way to the University and the Hadassah Hospital was subjected to a murderous Arab attack, and seventy-seven persons lost their lives—a disaster which robbed the University of some of its most outstanding scientists and scholars. This catastrophe put an end, for the time being, to all efforts to work on Mount Scopus.

The University, under attack, was defended by students and members of its academic and administrative staffs. By the time the siege of Jerusalem began in 1948, they were virtually cut off from the city. When the truce was reached and, some time later, communications were restored, it

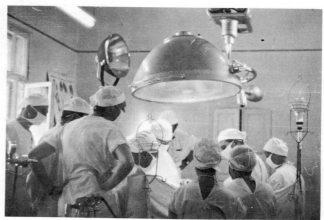

Surgeons perform an operation at the medical school while students observe.

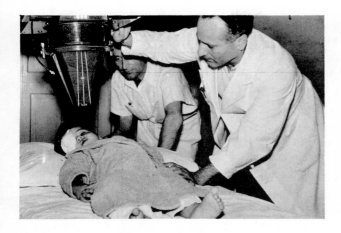

Taking an X-ray in the medical school's Department for Children.

Student nurses at the Hebrew University.

American students exchange notes on the terrace of the Abraham Mazer Building of the Hebrew University's Institute of Jewish Studies.

Relics of ancient Israel in the Archaeological Department of the Hebrew University.

was revealed that the damage sustained by the University buildings through Arab shelling was, on the whole, not severe and that the contents of the Jewish National and University Library had remained intact.

The Jewish National and University Library with its more than half a million volumes, and the valuable laboratory equipment were frozen on the hill. The Jordanians would not allow the University officials to transfer them to the city. These impediments did not, however, stop the rapid and extensive development of the University.

The name of the Jewish National and University Library indicates its two-fold function—it is both the National Library of the Jewish people and the Library of the Hebrew University. Acting in the former capacity, it collects books, manuscripts, periodicals, and other material reflecting the life and culture of the Jewish people. As the central library of the University it collects works in all fields of study, with particular reference to

Two of the jars in which the Dead Sea Scrolls were found.

Fragment of the Dead Sea Scrolls in the Hebrew University's Archaeological Department.

the subjects of instruction and research in the University's program. In addition, the Library also serves as the central library of Israel, its facilities being at the disposal of the population as a whole. Its collection of Hebraica and Judaica is among the largest in the world.

A new campus is being built at Givat Ram (Steep Hill), in the western part of Jerusalem, and some departments have already been transferred there. This campus is not intended to replace the one on Mount Scopus, but to supplement it. A new library has been established with a range of books almost equal to the one on Mount Scopus, still virtually inaccessible. As of 1957, the growing University comprised the following departments and schools: Department of Humanities, School of Oriental Studies, School of Education, The Eliezer Kaplan School of Economics and Social Sciences, Department of Science, School of Agriculture, School of Law, School of Medicine, School of Dentistry, School of Pharmacy, and the Graduate Librarian School.

University geologists are engaged in a continuous search for new resources that will promote a self-sufficient economy for the country. These experts are in the vanguard of the endeavor to find

Archaeological excavation near Beersheba.

An ancient Chanukah lamp of the Roman period.

Ivory plaque found at the palace of Ahab, King of Israel during the eighth century B.C.E.

A mosaic depicting the signs of the zodiac, from the ancient synagogue in Bet Alpha.

new water, oil, mineral, and chemical resources to facilitate the country's growth.

Under the direction of the University's physicists and other experts concerned with nuclear energy, a corps of alert, young Israeli scientists, trained at the University, are engaged in a program of nuclear energy research which is expected to produce sufficient power in a few years to turn the wheels of Israel's industry, supply its electric power, now dependent upon oil and inadequate water resources, light and heat its homes, and add new miracles to the annals of medical science.

In medicine, dentistry, and pharmacy, Hebrew University scientists are winning new laurels for research on cancer, polio, and tuberculosis. The University's experts on tropical medicine have succeeded in drastically checking and practically conquering such dread scourges endemic to the Middle East as malaria, trachoma, leprosy, and filariasis. In contrast to Israel, medical progress in neighboring Arab countries is still negligible. The good work of Hebrew University scientists has resulted in excellent health standards for the entire Israeli population. The life expectancy of its citizenry has now reached an average of seventy years.

Faculty, Students, and Graduates. In 1959-60 the faculty numbered 700 professors, lecturers, instructors, and assistants, drawn from almost every part of the world. An increasing proportion of the faculty are Hebrew University graduates.

The 6,500 students who were enrolled in 1959-60 came from some forty-five countries. Most of them, however, received their secondary education in Israel. Of these, 83 students came from the United States and Canada. By the end of 1948, the Hebrew University had awarded degrees to 842 students, and by the spring of 1957, the number had risen to 3,590.

With the aim of encouraging foreign students to study at the Hebrew University, a special one-year course for students abroad was introduced in the academic year 1955-56. The course is primarily designed to answer the needs of college and university students from the United States and Canada, who receive credits at their home university for the work done in Jerusalem. The twelve-month course is divided into two parts. The first part, of four months duration, is devoted to an intensive study of Hebrew at a special training center where they receive twenty-four hours of instruction a week at a level appropriate to their individual background in the language.

An extremely rare pottery mask of a bearded man, found on Mount Herodium near Bethlehem, dates back to the Roman occupation of Judea.

238

Adult Education. Two main factors have determined the character of adult education activities in Israel—the keen and widespread desire for learning among men and women of all classes and ages, and the great need for assistance in implementing the cultural orientation of the new immigrants. The Hebrew University, which has for many years been among the foremost institutions engaged in adult education, organizes and directs extra-mural courses of study on a university level in towns, villages, and immigrant settlements in cooperation with the Ministry of Education and Culture, the Cultural Center of the General Federation of Jewish Labor, and the local authorities. The Hebrew University Adult Education Center is responsible for two high schools (in Tel Aviv and Haifa), the graduates of which receive credit at the University; three Institutions for Advanced Studies (in Tel Aviv, Jerusalem, and Beersheba) in which one-year courses are given (in Jewish studies, general sciences, and the Humanities); and seminars, series of lectures, and single lectures in towns and villages. During the year 1954-55, 8,433 lectures were given.

The lecturers are Hebrew University teachers, or teachers whose academic standing has been approved by the University. In view of the difficulties of securing a sufficient number of lecturers from the ranks of those at the Hebrew University, it was recently decided to create a special group of teachers who will be at the service of the Adult Education Center.

The University also conducts research and study in connection with problems of adult education in general and in Israel in particular. The Department of Education offers one-year courses and seminars on basic problems of adult education. In the year 1955-56, sixty-five students took advantage of these courses. Training of adult education teachers is devised with a view to the special needs of new immigrants and is offered to selected students of the University's Department of Education.

Ben Zvi Institute for Research. In 1947, an Institute for Research on the Jewish communities in the Middle East was established under the auspices of the Hebrew University with the aim of collecting information and documents regarding the political, cultural, and economic conditions of the Jews in the Near and Middle East, and of compiling and publishing material on these subjects.

Ceremony opening a new semester at the George and Florence Wise Auditorium, the Hebrew University.

The Institute has been named after Itzhak Ben Zvi, who has headed the institution from the time of its inception.

The Institute has acquired over one hundred and fifty manuscripts and possesses the largest library of Ladino (mixed Spanish and Hebrew dialects spoken by Sephardic Jews) literature in Israel. Many scholarly works have been published by scientific bodies in Israel and abroad on the basis of the material it has collected.

The Magnes University Press. The Hebrew University Press (now the Magnes University Press) was established in 1929 to publish original Hebrew works and Hebrew translations of ancient and modern classics for the use of teachers and students of the University and for readers interested in scientific subjects.

Williams Planetarium of the Hebrew University. The Williams Planetarium in Jerusalem has introduced a new program which, in addition to showing the movements of celestial bodies, explains the astronomical problems involved in the dispatch of artificial satellites and demonstrates the orbits.

During the past sixteen months, since the inauguration of the planetarium, three hundred and forty illustrated lectures have been given to over eighteen thousand persons. As a result of the efforts of the Williams Planetarium scientists,

The Hebrew University synagogue erected in honor of Rabbi Israel Goldstein.

astronomical information now reaches the general and student public in a popular form for the first time. The planetarium not only offers instruction, but also arouses interest in astronomical subjects and attracts new members to the Israel Amateur Astronomers' Association.

Schools of higher education normally measure their existence in terms of centuries. It is, therefore, all the more remarkable that, in a little over three decades, this great Israeli center of science and culture has managed to make so much progress. Today, despite the fact that the Hebrew University has been exiled from its original campus on Mount Scopus for over nine years—since the Israeli War of Liberation—the University is flourishing. The increasing number of stu-

dents is an indication of the expanding economy and the growing desire for education.

TEL AVIV UNIVERSITY

On August 16, 1953, the municipality of Tel Aviv planned to establish the first institute of higher learning in that city. The decision was followed by the statement that "this institute would form the embryo of a future university." On December 1, 1953, the institute was opened and regular studies began.

On June 24, 1954, it was decided to open a second institute devoted to the humanities and particularly to Jewish studies. In June, 1956, these two institutions were joined within one academic framework with five departments: Natural Sciences, Arts, Law, Economics, and Social and Political Science.

In its combined form the Institute will be known as The Tel Aviv University. Professor Israel Ephrat has been appointed Rector of the University and Dr. Augusto Levy, Chairman of the Academic Presidium. The merger of administrations has been deferred for two years, so that the Tel Aviv Municipality continues to maintain the faculties of Natural Sciences and of Arts.

BAR-ILAN UNIVERSITY

The opening of Israel's 1955-56 academic year was highlighted by the inauguration of the Bar-Ilan University, the newest institution of higher learning in the country.

A project of the Mizrachi Organization of America, this new coeducational institution is designed to ease the growing need for additional university facilities. In addition, the Bar-Ilan University is expected to train Israeli youth in the arts and sciences, provide a comprehensive understanding of Jewish religious teaching and literature, and enable potential leaders of Jewish community affairs in the United States, Canada, and other parts of the world to obtain part of their college training in Israel, without losing credits in their local colleges.

A number of buildings in a semicircle connected by a covered walk were ready for the dedication of the Bar-Ilan University on August 7, 1955. They include a synagogue, auditorium, administration building, dormitory, restaurant, lecture hall, laboratory building, and a one-hundred-foot-high water tower which also serves as an astronomy observatory. When completed, the school will have twenty-four buildings.

In accordance with American principles, Bar-Ilan University enjoys complete academic freedom. The President of the University and the faculty have full and exclusive authority in internal academic matters. A Board of Trustees in New York handles all financial and welfare matters.

ISRAEL INSTITUTE OF TECHNOLOGY: THE TECHNION

Situated in Hadar Hacarmel, one of the central districts of Haifa, the Technion is the only engineering school of university standard in Israel, and it is the leading institute of technology in the Middle East. Although it was founded in 1912, the intervention of World War I delayed a regular program of activities until 1924, after which it developed rapidly. As the only college of engineering and applied science in the country, it bears the responsibility for providing the growing country with technologically trained manpower, and at the same time serves as a center of industrial research.

Throughout the world today, there is a new awareness of the significant role of the engineer and the scientist. In the free world, and behind the totalitarian curtains, government leaders and educators are constantly seeking ways and means to attract young people to the rapidly expanding opportunities that await them in these fields. By contrast, Israel has no shortage of talented and determined youths who wish to build Israel through engineering and science. But, Israel does lack adequate facilities and accommodations.

The Technion, while continuing to maintain its high standards of scholarship and research, has been waging a valiant struggle against inadequate classrooms, laboratories, research facilities, and other equipment so vital to a modern institution of engineering. Members of the faculty, who include some of the world's foremost scientists, have been compelled to conduct classes in basements and makeshift classrooms. Nevertheless, with a determination that is exemplary of the entire country, the Technion has forged ahead scholastically, adding new faculties and departments.

The student body at the Technion numbers over two thousand, and with one thousand stu-

Graduation exercises at the Hebrew University (1957).

Chaim Weizmann places a scroll in the cornerstone of the Weizmann Institute of Science (June, 1946).

dents enrolled in its affiliated Technical High School it has a total enrollment of more than three thousand. Four years ago, the Government of Israel deeded a tract of three hundred acres on the slopes of Mount Carmel to the Technion as the site of its new twenty-million dollar campus. Plans were immediately prepared for the construction of classrooms, laboratories, lecture halls, dormitories, and administrative offices. The growth and development of the Technion has been a heartening milestone in the development of Israel. The Technion is regarded as the country's catalytic agent, bringing modern science and technology into every aspect of Israel's life. Friends of the Technion abroad have promised to cover 50 per cent of the cost of the new campus; the other half will be covered by the Government of Israel out of its development budget.

The Technion offers instruction and engages in research in architecture, civil engineering, electrical engineering, mechanical engineering, aeronautical engineering, agricultural engineering, chemical technology and science.

The Technion has top level scholastic standards. Its curriculum is by no means simple. The students are serious-minded and dedicated, for they know that they are charged with the momentous task of charting a course for national survival.

The staff of professors, associate professors, senior lecturers, and instructors is among the best in the world—a faculty which has helped to win for the Technion the appellation, "M.I.T. of Israel." Among the eminent members of the teaching staff are many Americans who left positions in leading universities in the United States to help educate the technical students of Israel.

THE WEIZMANN INSTITUTE OF SCIENCE

The scope of the Weizmann Institute of Science embraces over eighty different projects distributed among a dozen departments and sections in physics, chemistry, and biology. The Institute perpetuates the work, spirit, and vision of Chaim Weizmann, statesman and scientist, who strove to create in Israel centers where scientific inquiry could be freely pursued. His purpose was the development of agriculture, industry, and social progress in Israel and the Middle East in order to advance science for the benefit of mankind. The result was the Weizmann Institute, its cornerstone laid on June 3, 1946. The Institute was actually in operation over a year before its dedication and played an important part in the Israel War of Liberation by putting all its facilities at the disposal of the war effort. On November 2, 1949, the cornerstone was laid for the Isaac Wolfson Building to house the department of experimental biology.

The Institute is devoted primarily to pure scientific research. Applied science, chiefly in the fields of agriculture and the chemical industry, has, however, been included in its research activities. Post-graduate students of the Hebrew University and the Technion may do research for their doctoral theses at the Institute. At the end of 1959, the Institute had a staff of 350 engaged in research in the departments of applied mathematics, nuclear physics, electronics, geophysics, optics, isotope research, polymer research, bio-

The dedication ceremony at the opening of the Weizmann Institute of Science (November 2, 1949). Left to right: Mrs. Weizmann, Dr. Weizmann, David Ben Gurion, and Mrs. Ben Gurion.

Lunch break for the team building the electronic "brain" at the Weizmann Institute.

Preparing a radioactive sample for analysis in the Isotope Department, the Weizmann Institute.

Dr. David Dannon at the electronic microscope of the Weizmann Institute where he is doing research on blood cells.

Members of the Electronic Computer Group at the Weizmann Institute check their instruments.

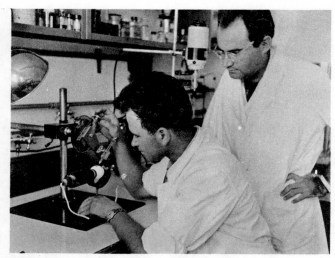

Biologists study immunological aspects of tissue development in the Cancer Research Department of the Weizmann Institute.

physics, organic chemistry, experimental biology, biochemistry and microbiology, microanalysis and plant genetics.

Daniel Wolf Building. This unit was founded as part of the Daniel Sieff Research Institute with funds donated by the late Daniel Wolf of Holland, for the development of industrial research. In this laboratory, studies in medicinal chemistry are mainly concerned with hypnotic, anti-conclusive, and anti-inflammatory drugs. Laboratories outside Israel cooperate with this branch of the Weizmann Institute by testing the drugs for their pharmaceutical value.

Libraries. Before a scientist begins a research project, he studies the literature written on his subject. Otherwise time, effort, and money might be wasted on a problem solved long ago. The importance of a complete, up-to-date library of books and journals from all over the world is evident. There are now three libraries housing a total of fifteen thousand volumes (books and bound periodicals). In addition, small libraries containing textbooks and handbooks are kept in the various departments of the Institute.

Workshop. Dr. Weizmann said that a scientific workshop should be capable of producing anything from "a bolt to a battleship." No laboratory is complete without a workshop, since new experiments often call for specially designed apparatus. Scientific development is therefore closely connected with technological development. This workshop, built to be self-sufficient, able to offset the disadvantage of being far from supply centers,

is now not only entirely independent, but also extends aid to other institutions and industries.

The International Conference on Nuclear Structure. The International Conference on Nuclear Structure was held, under the joint auspices of UNESCO (the cultural agency of the United Nations), the International Union of Pure and Applied Physics, and the Weizmann Institute of Science. Over one hundred fifty distinguished scientists from eighteen countries participated. The largest delegation, from the United States, numbered thirty-seven. The sessions took place at the Anna and Michael Wix Auditorium, September 8-14, 1957.

Chaim Weizmann and the Weizmann Institute of Science. Great men are honored by monuments which bear their names. The Weizmann Institute of Science is a singular testimonial which not only embodies the soul and spirit of the man for whom it is named, but carries on his life and work.

Most of the projects Weizmann directed at the Institute are still being developed. Weizmann revolutionized modern chemical industry when he discovered that the fundamental industrial chemical, acetone, as well as butyl alcohol, could be produced cheaply and in unheard-of quantities by a fermentation process—a method in which a bacterium breaks up carbohydrates into various chemical products. Weizmann's most timely discovery, during World War I, answered the serious shortage of acetone used in manufacturing smokeless gunpowder and opened up new vistas in the output of lacquers and varnishes, petroleum

Speakers' table at the International Conference on Nuclear Structure held at the Weizmann Institute (September, 1957). Left to right: A. C. G. Mitchell, Wolfgang Pauli, Golda Meir, Meyer Weisgal, David Ben Gurion, and Y. Racah.

Main building of the Technion, the most advanced and modern college of engineering in the Middle East.

chemicals, plastics, and the originally projected synthetic rubbers.

On November 16, 1952, one week after Weizmann's death, the government of Israel and the Jewish Agency created a national memorial site in Rehovot, to be called Yad Chaim Weizmann, and to include the residence of the late President, the site of his grave, the Weizmann Institute of Science, the Daniel Sieff Research Institute, and the Agricultural Research Station.

RABBINICAL COLLEGES AND TALMUD TORAHS

The *yeshivot* (rabbinical colleges and Torah research centers) have always been the great source and backbone of Jewish religious life. They offered courses not only in the Bible and Talmud, but also in law, philosophy, astronomy, and Jewish culture.

As such they did more to perpetuate Jewishness—tradition, culture, and religion—than any other single factor in the long years of exile. Jewish leaders throughout the years carried the Torah to every country of the Diaspora, and the living spirit of this great book gave the Jewish people strength to hold out against persecution and assimilation—the strength to live. There have always been some *yeshivot* in Palestine, the most notable of which was Yeshiva Etz Chaim, which had a Talmud Torah (Hebrew school), and a *yeshiva* with a large enrollment. When the Zionist movement gained momentum, Jewish religious leaders became more and more determined that the centers of Torah must also return to Eretz Israel. The pioneer among the *yeshivot* from the Diaspora was the Yeshiva Knesset Israel from Slobodka,

Lithuania, which was re-established in Hebron in 1924 with several hundred rabbinical students under the leadership of their dean, Rabbi Moishe Mordecai Epstein. This is the same Rabbi Epstein who was a staunch supporter of Chibat Zion, who went to Palestine in 1890, and helped found the colony of Hedera. After the pogrom of 1929, when the Arabs killed sixty-eight Jews in Hebron, among them many students, the Rabbinical College moved to Jerusalem.

At about this time, the Chief Rabbi of the Holy Land, Rabbi A. I. Kook, established the Central Yeshiva in Jerusalem where, in addition to Talmud, the philosophy of Judaism was taught. In 1932, Rabbi Kook also founded the Harry Fischel Higher Institute for Research in Talmud and Jewish law. The Yeshiva Tel Aviv was established by Rabbi Aronson, the Chief Rabbi of Tel Aviv in 1926. When his successor, Rabbi Amiel, enlarged the institution in 1938, he renamed it the Yeshiva of the New Yishuv and added a secular curriculum to the religious studies.

With the influx of immigration after the independence of the State, many of the rabbinical colleges, which escaped from the Nazis and via Russia and Siberia, found temporary refuge in Shanghai and Kobe during World War II, were brought to Israel. The rabbinical colleges of Mir and Kamenetz were re-established in Jerusalem; and the *yeshiva* from Slobodka, Lithuania, in B'nai Brak.

Rabbi Cahneman, the Dean of the *yeshiva* in

A group of students in the Architecture Department of the Technion plan for Israel's future.

The Technion's laboratory of chemical engineering.

Poneves, Lithuania, came to America on behalf of his school. Detained by the outbreak of World War II, he devoted himself to rescuing as many students as he could and arranged for their post-war transfer to Israel. He also founded a special institution for orphaned children under the name of Botei Avot. The two institutions were later re-established in Zichron Meir. Another *yeshiva* from the exile, the Lomzer Yeshiva, found a new home in Petach Tikva.

The religious youth organization of the Mizrachi, B'nai Akiva, established several smaller *yeshivot* in a few colonies where some secular courses are also offered. They also opened a postgraduate school. This organization inaugurated a new chapter in *yeshivot* in Israel—schools in which agriculture and trade were taught along with Torah and Talmud.

Yeshiva Hadorom from Kleck, Poland, which offers a regular secular high-school education, in addition to the usual religious courses, is under the auspices of the Orthodox Rabbis of the United States of America. There are now 150 rabbinical colleges in Israel, as well as smaller *yeshivots* and Talmud Torahs with an enrollment of approximately seven thousand students. The *yeshivots*, which followed their people all over the world, have finally come home to make the land of Israel once again the greatest religious study center in the world—a spiritual tower of light for Jews everywhere.

Related Institutions. Mifal Hatorah acts as the coordinating body for more than fifty *yeshivot* all

The Albert Einstein Institute of Physics at the Technion.

Students in the mechanical engineering laboratory of the Technion.

over the country and as a liaison agent between the State and various welfare institutions. Its main activity is the administration of medical insurance to all the students of the *yeshivot* and their families.

Vaad Hayeshivot, the central organization of Torah institutions in the State of Israel, is under the leadership of Dr. Isaac Halevi Herzog, Chief Rabbi of the Holy Land. Its work has so expanded since its inception that it now has under its jurisdiction 89 *yeshivot* and 76 Talmud Torahs spread all over the country from Dan to Beersheeba. All member institutions are the recipients of permanent monthly grants and subsidies as well as food and clothing. Other important functions of Vaad Hayeshivot include a convalescent home for sick and ailing *yeshiva* students in Ramat Gan and the publication of Talmudic literature.

PHYSICAL CULTURE EDUCATION

The School for Physical Culture in Tel Aviv was established in 1946, and trains teachers for physical education. The school provides a two-year course of theory and practical application and is directed by the Teacher Training Division of the Ministry of Education and Culture.

In 1956, training activities were begun at the Wingate Physical Culture Institute at Herzlia. These include post-graduate courses for physical-education teachers, courses for instructors in various athletic activities, and advanced training for champions of national teams.

SCIENTIFIC RESEARCH

The Israel Scientific Research Council, attached to the Prime Minister's Office, organizes and coordinates research work in natural sciences and all branches of technology and stimulates as well as carries out scientific studies calculated to lead to the development of industry and agriculture and the exploitation of the country's natural resources. It acts as adviser to the Government on plans related to natural sciences and technology. Among its committees are the Committee for Basic Research, with sub-committees dealing with such subjects as minerals and fuel, experimental medicine, subterranean water, and general biology; the Industrial Research Committee, with sub-committees dealing with cytology, problems of citrus and related industries, industrial exploitation of petroleum, and meteorological problems; and the

Technion students conduct an experiment in physics.

Building Research Committee, with sub-committees dealing with road construction, housing problems, general building, and the use of materials and methods.

A Department of Scientific Information publishes scientific literature, including a quarterly, *Bulletin of the Research Council of Israel*, maintains a library, and generally assists research workers in industry and agriculture.

The Productivity and Production Research Institute, established by the Israel Engineers' and Architects' Association, operates under the auspices of the Research Council.

The Israel Atomic Energy Commission was established in 1952 with powers to supervise, coordinate, and promote nuclear research. The foundation of Israel's nuclear research was laid in 1950, with the opening of the Department of Isotope Research in the Weizmann Institute of Science. The work of the Department has led to the construction of a pilot plant already producing heavy water through a method of production originated by Dr. Israel Dostrovsky, head of the Department. The Department has also been successful in the exploitation of low grade uranium ores, such as phosphates, of which Israel has large deposits. The cost of uranium extracted from phosphates in an Israel pilot plant by a special method is commensurate with the cost of that produced from rich ores by the usual methods.

In 1953, France and Israel concluded an agreement for cooperation in the development of nuclear energy for peaceful purposes.

On June 3, 1955, the United States and Israel

At a training center for soil conservation, set up under the United Nations program for technical assistance to Israel, students watch a demonstration of soil suspension in water.

initiated an agreement whereby the United States will lease to Israel 13.2 pounds of uranium enriched to a maximum of 20 per cent of the isotope U235 for the development of peaceful uses for atomic energy. This atomic fuel will be used for the reactor to be constructed in Israel.

ARCHAEOLOGY

For over a century, the Holy Land has been an inexhaustible treasure house of the past and has drawn archaeologists from afar. Owing to conditions in the country under Turkish rule, most of the excavation work was carried out by foreign expeditions, which deserve credit for the early efforts of archaeological exploration. Things began to change during the British Mandate and, today, most of the archaeological work in Israel is carried out by three local institutions, the Department of Antiquities of the Government, the Hebrew University, and the Israel Exploration Society, whose work is coordinated by a joint board composed of two representatives of each body, under the chairmanship of the Minister of Education.

Foreign expeditions, which had neglected Israel during the War of Independence, have since resumed their work, though on a limited scale. Dr. J. Bowman, on behalf of the Semitic Department of the University of Leeds, undertook a trial excavation in the soil of ancient Jaffa in the summer of 1952. In October of the same year, Professor P. Delougaz, of the Oriental Institute of the University of Chicago, started excavations in the northern part of Bet Yerah on the shores of Lake Kinneret, and continued them until spring 1953. Jean Perrot, on behalf of the French Centre National des Récherches Scientifique, is continuing his excavation of chalcolithic sites in the Negev in the vicinity of Beersheba, which started in the summer of 1953, and Professor Nelson Glueck of the Hebrew Union College, Cincinnati, has paid his third consecutive visit to the country in connection with an archaeological survey of the Negev.

Local institutions are also active. The Israel Exploration Society has resumed its excavations in Bet She'arim, which were interrupted in 1940, after four seasons, and the Department of Antiquities has been busy with a series of excavations, the most important of which, since 1953, were conducted in the vicinity of Beersheba, in Naharia, in the southern part of Bet Yerah, and in the tumuli west of Jerusalem. And lastly, work has already started on the excavation of ancient Massada, which will take several years and will be carried out jointly by the Department of Antiquities, the Exploration Society, and the University, with the cooperation of the youth movements.

It is impossible in this limited space to give a report of the results achieved by these excavations, but a cursory glance at the yield of the most important of them will provide some indication of their range.

The Department of Pre-History of the Hebrew University undertook excavations in the Kabbara Cave near Zichron Yaakov with the participation of the Department of Antiquities. Remains of the Mousterian Middle Palaeolithic Culture were uncovered.

The excavations of M. Perrot and of the Department of Antiquities have rendered irrefutable proof of late Chalcolithic settlement (end of the fourth millennium B.C.E.) in the region of Beersheba. Those early inhabitants of the area lived in subterranean houses clustered together and derived their livelihood from agriculture and sheep- and cattle-breeding, as proved by great quantities of animal bones and remains of cereals. Pottery, basalt of fine workmanship, stone querns, amulets, and ornaments of bone have been found, but the most interesting discovery is doubtless the evidence of copper-working, the metal having been brought from the mines of the southern Negev later exploited by King Solomon.

To more or less the same period (late Chalcolithic period) belongs the lowest and most interesting stratum of a mass tomb excavated by the Department of Antiquities in 1953 a few hundred yards from Tel Assawir, near Kibbutz Barkai. More than two hundred pottery vessels have been found intact, as well as quantities of beads and amulets of semi-precious stones, one of them reflecting early cultural relations with Egypt. With the exception of the Hyksos graves excavated in Jericho, this is the richest tomb discovered so far in Palestine, and is probably related to Tel Assawir, which seems to have been an important site from very early times because of its proximity to the Wadi 'Ara Highway, later used by Thotmes III in his campaigns.

The excavations of southern Bet Yerah revealed a full-fledged urban civilization. Sixteen different strata were discovered, ranging from late Chalcolithic to early Arabic. Some of them—EB (Early Bronze) II, MB (Middle Bronze) I-II, and Persian —were established at Bet Yerah for the first time, thus narrowing the gaps in our information about occupation of the site by about a thousand years.

Special mention should be made of the ancient city walls. The mud-brick wall erected about 3000–2600 B.C.E. (EBI or II) surrounding the city from the south (from the west, north, and east it was protected by Lake Kinneret and the River Jordan, then flowing along a different

Meteorologists release a balloon to study wind currents at high altitudes.

An open-air class at Bar-Ilan University.

course) was about 32 feet wide including additions, and has been preserved to a height of 16 feet. A slightly later city-gate (EB III) was about 10 feet wide and flanked on both sides by guard-rooms. Later, about 1900 B.C.E. (M.B. I) another wall was constructed which continued to be in use in Hellenistic times. Unlike the earlier wall, of which only segments have survived, this wall has been excavated over an almost continuous length of about two miles on the south and west of the site. It is about 32 feet wide, its stone foundations about 11 feet high, and on it a mud-brick superstructure about 6.4 feet high; six rectangular and seven round towers alternate along this wall; there are two gates on the south and on the west. The western gate, which is better preserved, is protected by two rectangular towers projecting from the wall and its entrance is similar to the contemporary (MB I) Meggido gate. There is a fascinating secret passage through the wall in the form of a narrow-arched doorway.

Outstanding among discoveries of later epochs at Bet Yerah are a fortified synagogue of the fourth or fifth century C.E., the largest so far discovered in Palestine (12 feet by 6½ feet with three adjoining rooms of 33 feet by 25 feet each) and irrigation and canalization installations.

Most interesting for the study of ancient religions is a Canaanite "high place" on the shore of Naharia, excavated in 1954 and 1955. It was discovered near a Canaanite temple of MB II, excavated in 1947, and together they apparently formed a shrine dedicated to Astarte or Asherat-Yam. The "high place" consists of a roughly semi-

Two youngsters study the alphabet at one of the thirteen Talmud Torahs conducted by the Etz Chaim Institute in Jerusalem.

circular stone building of about 16 feet radius, with three steps ascending to it. Remains of animal sacrifices, cinders, and votive offerings testify to its use in about 1650 B.C.E. A most common votive offering is a sort of small saucer with seven tiny cups on top of it—the remote ancestor of the seven-branched Menorah. Animal figurines of clay, flat silver figurines of the goddess Astarte, and various ornaments were found. This is the first "high place" complete with votive offerings ever discovered in Palestine.

Several important discoveries have been made relating to the time of the Hebrew monarchy. At Ramat Rahel, on the southern outskirts of Jerusalem, the Department of Antiquities excavated part of a fortress of about eighth century B.C.E., with a double wall, guard rooms, and stores.

Of slightly later date (seventh or eighth cen-

tury B.C.E.) is a suburb of ancient Hatsor excavated by the director of the Department of Antiquities, east of Ayelet Hashahar in the upper Galilee. Apparently, it contained nothing but store houses but the existence of a special suburb of stores testifies to the great commercial or administrative importance of Hatsor.

Contemporary with the Hatsor suburb are the mysterious tumuli in the vicinity of Jerusalem. There are about twenty of them, from about 8½ feet to about 24½ feet high and from about 49½ feet to about 132 feet in diameter. They were found to be artificial mounds consisting of a solid filling of stones covered with a thin layer of earth and surrounded at their base by a stone ring wall. In the circular enclosure inside the wall there is a regularly elevated area, characterized by a pavement, a pit, and a burning place with cinders.

The entrance to these clearly testifies to special intentions on the part of the builders. All these are covered up by the stone tumulus, and it is obvious that the tumulus was put up specifically for this purpose. It has been suggested that the elevated areas covered by the mounds might have been "high places" as mentioned in the Scripture, and that the stone mounds served only to cover up and destroy these places of pagan worship but, as yet, the mystery remains unsolved.

The ancient fortress Massada, the scene of the last Jewish stand in the First Revolt of 66 C.E. has been the site of a joint excavation recently undertaken by the Department, the Hebrew University, and the Israel Exploration Society. They have uncovered the magnificent comples of the Herodian palace, built on three steep rock steps on a preci-pice, and interesting remnants of bread, salt, textiles, and shoe soles.

Finds similar to those of Massada were discovered in the Hefer Valley by the Department. They discovered two Roman camps, on either side of the valley, which guarded the entrances to the caves below. One cave, below the northern camp, contains three halls whose combined length is about 37 feet. In them were found numerous big vessels of Roman times, pieces of wooden bowls, parts of shoes (among them a woman's and a child's shoe), and many textile shreds. This archaeological evidence makes it clear that, during Bar Kochba's revolt a large crowd, with women and children among them, sought refuge in this cave and were besieged by the Romans. The other cave, below the southern camp, explored this year,

Lunch time in the dining room of an Etz Chaim Talmud Torah.

Headquarters of Yeshivat B'nei Akiba run by the Mizrachi movement in Jerusalem.

yielded a considerable quantity of shoes, more textiles, remains of ropes, baskets, some dried up food (olives, barley corns, a pomegranate), and many skeletons, mostly of women and children. This group was apparently besieged and starved to death by the Roman garrison above during this revolt.

In 1954 and 1955, Dr. N. Avigad, on behalf of the Israel Exploration Society, resumed the excavations interrupted in 1940 in the Necropolis of Bet She'arim, of the second to fourth century C.E. The two seasons' work on the spot have added several new catacombs to the eleven already known, one of them differing from all others in plan and in design. Three masonry arches are applied to its rock-cut face, it is marked by a semicircular terrace structure on top and its whole lay-out suggests the burial ground of a particularly wealthy and dignified family. Since two of its graves are defined as those of Rabbi Simeon and Rabbi Gamaliel, it is probable that they represent the resting places of the two well-known sages of these names—the sons of Rabbi Yehuda the Prince, the famous Patriarch codifier of the Mishna—and in this case, the whole catacomb may well be the one belonging to the patriarchal family. It is even possible that a double grave sunk in the floor of this catacomb may prove one day to be the resting place of Rabbi Yehuda and his wife. At any rate, the patriarchal catacomb belongs to the end of the eleventh century, C.E., the arched masonry façade having been added to it during the first half of the third.

Mention should also be made of another three-story catacomb with over three hundred graves—obviously of humbler folk—as well as of several scores of new funerary inscriptions, mostly in Greek, which were also discovered in the latest excavations at Bet She'arim.

This brief, chronological survey includes only the principal features of the most spectacular finds made during the last years in Israel. Many smaller excavations (for instance at Bet She'an and Tiberias) have also contributed to knowledge of Israel's past.

Apart from actual excavations, the most important archaeological item from Israel is undoubtedly the recent purchase in the United States of the four Dead Sea Scrolls by Israeli National Institutions, made possible by the offices of Professor W. F. Albright and Dr. Y. Yadin. Since the three other scrolls were already acquired in 1947 by the late Professor E. L. Sukenik for the Hebrew Uni-

Talmud study in the Tiferet Zion Synagogue, Jerusalem.

versity, the whole treasure is now assembled in Israel. The University has recently published a full edition of the latter three scrolls and Dr. N. Avigad of the University is now working on the only one of the four scrolls which has not yet been opened and deciphered, owing to its poor state of preservation (the three others were published by the American School of Oriental Research). In the meantime, Dr. Avigad has published the first comprehensive and detailed study of the well-known monuments in the Kidron valley east of Jerusalem (Absalom's tomb, etc.) now in Jordan territory.

Another archaeological treasure is the splendid collection of ancient art (especially rich in ancient glass) of the late Dr. W. Moses, turned over by him to the municipality of Tel Aviv. A similar collection was given to the municipality of Haifa a few years ago by Mr. A. Roche. The museum of the Department of Antiquities, established in 1951, has been considerably enlarged and enriched by new acquisitions and, in Acre, Tiberias, and other places, local museums have been set up.

Despite a shortage of trained personnel and funds, the Department of Antiquities maintains a large degree of control over antiquities and ancient sites, and supervises the restoration and preservation work on ancient monuments. Various publications and periodicals are issued by the Israel Exploration Society, a quarterly on current news, the annual for more detailed studies and reports, and another quarterly in English, *Israel Exploration Journal,* aimed at acquainting the English-speaking public abroad with the results of Israel archaeology, which has achieved a fine reputation in the scientific world. Similarly, the Department of Antiquities is preparing the first volume of an annual of its own, in both Hebrew and in English.

The annual convention of the Israel Exploration Society, held traditionally during the week of the Feast of Tabernacles and, on each occasion, in another part of the country, is a special event in the Society's annals and the country as a whole. The theme of the convention is linked to that particular region in which the convention takes place and hundreds of people attend the lectures and participate in the archaeological trips arranged by it.

11 CULTURE AND SPORTS

LITERATURE

Modern Israeli literature should be evaluated against the background of the continuous growth of the Hebrew language. The revival of Hebrew as a spoken language is attributable mainly to the tireless efforts of Eliezer Ben Yehuda. Today, modern Hebrew has a vocabulary, including technical terms, of perhaps sixty thousand words, and hundreds of new words are being added every month. As a result many Hebrew writers are concerned more with form than substance—yet there are many who have achieved success and fame.

The earliest of the modern writers, Abraham Mapu, wrote love novels in Biblical style. But more recent writers are breaking away from the themes of exile, persecution, squalor, inbred inferiority, and hypersensitiveness; the Jewish National renascence is apparent nowhere more than in its publications.

Of those who have received recognition so far, the older generation is notably represented—Chaim Nachman Bialik, the Hebrew poet laureate, and poets S. Tchernichovsky, Uri Zvi Greenberg, J. Cohen, and D. Shimoni. S. J. Agnon is perhaps the greatest living novelist in contemporary Hebrew, and there are Hazaz, Shofman, Berkovitch and others who write of the new State but, nevertheless, represent the influence of the Continent.

The War of Liberation and the establishment of the State have brought younger people to the fore. Their own participation in these events and the different approach of youth to the stirring and momentous history being made could not but prove inspiring.

Itzhak Shenhar (Shenberg), possesses exquisite Hebrew style and he tells of the present-day Jerusalem with color and subtlety. Then there is Yehoshua Bar-Yosef of Safed, the cradle of Cabala. S. Izhar (Smilansky) shows his age and generation in the use of jargon, slang, and his knowledge of Israel.

Not to be overlooked is the monumental work which has been done by those who have translated, not only the classics, but important contemporary books into modern Hebrew. This in turn helps in the development and background of the active and rising young authors.

Literature in Israel is rapidly achieving maturity, offering promise of greater work to come.

PRESS

A recent survey of publications appearing regularly in Israel shows that there are over 350 in existence, exclusive of bulletins and organization periodicals. There is as yet no Audit Bureau of Circulation so the figure cannot be accurately determined.

The Israeli population (about 1,950,000) is made up of citizens from all the nations of the world, and each group has contributed to and found a voice in the press. As a result, the publications of this small State, appearing in more than a dozen languages, are perhaps more varied than in any country:

Hebrew	216
Hebrew with foreign or summary	25
Arabic	15
English	35
Yiddish	12
French	10
Bulgarian	8

Eliezer Ben Yehuda (1858-1922) who almost single-handedly revived Hebrew as a spoken language.

Rumanian	9
Ladino (Spaniolit)	8
Hungarian	4
Polish	3
Persian	1

Of the 23 daily newspapers, 16 appear in Hebrew and 1 in Arabic. Six are published in English, French, German (2), Bulgarian, and Hungarian. One, *Omer*, is printed in simple and voweled Hebrew for the benefit of new immigrants. It should be added that many foreign-language dailies now publish a Hebrew column. Several Yiddish, Rumanian, and Polish papers appear three times a week on alternate days, providing daily reading matter in these languages as well.

According to their periodicity, the 357 publications can be classified as follows:

Dailies	23
Three times a week	10
Weeklies	70
Bi-weeklies	16
Monthlies	105
Bi-monthlies	20
Quarterlies	45
Annuals	12
Irregulars	55

Of the 70 weeklies, at least 41 are dedicated to politics; the same is proportionately true of 4 bi-weeklies and 14 monthlies. It is of further interest to note that at least 21 publications deal with art, literature, music, and theater, 15 with trade and economics (not including purely statistical reports), 16 with labor problems and the cooperative movement, 17 with education, and not less than 15 are concerned with history and archaeology. Medicine is represented by 6 publications, the natural sciences and engineering by 4 each, and philately by 3; 8 deal exclusively with religious affairs and 2 with sports. There is a total of 30 youth publications (several sponsored by the Jewish Agency), 5 women's magazines, and over 50 major Government publications.

Only 10 of the 23 daily newspapers appearing now were established prior to 1948. The oldest existing Israel daily is the *Ha'aretz*. Only 3 papers of the 23, among them *The Jerusalem Post*, in English, are published in Jerusalem. The other 20 appear in Tel Aviv, but all the papers enjoy countrywide distribution. The legal ownership rests with limited companies in most cases but, in several instances, the shares are concentrated within family groups or owned by a few individuals. The

Chaim Nachman Bialik (1873-1934), revered Hebrew poet.

evening paper, *Ma'ariv*, has been established and is cooperatively published by a group of working journalists and printers. There are no newspaper chains although many of the dailies are party organs. Two—*Davar* and *Omer*—are published by the labor federation, Histadrut.

The size of the newspapers is limited to four pages on weekdays and eight pages on Fridays and on the eve of festivals, since no papers are published on festival days. The circulation figures are low in comparison with those of many other countries. However, the number of readers per copy is often appreciably higher, e.g., a communal settlement might subscribe to a few copies of a paper which are then read by a large number of the settlement's members. The highest average daily circulation is that of the *Maariv* which, in 1954, was estimated at about fifty-two thousand.

Israeli papers and magazines are more "solid," that is less frivolous, than those to which we have become accustomed in the United States. There is little room for sensationalism in a country where daily living and minute-by-minute difficulties produce such exciting situations. The proportion of articles on timely subjects, educational disserta-

The new Habimah Theater, Tel Aviv.

Interior of Habimah.

Habimah presents Ibsen's *Peer Gynt*.

Marcel Marceau (knife in hand), brilliant French performer, and Shai K. Ophir, outstanding Israeli mime, at the Chamber Theater.

Teahouse of the August Moon at the Habimah Theater.

Habimah players in *The Brothers Karamazov*.

The Histadrut Theater, Ohel, presents Theodor Herzl's *Solon in Lydia.*

tions, and informational notes is much greater. Oddly enough, the arts fill a larger quota of space, though there are fewer photographs and no comic strips. There are, however, cartoons, political and otherwise. The dailies have magazine sections and youth supplements weekly.

Many newspapers have their own foreign correspondents. Some publications subscribe to the A.P., Reuters, etc., and the Jewish Telegraphic Agency (covering the world) and ITIM (locally) provide items of special Jewish interest.

Government news appears in the *Government Press Bulletin* and is distributed by the Government Press Office.

As a tribute to newsmen, Israel has constructed a Journalists' House in Tel Aviv, and there is a chair of Journalism at Tel Aviv School of Law and Economics which was established only three years ago.

THE AMERICAN FUND FOR ISRAEL INSTITUTIONS

The American Fund for Israel Institutions was established early in 1940 for the purpose of centralizing funds for Palestine institutions and dis-

Children of a Jordan Valley settlement watch the members of Ohel erect a stage for an outdoor presentation.

seminating information about them. When operations began there were seven beneficiaries—there are now more than fifty—music and theater, language and literature, art and archaeology, sea and air, agriculture and vocational training, sports, cultural centers, research, traditional, and social-welfare institutions.

During the ten years of its operation, from 1941 to 1951, close to seven million dollars was raised. Of the four hundred organized welfare drives in the United States and Canada, representing about three thousand communities, the Fund has received contributions from 373 drives in the United States, 14 in Canada, and 2 in Latin America.

A scene from Steinbeck's *Of Mice and Men* performed by the Chamber Theater.

Since the inception of the State, the Fund has been serving as a two-way street promoting cultural relations from Israel to America, as well as within Israel itself. A cultural periodical, *Israel Life and Letters*, is issued regularly. The tours of the Philharmonic Orchestra and Habimah in the United States were sponsored by the Fund.

THE BIALIK FOUNDATION

The Bialik Foundation was established by the Jewish Agency Executive in 1935 in memory of the great Hebrew poet, Ch. N. Bialik. Its functions are to encourage original literary and scholarly work in Hebrew, to bridge modern Hebrew literature with that of past ages and with world literature in general, and to promote the development and study of the Hebrew language. Its affairs are conducted by a curatorium of writers, scholars, and scientists.

The Foundation re-edits and re-issues the classics of Hebrew literature, publishes valuable source material and studies, *belles lettres*, and scholarly works, promotes research into the Jewish language, culture, history, and country, and translates outstanding literary works in general.

In addition to the Bialik Foundation, the Jewish Agency also maintains a special foundation in memory of Rabbi A. I. Kook. The Rabbi Kook Foundation devotes itself mainly to underwriting the publications of rabbinnical texts in Hebrew and works of Orthodox Jewish scholarship.

David Ben Gurion toasts actor-director Joseph Milo and Orna Porath after the première of the Chamber Theater production of *Joan of Arc*.

MOADIM

Moadim Play Publishers and Literary Agents, founded in 1936, is a private firm engaging in semi-public cultural activities. It supplies the Hebrew professional theater and amateur groups with suitable literary material, acts as representative for authors living in the country, more particularly those who immigrated after 1933, and promotes the production of their plays in Israel and abroad.

A number of local plays have been widely produced abroad, in Europe, and elsewhere through the activities of this firm. In addition it has published many plays, some in Hebrew and some in other languages, by the late Dr. S. Gronemann, Shulamit, Bat-Ori, Max Brod, Margot Klausner-Brandstatter, C. C. Boschwitz, Max Zweig, and Freidrich Lobe.

The ballet from *Faust* at the National Opera of Israel.

As a literary agency, Moadim is one of the few enterprises devoted to finding a market abroad for works written by Israeli authors.

THE OVER-ALL PUBLISHING PICTURE

During 1953 a total of 977 Hebrew books were published. Of these 205 were fiction—including drama and poetry (70 originals and 135 translations of both classics and modern writers), 108 (49 originals and 59 translations) were published for children and young people, 63 (of which only two were translations) dealt with Jewish scholarship, 20 (one translation) were on the history of the Land of Israel, 19 were devoted to general history and 11 to Jewish history. Today, the annual book publishing rate is about one thousand books per year.

The cast of *Thaïs* at the Israeli Folk Opera.

An outdoor performance of the Ellisheva Mona Ballet in Independence Park, Tel Aviv.

LIBRARIES

The largest library is the Jewish National and University Library in Jerusalem. Others include the Municipal Library of Tel Aviv, the Knesset (Parliament) Library, and the nationwide library chain of the *Histadrut* (General Federation of Labor). "Book Mobiles" have been organized to serve immigrants and settlers living in outlying districts.

For more specific interests, there exist the Art Library of the Bezalel Museum in Jerusalem, the Botanical Library of Bet Gordon in Dagania, the Bet Sturman Library of Archaeology and Natural Sciences at Ein Harod, and the Index Library of the Scientific Research Council of Israel. A central library for the blind, the only one of its type in Israel, was set up in Natanya.

RADIO

Kol Israel (the Voice of Israel) is on the air for seventeen hours a day broadcasting from its studio in Jerusalem, with parts of the program transmitted from Tel Aviv. In 1953, a new fifty-kilowatt transmitter, on a medium wave length, was put into operation, serving the entire country. The new transmitter also made possible the introduction of a cultural program.

There are six regular daily news broadcasts in Hebrew, three in Arabic, two in English, and one in French. Two hours daily are devoted to Arabic programs.

In the evening, *Kol Israel* broadcasts on a special wave length for new immigrants. There are daily programs in Yiddish, French, and Ladino; four times a week in Rumanian and Hungarian; three times a week in Turkish; and twice a week in Persian.

There are two smaller stations as well. The station of the Defense Forces, *Galei Zahall*, is on the air for three and a half hours daily, broadcasting lighter programs for the armed forces. *Kol Zion Lagola* (The Voice of Zion) broadcasts daily on short wave in Hebrew, Yiddish, English, and French and is beamed to Europe, North Africa, and the Americas.

At the end of 1953 there were 244,622 radio receiving sets in the country as compared with 146,489 in 1950.

THEATER

Many Jews in the Diaspora have achieved fame in the world of the theater, but drama has not been a significant factor in the cultural history of the people of the Book. There was too much real pain and suffering, and too little time for play-acting.

When the people began to return to the homeland, long before the creation of the State, they found a measure of security despite hardship, and with it came the desire to entertain and be entertained. As early as 1908, when Tel Aviv was founded, Israel's city of art and the mother of its theater witnessed the creation of the first dramatic troupes. Whole evenings were devoted to amateur recitations and readings of both Hebrew poets and writers and world renowned literary works. There were cafes where writers, actors, painters, and others of the *avant garde* discussed the theater, which was just coming into being in most unsuitable substitutes for a stage. In these early days, long before the famous Habimah settled in Palestine, there were numerous attempts to establish troupes of actors, the most important of which were the Hebrew Theater, the Popular Theater,

The annual dance festival at Dahlia.

Members of Inbal, the National Dance Theater of Israel, in a scene from the Shepherd Dance, which dates from ancient times.

Students at Kfar Silver, ZOA's Agricultural Training Institute, perform the Dance of the Exodus.

The Rachel Nadav troupe, one of the most famous Yemenite dance groups in Israel, in their colorful traditional dress.

Young Israelis perform a *Hassidic* wedding dance.

Fascinated children watch Hanso Ben Shalom, founder of the traveling puppet theater, Bubatron, painting an "actor's" head in his workshop.

A children's troupe performs in Dagania.

Hakumkum (The Kettle, a satirical group), and the Eretz Israel Theater, Hatai.

Although none of these early groups survived, they were pioneers. Some of their founders are now leading actors in Israel although others have long since left the country, and it is to them that credit must be given for the contemporary professional Israeli theater which is represented by three permanent companies—Habimah, Ohel, and Teatron Kameri (Chamber Theater).

Habimah, the oldest of the Hebrew companies, originated in Russia in 1918 as the Moscow Hebrew Theater under the direction of Stanislavsky and Wachtangoff, two of the greatest stage producers of their time. These two wanted their new company to be a daring vehicle of stark realism combined with expressionism. This famous company won acclaim both in Europe and the

A sword dance in a Druse village.

United States for its interpretations of *The Dybbuk, Golem,* and *The Eternal Jew*—for proving that Hebrew was a living language, when it settled in the Holy Land in 1928. Today it has a hall of its own, a building of its own, and the largest theater in the country.

Ohel, the workingman's theater, was started even before the arrival of Habimah, when Moshe Halevi, a former member of Habimah, opened a studio in 1925 which was sponsored by the Histadrut. Halevi, who directed the company for twenty-five years, recruited his first performers by interviewing the young people of both the agricultural settlements and the urban factories.

Israel's first circus performs at Ramat Gan.

In the early days, Habimah and Ohel performed on alternate nights for there was only one sizable theater in all of Tel Aviv—the Mograbi, with 650 seats. In 1940, however, when the Histadrut opened its own building, Ohel had its own home with a seating-capacity equal to the old Mograbi.

Teatron Kameri (The Chamber Theater), the third permanent dramatic company, and the most

266

Entrance to a new movie house in Tel Aviv.

A movie theater erected for settlers in the Dead Sea region.

modern and lively of all, was founded by Joseph Milo in 1945, at a most auspicious time. Mograbi was vacant—Ohel had permanent quarters, and Habimah had just moved into its new one thousand-seat theater. More important, however, the Teatron Kameri acted as a challenge to the over-conservative attitude which the older groups were beginning to manifest. These two companies were finally forced to admit young actors, to enlarge their repertoires, to invite famous foreign guest directors—in actual fact, to modernize and re-adapt the entire Hebrew theater. Special children's performances are regularly scheduled by Ohel and occasionally by Habimah and Teatron Kameri.

There are all kinds of theatrical presentations in addition to those offered by the "Big Three." The American Negro ensemble won a tremendous ovation when it presented Gershwin's *Porgy and Bess* in the Habimah theater. Two small institutions in Tel Aviv, which provide regular amusement, are Li-La-Lo, under the management of Moshe Wallin, which is a literary cabaret, and Do-Re-Mi, George Val's operetta theater. The

Wooden Troupe, the excellent marionette theater, which was forced to suspend activity for several years because it did not have a suitable hall, is once again functioning under the celebrated Dr. Paul Loewy in a new center in the Teatron Kameri building.

Finally, there are the numerous amateur groups which are active in agricultural settlements, schools, and youth organizations. Some of their performances of local and foreign works have been so outstanding that they have been repeated on professional stages and in open-air performances in many parts of the country.

Although inactive now, mention should be made of the famous Matate Satirical Theater which had been in existence twenty-five years when it fell by the wayside in 1955—partly because the *Bet Haam* (People's House) in which it operated was on the verge of collapse, and partly because of the dearth of writers who could feed it the type of sketches of current events and personalities which the Israelis so loved. This was the theater which had "played" the High Commissioner of the Mandatory Power, Ben Gurion, Stalin, Churchill, Roosevelt, workers and factory owners, *kibbutzim*, and American tourists.

All these activities are especially commendable in view of the very real problems which the theater in Israel is facing. The organizational difficulties

Settlers in a remote area watch an outdoor movie brought to them by a touring projection truck.

Arturo Toscanini, with violinist Bronislaw Hubermann *(left)* and Chaim Weizmann, during his visit to Palestine in 1937 to help organize the new symphony orchestra.

alone are staggering. There are no "angels" to finance productions and there are no State or Municipal theaters to guarantee operating costs. The people must aid the efforts of these self-supporting companies which are organized on a co-operative basis. The people are everywhere, from Dan to Eilat, not only at home in Tel Aviv, and so the troupes take to the road, where the cost of rent, transportation, personnel, and costumes are so high that there must be at least thirty "sold-out" houses before the break-even point is reached. Happily, theatrical enthusiasm is so great in these starved centers that this figure is often exceeded. Foreign authors alone can bear witness to this, for they, the only ones who might conceivably be considered "angels" (they have lowered their usual royalty scales to help promote the struggling theatrical life of young Israel), are often surprised by their checks which are frequently much larger than those from bigger and more prosperous countries.

Theatrical enthusiasm alone is not a sure-fire guarantee of success, even in the hinterland. The troupes are good, their producers gifted, their set designers excellent, their translators and composers highly professional, and their actors dedicated. The latter often leave Tel Aviv after a morning of exhausting rehearsals, even in the heat of summer, to present their plays in outlying communities, return home late at night, and arrive in time for rehearsal at ten the next morning. Recently such arduous schedules were reduced and

dissatisfaction flared in the provinces. As a result there is talk of creating permanent professional companies outside of Tel Aviv. The established groups are expected to train these new candidates, but the municipal authorities must also help. They must provide physical accommodations, but to date the only aid they have given the legitimate theater is an exemption from the heavy entertainment tax which the movie houses are still forced to levy. In time these problems will resolve themselves. The State of Israel is new and dynamic.

Far more serious is the immediate problem of the Israeli theater. Each of the three troupes has its established repertoire. Habimah has Shakespeare, Molière, Shaw, Capek, Romain Rolland, Gogol, Schiller, Stefan Zweig, Chekhov, Ibsen, Dostoevski, Racine, Sophocles, Lope de Vega, Brecht, Federico García Lorca, Strindberg, and Maeterlinck and such Jewish writers as Sholom Aleichem, Leivick, Sh. Asch, Goldfaden, Ch. N. Bialik, Hayim Hazaz, Aaron Ashman, Nathan Agmon, Yigal Mossenson, and Moshe Shamir. Its successes include Ansky's *Dibbuk*; Sholom Aleichem's *Treasure*; Calderons' *David's Crown*; Leivick's *Golem*; Capek's *Mother*; Dostoevski's *Crime and Punishment*; Ashman's *This Land*; Sholom Aleichem's *Tuvia the Dairyman*; Sophocles' *Oedipus Rex*; Mossenson's *In the Negev Plains*; Emmanuel Roblas' *Hostages*; Shakespeare's *Othello*; Ibsen's *Peer Gynt*; Maxwell Anderson's *Lost in the Stars*; Arthur Miller's *The Crucible*

Serge Koussevitzky and Edward G. Robinson arrive in Israel, the former to conduct the Israel Philharmonic Orchestra and Mr. Robinson to dedicate the Press Center of the Israel Journalists Association.

Danny Kaye conducts the Israel Symphony Orchestra in his own inimitable way during his tour of the country.

and *Death of a Salesman*; and, recently, the F. Goodrich and A. Hackett adaptation of *The Diary of Anne Frank*.

Ohel has "Peretz Evenings"; Heyerman's *The Fishers*; Krasnenikov's *Jacob and Rachel*; Stefan Zweig's *Jeremiah*; the Ben Jonson adaptation of *Volpone*; Gorki's *Lower Depths*; Max Brod's adaptation of Hayek's *Good Soldier Schweik;* Gronemann's witty verse comedy, *King Solomon and the Cobbler*; Goldfaden's *The Witch*; Giradoux's *The Madwoman of Chaillot*; Sartre's *The Respectful Prostitute*; Emlyn Williams' *The Corn Is Green*; and Alexander Kirkland's *Tobacco Road* (based on Caldwell's novel).

The Teatron Kameri has presented over forty-five plays since its inception. Although its repertoire includes room for modern French, English, and American drama it also presents interpreta-tions of classical pieces. Armand Salacroux is presented along with Leonid Leonow, Carlo Goldoni with Karel Capek, Jean Anouilh and Franz Werfel follow one another, Priestley comes with Moshe Shamir, and Nathan Shoham falls between Gogol and Molière. The Brothers Cointrau, Bernard Shaw, Eugene O'Neill, Shakespeare, Oscar Wilde, and Shulamit Bat-Dori all have their place. Its 1957 production of *No Time for Sergeants* was not a success. This failure was important because it served so well to emphasize the particular needs and problems of the contemporary Israeli theater. The audience in the Holy Land is a heterogeneous one, composed of the old inhabitants who came from Eastern Europe more than three decades ago, the immigrants from Germany and Central Europe who came after 1933, the new settlers from the Asiatic and Oriental countries, and the native

Artur Rubenstein *(center)* after conducting the Israel Symphony Orchestra in its first concert in the Cultural Center in Tel Aviv.

The Israel Philharmonic Orchestra gives a private concert in the Vatican for Pope Pius XII in 1955.

The Israel Philharmonic Orchestra at the dedication of the Frederick Mann Auditorium in Tel Aviv.

An amateur orchestral group gives an Oneg Shabbat concert in one of the settlements.

Israeli composer Marc Lavri rehearses Hazel Scott in a rendition of his song, *Kinneret*.

A recorder concert by school children.

born. They cannot be satisfied by just the world classics or popular foreign plays. They want theater and drama which reflects the life of their country and its people; a truly national theater where original Hebrew plays are presented. And, although the Israeli theater has not yet found itself in this respect, there are straws in the wind which indicate that their direction is right.

At one time the only worthwhile original drama was a cycle based on Biblical stories by Ashman centering around the romantic and heroic figure of King David. More recently, Moshe Shamir dramatized his best-selling novel, *He Walks Through the Fields,* which received laudatory acclaim in Israel and at the Paris Theater Festival. One of the most original and profound plays is Leah Goldberg's *The Lady of the Palace,* which is beautifully poetic and timely. Yigal Mossenson, Aaron Meged, and Ephraim Kishon are other important playwrights dedicated to the native stage. Although the bulk of productions are still translations of the classics and imports from Europe and the United States, the theater is still young, and it has just begun to assert itself. The theater meets an important need and is finally receiving recognition. Prizes, which have always been awarded for productivity in every field from onions to babies, are presented in the name of Ramhal (Rabbi Moshe Haim Luzzatto), an early eighteenth-century Hebrew cabalist and dramatist. Although, to date, awards have only been given to actresses and actors of well-known roles, it is hoped that new impetus provided by this recognition will serve as a spur to future natural dramatists.

FILMS AND CINEMA

Motion picture production, still in its initial stage, has expanded greatly in the last ten years and has become an important factor in Israeli entertainment. The screen opens a window to the outside world for many who never have seen other countries and ways of life. According to a UNESCO survey, more Israel residents frequent the cinema than in any other picture-showing country. The average attendance per person is thirty-eight times a year.

In this country with its population of about two million, the number of cinemas totals one hundred sixty, with an approximate seating capacity of over one hundred ten thousand. In addition, there are three hundred theaters with sixteen-

The Bezalel National Museum and School of Art in Jerusalem.

millimeter sound tracks in rural areas. The season for open-air performances is six to eight months, with an average attendance (one performance weekly) of about four to five million per year. The urban cinemas alone were attended by twenty-seven million viewers in the last year.

Twelve large theaters have been built recently: two in Tel Aviv, one with twenty-five hundred and the other with eighteen hundred seats. The most modern house, with a theatrical stage, is in Natanya. Six hundred fifty-four films were presented for censorship in 1956-57.

Long films	341
Short films	144
Newsreels	180

The composition, by countries of origin:

From Israel	2
United States	204
Britain	22
Italy	31
France	51
and from other countries	31
Total	341

A class in the Bezalel School of Art.

Haaretz Museum of Archaeology in Tel Aviv.

An ancient handwritten scroll, on exhibit in the Bezalel Museum of Jewish Arts and Crafts, tells the story of Queen Esther.

**Blind children study the sculpture of Moses by
Mestrovic.**

Sculpture representing Art, Music, and the Dance at the Hebrew University.

The linguistic problem is remedied with dialogue translations in Hebrew and other languages shown on side screens. Subtitles in Hebrew are coming more and more into use, Hebrew synchronization is already employed for newsreels, and will soon be used in feature films.

A law promulgated in 1954, obliging all cinema theaters to regularly present Israeli newsreels, has afforded newsreel production a sound financial basis and led to improved quality. The shorts are sponsored by various public bodies. A portion of these films are intended for presentation abroad, while others serve educational and cultural purposes at home. Only a few full-length pictures are produced locally.

The oldest film-producing company is Carmel Film. It produced its first action picture in 1932, but now is limited to newsreels and shorts. The Israel Motion Pictures Studio in Herzlia was founded by Klausner and Brandstaetter in 1949, and is the largest and best equipped in the country. Production started in 1952 on several films lasting half an hour (*The Tent City, 2003, Jonathan and Tali*), a number of shorts, and documentaries for the Government Information Cen-

ter, the Army, and other public institutions. In 1957, this company entered into agreement with Carmel Film for the joint production of the regular newsreel. Thus, through a full utilization of the combined equipment of both companies, the technical quality of the newsreel will be highly improved.

The Geva Company was founded in 1950. The young company has produced some sixty shorts and over one hundred thirty bi-weekly newsreels, accounting for the greater part of the country's total film output. Geva also produces a monthly film magazine regularly issued in several countries. The first full-length picture, *A Tale of a Taxi*, was produced in 1956 and, with a new studio and laboratory under construction, this appears to be just the beginning.

Many other companies have produced full-length films. *Hill 24 Does Not Answer*, which has enjoyed wide audience in Israel and in cities abroad, was produced by Zik-Or Films Limited under the management of R. Sieff and Z. Kolitz; *Every Mile a Stone* was produced by the Sadot Company; *The Golden Key* was filmed by S. Alexander, one of the country's best known photographers; and *Without*

Delegates at a session of the International Philatelic Congress held in Jerusalem in 1957.

Fatherland, produced by N. Habib, was Israel's first color film.

The film industry's annual turnover exceeds almost five and a half million dollars, not including about a million and a half dollars collected in entertainment taxes. The Cinema Owners Association acts as liaison between the industry and the Government and is a member of the International Organization of Cinema Owners, whose main office is in Paris. It was also instrumental in organizing two film festivals in Israel.

MUSIC

For these thousands of years in exile, music of Jewish origin has been kept alive and been affected by its surroundings. Everywhere the world over, one could hear strains of Jewish music, and now for the past ten years these historically related sounds, strangers to each other, are meeting once again. The marriage is bringing forth a new era of music, something different, vigorous, and compelling.

God's Chosen People built their Temple and sang. Centuries later these same chants healed their Ghetto-imprisoned spirits, made their sorrows more bearable, gave expression to their joy.

Some of these impassioned composers became famous—Salomone Rossi, Mantua, Mendelssohn, Meyerbeer, Mahler, Offenbach, Saint Saens, the Rubinsteins, George Gershwin, Irving Berlin, Serge Koussevitzky, and Benny Goodman.

It was not until the end of the nineteenth century, with the general upsurge of Zionism, that national identity and consciousness caused an influx of musicians to Israel, among them distinguished concert artists, conductors, and teachers who accelerated the development of a new type of music in the homeland. Symphony orchestras and chamber ensembles were formed; composers and producers of musical shows gave Israel music in great quantity, and its quality compares favorably everywhere.

Erich Walter Sterneber, Joseph Gruenthal, Mark Lavry, Menahem Avidom, Alexander U. Boxcovitz, Karel Salomons, Hannah Schlesinger, Paul Ben Haim, Odeon Partos, Joseph Kaminsky, M. Mahler, Kalkstein, Yitzchak Edel, Verdina Shlonsky, Frank Pelleg, and Ben Zions Orgad, are widely acclaimed Israeli composers whose works portray Biblical subjects, the new life in the homeland, and Oriental motifs. Some of the older, of course, follow the European pattern, but it is new music, a different use of the medium, that emerges.

The Israeli Composers Association represents over four hundred fifty composers, authors, and publishers of music in Israel. It was founded in 1936, and became a member of the International Confederation in 1949, only a year after the independence of the State. It now represents foreign societies in Israel, and collects royalties for its members' performances and broadcasts there and abroad. A few writers of popular music are organized separately; their society is known as ISGAM.

Unusual commemorative stamp issued for Israel's International Philatelic Congress.

278

Premier U Nu of Burma attends the "Conquest of the Desert" exhibition held in Jerusalem in 1955.

But, nevertheless, music publication is still very limited in Israel.

The airwaves in Israel are well supplied by *Kol Israel* and continuous programs are broadcast to the Diaspora over Kolzionlagola (under the sponsorship of the World Zionist Organization).

The Israel Philharmonic Orchestra, founded by the late Bronislaw Hubermann and given its first impetus by Arturo Toscanini, is world famous and known everywhere. Its eighty-three members, only eleven of whom were born in Israel, are all artists in their own right. Twelve years ago it had five thousand subscribers and now having given thirty-two hundred concerts it has more than seventeen thousand annual subscribers.

The orchestra toured and performed in forty-two North American cities in 1951. Its only criticism came from those who were disappointed that more music from the new Israel was not included in the programs.

While on the subject of awards, let us not fail to mention that two young composers won awards from the International Arts Institute of the United States and the UNESCO Music Council (Paris). Once a year, the Joel Engel Prize is awarded for a significant contribution to Israel's music in memory of this popular composer of Hebrew songs. In 1957, after being forced to play in inadequate halls, the Israel Philharmonic Orchestra moved to its own quarters in the new Cultural Center in Tel Aviv, built with the assistance of the American Fund for Israel Institutions. The Center opened with great fanfare. The hall seats five thousand and programs of classical and modern chamber music can be heard there the year round.

Concerts of chamber music take place each Saturday evening from October through May in the Tel Aviv Museum. They are so popular that most concerts are given at least twice. Similar chamber music societies prosper in Jerusalem and Haifa.

Operas and operettas can be heard every week throughout the year. During the winter season regular concerts are given by the Israel section of the International Society of Contemporary Music, and broadcast over *Kol Israel*.

An Institute for Music—Ethnological Studies is supervised by the Ministry of Education and Culture. Folk music is transcribed into print so that the music of the Orient from ancient Jordan will not disappear under the bombardment of the newer more arresting music of the West.

Everyone in Israel finds expression in music, whether in singing at work, attending a religious

The Bialik House in Tel Aviv, home of the famous Hebrew poet, is now a cultural center.

This mural by Argentina's Manuel Kantor in the lobby of the ZOA House in Tel Aviv depicts the elders of B'nei Brak discussing the Exodus from Egypt.

A Chanukah program at the ZOA House, filmed for television showing in the United States.

ויקא את יונה לדני

A Purim carnival float in Tel Aviv depicts Jonah and the Whale.

An Israeli newsstand offers publications in many languages.

Broadcasting over _Kol Israel_.

The Traclin Art Gallery in Haifa.

Soccer—Israel's national sport.

Nat Holman, the first American basketball coach to visit Israel, demonstrates a fine point to Israeli players.

service, at group gatherings, or in the theater. Such general appreciation cannot help but inspire the musically gifted and help to unite all these newly transplanted peoples who can find a universal language in music. Israel's music institutions include the Israel Philharmonic Orchestra, the Haifa Orchestra (established 1950), the *Kol Israel* Orchestra (established 1936), The Army Orchestra, the Musical Theater (light opera and operetta), the Hebrew National Opera, the Opera Workshop, and the Tel Aviv Chamber Choir.

Music Schools:

> The Israel Conservatoire of Music—Jerusalem
> The Israel Conservatoire of Music—Tel Aviv
> The Israel Academy of Music
> The New Jerusalem Conservatoire of Music
> The New Conservatoire of Music—Tel Aviv
> The Jerusalem Academy of Music
> The Israel Conservatoire of Music—Haifa
> The Music Teachers' Seminary, Carmel School —Tel Aviv
> Shulamith Conservatoire—Tel Aviv
> Music Institute—Haifa
> Hasharon Conservatoire—Raanana
> The Joel Engel Conservatoire—Jaffa
> The Folk Conservatoire (established, by the Histadrut in various centers)

Small private music schools:

There are nearly three thousand students attending the schools which are under Government supervision, and these schools have over four hundred teachers.

About seven thousand students are attending private schools or are under private tutors.

Special Music Institutions. The Ethnological In-

stitute for Jewish Music, attached to the Ministry of Education and Culture, systematically records songs and melodies, and collects and studies music brought to Israel by the Oriental communities and East European Jewry.

An Institute for Research in Sacred Music is sponsored by the Ministries of Education and Culture and Religious Affairs.

A Central Music Library has been established in Tel Aviv. There are two music record libraries, established by the Music Division, in Jerusalem and Tel Aviv.

Music Festivals. A music festival, comparable to the Tanglewood Festival in the United States, is held annually during Passover at Ein Gev, on the eastern shores of the Sea of Galilee.

The Zimriah, a new song festival, took place for the first time in 1952, with a participation of some 740 persons from ten different countries.

THE DANCE AND THE BALLET

Before the Government of the new State established its unique sociological plan which generated

Israel's first victory in the Olympics flashes on the scoreboard at Helsinki.

284

The Israeli Olympic team strides into the arena at Helsinki in 1952.

Nachum Buch, of B'rith Maccabee Atid, Israel's free-style champion.

native expression, there was little means for co-operative entertainment except dancing. But today, not only does everyone dance, and go to the dance, but there are huge attendances at all dance performances.

From ancient times the people of Judea knew the ritualistic dances of the shepherds, joyously celebrating the birth of a son, or rain in the desert. The earliest of the modern developments of the Jewish dance was the *Hassidic* movement among the Jews of eastern Europe. Its traces remained even while Hitler was in power. There was only one other purely Jewish dance form which emerged and withstood the ages; the rhythmic dance of the Yemenites, replete with dramatic expression, is deeply influencing the dance in modern Israel.

The Jewish creative process now expresses itself in all phases of Israel's life, but in none so vividly as in the dance. The early pioneers brought the rhythms and songs of the lands of their origin. Of these, one of the most popular was the Krakoviak from Poland, the tune played breathily on the harmonica by one of the couples inside the circle of dancers. From Russia's southern mountains came the Tcherkessia, a wild, stamping dance with varying steps, in which the dancers hold each other round the waist in a long snake line. The best loved of all the dances, the Hora, came from the depths of Bessarabia. Words were put to the dance tunes, creating songs of labor, of brotherhood, and of building Israel. These dances accompanied the early youthful settlers in their conquest of the wasteland, while Israeli songs and dances were slowly coming into being.

Planting, harvesting, and homecoming holidays infringed upon the territory of religious festivals. Settlements celebrated anniversaries, the birth of the first child, the gushing of water in a new well through symbolic dance movement. Visitors from all over the country mingled with the settlers on these occasions, carrying the choreography back to their own communities. By word of mouth, and by individual teaching, these rhythms were woven into a true dance pattern, until few remembered their source of origin. The Hebrew poetry of Bialik and Rachel were made into song, the same words set to music in various parts of the country and then transposed into dance form.

Much of the music accompanying these dances has a definite Oriental flavor. The Arab Debka, a traditional Eastern dance with many variations, has already blended into the local pattern. There are many modifications of these fast, snakelike dances which go on for hours to the accompaniment of the flute or pipe. These Israelis are costumed in long, flowing dresses with rich Yemenite embroidery for the girls, high collared blouses with

Mrs. Olga Wittenberg, Israel's outstanding woman discus thrower.

286

The opening of the 1953 Maccabiah games.

Gil of Israel leads in the first lap of the 800-meter race at Helsinski.

terranean Style—Eretz Israel was vocal, gloriously so.

No less joyful, if of better timbre and content, were the songs of the early *aliyot*, which contain the minor scales of the *Hassidic* tunes, and are often based on Russian and German melodies.

The Orient, and the Arab world in particular, struck the fancy of the immigrant from Europe. The *shomer* (watchman) who was the prototype of the period, rode his Arab horse and wore Arab dress and headgear. He could not very well sing Russian tunes, so he began to adapt Arabic tunes to Hebrew words. Typical among the songs whose tunes were taken from the Arabs were: *Bein Nehar Prat* by Bialik; *Yad Anuga* by Shneur; *Yaleil Yaleil,, Yaldah Neima,* and others. The influence of the Oriental Jews, especially Yemenite and Sephardic, can be traced in such songs as *Eshala Elohim* and *Ani Tsameh.*

The songs for the new occupations are closely linked with the land. Centuries-old yearnings found expression in songs of work like *Shir Ha'avoda,* the refrain of which is based on a

wide trousers and colorful sashes for the boys. They often dance barefoot or in thonged sandals (no Israeli dance costume has yet evolved). Dances often take place out of doors and in the fields, with each dancer carrying a symbol of the dance theme.

Eight hundred performers participated in the Third National Folk Dance Festival at Dahlia in the hills of Ephraim in 1953. Sixty thousand saw the final performance. The only national dances performed at that festival were Israeli, its theme was "The Ingathering of the Exiles." There were Yemenite dances, some Druse, and Arab compositions from the Carmel Hills. The Jewish pioneer outdid himself to express his memories, his sufferings, his hopes, and his present joy.

All over Israel people give release to their emotions in dance. Some use Bessarabian forms like the Hora, there are those group dances strongly influenced by the African and the Kurd, there is English ballroom dancing and American barn-dancing—some of the professionals show their training with the Lifar and Chalif or the Pavlova groups. But all are affected by their new life, the homogeneity of a far-flung people come home, to work and to enjoy, to live and to build. Little wonder that Israel has given birth to the only truly new artistic dance form.

SONGS OF ISRAEL

Immigrants to Israel have something new to say in word and song, something that had never been said before, and they had to develop a new style to say it. This came to be known as the Medi-

A skindiver in the warm waters near Eilat.

Sailing on Lake Kinneret.

Babylonian, and other Jewish folk music. Karchevsky had been a music teacher at the Gymnasia Herzlia. He wrote also in a sentimental vein. Today he is well known for his *Al Sfat Yam Kinnert*.

The period of song which followed the second *aliyah* might be called the Joel Engel period. Engel had a good musical education and was a well-known music critic in Moscow. When he arrived in Eretz Israel he immediately set about expressing his joy in song, and what he wrote captivated the people—*Agvania, Shnei Michravim, Halutz Bueh*, and *Hoy Hoy Naalayim* are sung today with all the affection with which they were sung in the twenties.

Bracha Zefira put in writing the songs of the Yemenites. With Nardi she arranged *Alei Giv'a* and *Bein Nehar Prat* which are of Arab origin. Together they wrote many popular songs and one of them even became an international hit.

Today there are many accomplished composers of glorious songs of the new State of Israel: Aviassaf Admon (Bernstein), Ephraim Ben Chaim, Moshe Bik, Yitshak Edel, Yariv Ezrahi, and Shmuel Fershko are just a few.

ART

General interest in art in the new State is intense, and it is little wonder that a new school of art is developing among the numerous young artists growing up there.

The accent is on modern art. Thirty years ago artists of the eastern Mediterranean broke away from the Bezalel influence. A new life, a new culture, a different way of thinking, unusual stimuli for the emotions—all these came as a gift to the young Israeli artist. He had the greatest tradition

The Israeli team is greeted at Melbourne's Olympic Village in 1956.

rhythmical ditty of the *fellahin* (Arab peasants). This rhythmical tune is well fitted to the motions of the hard worker.

Then comes the influence of the restored Hebrew language. Singing in Hebrew was nothing new in itself, but what was new for Ashkenazi Jews was the Sephardic pronunciation and stress. The difficulties of adaptation to this, the use of *a* instead of *o*, the last syllable stress of the local pronunciation instead of the penultimate one of the Ashkenazim, all affected the melodies. There was a period of adaptation when songs were sung in the penultimate accentuation of the Ashkenazim but with the Sephardic pronunciation. This led to a new rhythmic pattern in the melodies. Striking is the fact that Diaspora folk tunes of a minor character are relatively unimportant in the songs of Israel.

Most active as musicians at the time of the second *aliyah* were Idelsohn and Karchevsky. Idelsohn's compositions were entirely European; his songs were romantic and sentimental. But, he is best remembered for his research in Yemenite,

Working on model airplanes and gliders at the Boys' Aero Club.

and examples from the past, for instance the mosaic floors and frescos of the Dura Europos, and he brilliantly incorporated these into the new.

A great exhibition of modern art was opened in Jerusalem thirty years ago. Since then some of the greatest contemporary painters, sculptors, architects, engineers, and craftsmen have come to the Holy City. The most modern art came into being in the newest State, an art trend quite unique and autonomous, the plastic and visual arts, painting and sculpture, have flourished and art exhibitions have become a regular feature of the cultural life of the country. The Bezalel Museum in Jerusalem and the Municipal Museum in Tel Aviv had relatively small collections, but they have expanded rapidly. They now have outstanding works of art by Jewish and non-Jewish artists. Generally, the country has few art foundations, academies, and

Aviation Day at the Aero Club School of Aeronautics.

galleries. Nevertheless its whole population is art conscious to a degree quite out of proportion to its area and population. Hundreds of artists in all fields are members of the *kibbutzim* or are still living in *maabarot*. They exhibit their work all over the country, and the shows are well attended. Better known artists are making their living professionally, selling their work to institutions and private collectors.

Bitan Haomanim (Artist Pavilion), in Tel Aviv is the site of exhibitions by painters and sculptors who receive permission from the Israel Association of Painters and Sculptors to whom the Pavilion belongs. Exhibitions directly organized by the Association and its members are also held there. Their most important exhibits were those of Marc Chagall, Hanna Orloff, Issachar Ber Ribak, Albert Markuet, and Mane Katz. The "Fifty Years of French Painting" and "A Hundred

Boy Scouts of Israel.

Years of Dutch Art" exhibitions were also held there.

The directors of the Venice Biennale officially invited Israel to erect a permanent pavilion on the exhibition grounds for presenting the arts of Israel. The Ministry of Education and Culture then established a special department for arts under its first director, the Israeli painter, M. Mokady, to arrange exhibits at forthcoming art exhibitions. The new department did much to strengthen and organize artistic endeavor in Israel. It is to be hoped that the Ministry will soon expand to meet the growing needs of the country in art education and creative expression. The thirst of the Israelis for art is obvious from the abundance of Hebrew books dealing with general and local art subjects.

Israeli Sea Scouts in a semaphore drill.

There are many private galleries, the most famous of which are Mikra Studio, Katz Galleries, and the Tel Aviv Galleries. The first of these chiefly exhibits the work of modernists; the second is the oldest of the galleries. Some institutions permit their halls to be used for private exhibits.

Although Israel's political capital is Jerusalem, Tel Aviv is undoubtedly its artistic capital. Most of Israel's famous artists live in Tel Aviv, and this lends a Bohemian and artistic atmosphere to some of its neighborhoods, an atmosphere reminiscent of Montparnasse. One of the most notable artistic centers is the club frequented by writers and artists known as *Milo*, where there is always a discussion of cultural matters in progress, and sometimes a heated debate as to the merits of Picasso or Matisse.

The Ein Hod—an art colony on Mount Carmel —is the "Greenwich Village" of Israel, outstripping its American ancestor in liveliness and exuberance of artistic spirit.

In recent years, Israeli painters have been exhibiting in Europe and in America, and their work has been favorably received. Israeli's art, like the other activities of the new State, is achieving international recognition.

MUSEUMS, ART GALLERIES AND EXHIBITIONS

Israel's oldest museum is the Bezalel Museum in Jerusalem, named after the Biblical craftsman, and founded in 1906 by Professor Boris Schatz. It owns a fine collection of paintings, and is the main repository of Jewish art treasures. The Bezalel Museum holds special exhibitions four to six times a year, and organizes exhibits that are shown throughout the country. Other museums include the Tel Aviv Museum founded in 1926, the Haaretz Museum of Archaeology in Tel Aviv, the Museum of Antiquities in Jerusalem, the Archaeological Museum in Tel Aviv, and the Mishkan Leomanut (Temple of Art) in Ein Harod.

There are numerous art galleries in Jerusalem, the most prominent being the Artists' Pavilion of the Jerusalem Artists' Association, also in Tel Aviv and Haifa, and smaller collections in other towns, villages, and settlements.

The latest addition to these is the Permanent

Youngsters return home along the Tel Aviv beach after a National Maritime Day parade.

Israel Pavilion on the grounds of the National Convention Center in Jerusalem, which was part of the International Conquest of the Desert Exhibition in 1953.

BEZALEL SCHOOL OF ARTS AND CRAFTS

The oldest art school in the country is the Bezalel School of Arts and Crafts in Jerusalem. The School gives instruction in drawing and painting, sculpture and modeling, commercial art and book illustration, metal work, hand weaving and embroidery, writing and lettering, and applied graphic arts. An Art Teachers College is in the initial stages of development.

Upon the completion of a four-year course of study, graduates are awarded the B.A. degree. In 1955-56 the school had nearly three hundred students. Many contemporary Israel painters, sculptors, and commercial artists once studied at Bezalel.

The College for Arts and Crafts Teachers in Tel Aviv, the Women's College for Arts and Crafts in Nachlat Yitzhak, the College for Art Teachers in Tel Aviv, and the College for Arts and Crafts Teachers of Beit Zeirot Mizrahi in Tel Aviv, provide teacher personnel for arts and crafts instruction in the elementary and high schools.

PHYSICAL EDUCATION AND SPORTS

It is not surprising that the beginning of the national Jewish revival brought with it the problem of erasing the bitter memories of the suffering of Jews in many parts of the Diaspora. Physical culture and calisthenics were used as a means to a thorough physical education in the schools of Palestine. In the beginning, physical culture in these schools was of a strictly formal nature but the Zionist spirit made itself felt and physical education became the spirit and symbol of the national Jewish revival.

The first sports club, Rishon-le-Zion (the first in Zion), was organized in the year 1906, in the city of Jaffa. A second sports group, Bar Giora,

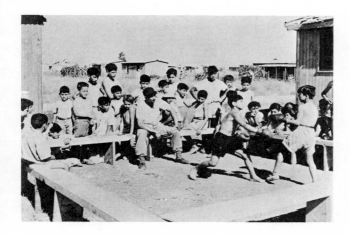

A makeshift boxing ring at Or Yehuda.

was started in the city of Jerusalem. Both of these groups later changed their names to the Maccabee Sports Club. During that same period another organization, Hashomer (the watchmen), came into being, symbolizing the heroic spirit of the new settlers of Palestine. At this time, all schools included physical culture and calisthenics in their regular curriculum. During this period, the first trade publications of sports were published in the Hebrew language.

In the year 1912, all the various sports clubs in Palestine held their first convention in the city of Nes-Zionah. They decided to merge into a national organization, Maccabee.

The beginning of World War I brought with it hard times for the growing Jewish community in Palestine. The worst tragedy that befell them was the mass exile of Jewish youths from Palestine organized by the then-ruling Turks. This, of course, brought the activities of all organizations, especially that of the Maccabees, to a standstill.

With the beginning of the British occupation of Palestine, the activities of the Jewish communities in Palestine, in particular youth organizations, began to blossom again. Many of the Jewish youths joined the British forces at that time, particularly the Jewish Legion created by Vladimir Jabotinsky, which fought side by side with the Allies to liberate the Middle East from the Turks. Many high-ranking members of the Jewish Legion were members of the Maccabees.

During the Jewish holiday of Succot in the year 1919, the first national conference of all Maccabee groups from all over Palestine was held in the city of Jerusalem. This was an especially important event in the life of the Jewish community for it marked the beginning of free Jewish national expression which was so long suppressed. Eleven Maccabee clubs from Palestine and one from Damascus took part in that conference.

Maccabee. In the years from 1920 to 1932 the Maccabees sport organization grew tremendously, and in 1925 they began to send selected teams to the various capitals of Europe as representatives of Jewish Palestine under the blue-and-white flag and singing the official national anthem, *Hatikvah.* The appearance of these Jewish athletes from Palestine awakened in the Jewish youths of European countries a love for sports and strengthened the Maccabee groups in Europe, spreading Zionist ideology among Jewish youths in the Diaspora.

The strongest influence on Jewish sport activities throughout the world was the Maccabiah held in Eretz Israel periodically. The Maccabiah brings together Jewish athletes from all over the world every three or four years. The first Maccabiah was

An international basketball match—Israel vs. the Philippines.

293

On the last stretch of the "March to Jerusalem"—
an annual national marching tournament.

held in Tel Aviv on March 28, 1932, with thirty thousand spectators at a sports arena especially erected for this event. For the first time in the history of the Jewish people, representatives of twenty-one countries in the Diaspora and members of the Maccabees from Eretz Israel joined together for eight days to make the first Maccabiah a success.

Now, the Maccabees, the oldest sport organization in Israel, has thirty-nine branches with active sports participation in calisthenics, soccer, basketball, water sports, tennis, table tennis, hockey, fencing, boxing, swimming and light athletics. The soccer teams and basketball teams of Tel Aviv were champions in many games in the State and the athletes of the Maccabees were outstanding in many sports events. Incorporated in the Maccabees is a youth organization called Maccabee Hazair (the young Maccabees).

Hapoel. The first branch of the Hapoel was organized in Haifa in 1924, and in 1926 a national organization was created with branches all over the country. It began with a soccer team and eventually incorporated all other sports.

In the year 1927, the Hapoel joined the Socialist International of Worker Athletes and four years later a large delegation from Hapoel went to the Olympic games of worker-athletes in Vienna. These Hapoel groups played an important part in the defense of the country in the Arab riots of 1936, and most of them took an active part in the Hagana.

With the emergence of the State of Israel, the Hapoel enlarged its activities and excelled at many sport events arranged by the Association of Sport

President Ben Zvi opens the fourth Maccabiah games at Ramat Gan Stadium.

Groups in Israel. At the marathon races held in celebration of Israel's Independence day, the Hapoel were often victors. In 1950, the Hapoel participated in the third Maccabiah and won fifty-six medals out of eighty-five which was the total won by Israeli athletes. At the International Worker's Sports event in Belgium, 1951, the basketball team of the Hapoel won the Europe Cup. In the year 1952, at the fifth Hapoel convention, six thousand athletes took part in group calisthenics and twenty-five thousand marched through the streets of Tel Aviv.

Betar. In 1924, the national youth organization B'rith Trumpeldor was founded in Palestine after many branches all over the world. This organization named itself after Captain Joseph Trumpeldor, the hero in the defense of Tel Hai and an associate of Vladimir Jabotinsky in organizing the Jewish Legion during World War I.

This organization became known by the abbreviated name of Betar. It devoted, a large part of its activities to competitive sports and physical culture, and excelled in boxing and soccer. In 1940, 1941, and 1942, some of the Betar soccer teams and boxing teams were champions, winning cups and medals. The Betar soccer and boxing teams competed many times against European teams with outstanding success. Youths from Betar also played a great part in the defense of Palestine against Arab rioters and participated in the fight of the Irgun in the liberation of the country. Betar, today, has some forty soccer teams, scores of boxing teams, and participates actively in all sports events in Israel.

Alizur. In the year 1938, a religious sport or-

The American delegation to the Maccabiah games enters the Ramat Gan Stadium.

Promotion is launched during National Baseball Week for an increasingly popular sport in Israel.

ganization, Alizur, set itself the task of bringing sports and physical culture to the religious youth in Israel. This group ran into difficulty because it would not participate in sport's events on the Sabbath, which is the only free day which most people in Israel have for such activities. However, in spite of their difficulties, a good sports organization developed, and their various activities include calisthenics, light athletics, basketball teams, with emphasis on rowing and other water sports. Like the other sports groups, Alizur belongs to the National Sport Association of Israel.

Assa. This is an academic sports organization incorporating students from universities and colleges. In the year 1952, they took part in the marathon on Independence Day; in 1954 they participated in the International games for students in Budapest, and in 1955, in San Sebastian.

THE OLYMPICS

The Israel Amateur Sports Federation was founded in 1931. Two years later, in 1933, the Israeli Olympic Committee was established. The Federation's international affiliations enables the committees for specific sports to participate in international events.

The Israel Football Association is affiliated directly with the Federation Internationale de Football (F.I.F.A.), making Israel eligible for the World Soccer Cup competition. In 1948, an Israeli soccer team went to America and played against the American All Star Olympic Team; the Israelis lost three to one, but in 1949, 1950, and 1953 they won in Cyprus, Turkey, and Greece, losing twice to Yugoslavia. The army has its own league, and a separate Cup Tournament.

The Israel Lawn Tennis Federation is also internationally affiliated, and Israel has entered world-wide tennis tournaments, including the Davis Cup competition.

In 1935, Israel received an invitation to the Olympic Games in Berlin, but refused because of Germany's persecution of the Jews. In 1947, Israel participated in the Tournament of the Mediterranean countries in Athens, and in 1948 Israel did not send its teams to London for the Olympics, because the British unjustifiably prevented their participation.

Since the establishment of the State of Israel, its international sports ties have steadily increased. An Israeli team played in Turkey and Yugoslavia, and was successful in a tournament in the Union of South Africa. Teams from England, the United States, Sweden, Scotland, Bulgaria, Brazil, and Uruguay have visited Israel.

The American Committee for Sports in Israel has sent several renowned coaches to Israel to train its athletes. The first was Nat Holman; in a short time, basketball became one of Israel's national sports. Robert Kipuht gave an intensive course in swimming. When, in 1952, Israel was officially invited to the Olympic games to be held in Helsinki, Finland, two famous instructors were sent from America—Irving Mundshein who worked in many branches of athletics, and S. Raskin, who trained the basketball team. In the preliminaries the Israeli basketball team scored over Denmark, Sweden, and Finland but in the Olympics the Israelis lost to the team from the Philippines, fifty-seven to forty-eight, and to Greece thirty-five to twenty-seven. However, on July 19, 1952, they were victorious over Switzerland. Israel was among the seventy delegations who marched in the Olympic Stadium at Helsinki, represented by twenty-six

Rafer Johnson, American decathlon champion, teaches the art of throwing the javelin at the Wingate Physical Culture Center in Tel Aviv.

The Israel soccer team, Hapoel, at New York's Yankee Stadium where they played the American All-Stars.

Two grandmasters in chess—Cherniak of Israel *(right)* and Reshevsky of the United States—meet in a championship game at Helsinki.

participants and eight managers. The Israelis participated in exhibitions, basketball, swimming, and marksmanship.

It should not be overlooked that Israel was invited, after the 1952 Olympics, to take part in the European championship games held in Moscow in May, 1953. It was then that the Soviets first saw Israeli teams. The flag of Israel was flown over the Stadium and they heard the National Anthem of the young Hebrew State. This appearance of the Israeli team in Moscow, where they won second place, was of great significance and most important to Israel for, at that time, diplomatic relations between Israel and Russia were cut off, and this was the first opportunity to establish good will. Competitors and spectators alike were impressed by the appearance, dignity, and behavior of the athletes from Israel.

Israel won a moral victory when the Egyptian team objected to appearing with them, for the spectators booed the Egyptians. Israel won acclaim from the world press—their democratic spirit and ability gained sympathy for their country's cause. A few days after the games, Russia renewed diplomatic relations with Israel, and at least one newspaper—in Poland—acknowledged that this had been achieved because of the fine impression the Israeli team had made.

An Israeli team under the direction of Jacob Saltiel won from Finland and Bulgaria but lost by the close score of fifty-seven to fifty-five to Yugoslavia. It was exciting to learn that the Israeli team was to be included in the finals for the European championship. There were other victories, over Czechoslovakia, and even Italy, one of the strongest teams in Europe. Israel finally lost to the French, the Russians, and the Hungarians, but their accomplishments nevertheless had made them a nation to be reckoned with in the world of sports.

Later, Israel participated in the tournament of the Asiatic Nations held in Manila, capital of the Republic of the Philippines in May, 1954. Nineteen countries took part. Israel had only a small delegation, but they scored great victories. Israel won three gold medals—one for the high jump, one for jumping in water, and the third for shooting. That same year, an Israeli basketball team competed for the world championship in Brazil. The Israelis scored victories over Chile and France, losing to Uruguay.

Almer Ripley, an American instructor, went to Israel to train the basketball team in anticipation of the Olympic games to be held at Melbourne, Australia in 1956. Their test game was played with Greece and they won, but only three delegates were free to go to Melbourne for the games because of the beginning of the Sinai operation. The political importance of Israel's successes in Melbourne was the greater because of the refusal of Egypt and the Arab states to participate.

In 1956, Israel sent a soccer team to America. It played a crack American League team and the score was one to two. The team later toured the United States, successfully awakening interest in Israel and building good will for their country.

Today, in Israel, there is a variety of sport—soccer, basketball, swimming, water polo, handball, volleyball, boxing, wrestling, weight-lifting, rowing, sailing, softball, fencing, riding, and shooting. There are annual events, league contests, and championship contests every Passover—for example, a sailing race from Haifa to Tel Aviv, and a swimming race on Lake Kinneret. Competition for the Jerusalem Cup (soccer) and the Independence Cup (for running), are held on Independence Day.

The largest, finest sports arena, accommodating sixty-five thousand spectators, is the Ramat-Gan Stadium near Tel Aviv. It is Israel's "Rose Bowl" and was completed in time for the Third Maccabiah in 1950; the opening and finish of the Fourth Maccabiah (1958) were also held there, as well as some of the international soccer games, in which Israel's champions proudly faced world-famous teams.

THE AVIATION COUNCIL FOR ISRAEL

The Aviation Council for Israel is the highest public institution dedicated to the task of fostering the spirit of airmindedness throughout the community, furthering the development of national aviation, and providing the means for flying and technical training.

The Aviation Council is composed of men and women representing all sectors of the *Yishuv* and Government officials of various ministries, directly or indirectly connected with aviation. The Council is not part of any party; by virtue of its unique composition it represents all political factions and none.

The Annual Budget is derived from Government funds and contributions from the Jewish people in Israel and abroad. The largest share of the annual budget goes to the Aero Club of Israel which forms an integral part of the Council and which is a member of the Federation Aeronautique Internationale.

The Aero Club of Israel. The Aero Club of Israel is a national movement which maintains a highly skilled nationwide organization for aviation training. The Aero Club has fifty branches spread out from Dan to Beersheba where over two thousand boys and girls from the age of twelve are taught the elements of aeronautics and aeromodeling.

The Aero Club maintains a central flying school at Tel Aviv Airport, a gliding school and workshops for the maintenance of its planes and for the construction of its own gliders. The Aviation Council and the Aero Club jointly publish a monthly Civil Aviation Journal *Hateufa* (Aviation) in Hebrew.

12 ISRAEL AND ITS NEIGHBORS

For Israel the word "neighbor" is euphemistic. The past actions of these "neighbors" suggest that a better word might be "enemies." These are formidable enemies who openly express their desire to liquidate the new Jewish nation, to "push Israel into the sea." Through the ten years of Israel's existence, the expressions of hatred have been constant. The Arab Secretary General, Abdul-Raham-Azam Pasha, said in 1948: "This will be a war of extermination and a momentous massacre, which will be compared to the Mongolian massacres and the Crusades." These threats were repeated time and again in increasingly virulent terms. In 1956, this message was broadcast by the Nasser-controlled radio of Egypt: "As far as we are concerned it is a matter of life and death, not a dispute over frontiers or interests. Nor is it a difference over viewpoints, which require mediation for settlement. The Middle East cannot hold both of us. It is either we or they. Steel bullets will realize our objectives." These are typical expressions of hostility.

This calculated line of propaganda has proved most rewarding to Arab world politics. It was the same Secretary General of the Arab League, Azam Pasha, who said to Abba Eban in September, 1947: "The Jews will have no State unless they obtain it and hold it. By the logic of our history we shall fight it. Unless you can first resist the entire Arab world you cannot ever be entitled to discuss agreement. We once had Spain and Persia. If anyone had come and asked us to surrender Spain or Persia he would have received the same negative response as I now give you."

This very enlightening statement was made almost a year before the inception of the State of Israel. It would seem that the Secretary General of the Arab League was implying that, like Spain and Persia, both non-Arabic countries, which the Arabs had ruled by doubtful virtue of conquest, Israel, also a non-Arabic country, would eventually have to be returned to its rightful owners. It is hard to believe that such an experienced political leader did not understand the full implications of

his statement. But one thing remains above any doubt: Israel completely fulfilled his condition for discussion. She did "resist the entire Arab world."

AGGRESSION UNDER PROTECTION OF THE ARMISTICE AGREEMENTS

The short period during and after the negotiation for the armistice agreements created ample opportunity for a peace settlement. It is now believed that with real statesmanship and resolution the three major Western Powers could have brought about a final settlement between Israel and the Arab states in 1949. The signing of the armistice agreements by the Arabs, a recognition *de facto* of the State of Israel, is sufficient proof that no special difficulties would have been encountered if a real attempt had been made to bring about a final peace settlement. Instead, various political forces started to encourage the Arab states, implying that they would be assisted in their struggle against Israel.

Within two comparatively peaceful years the Arab states renewed their military strength. A war was generated under the protection of the armistice agreements and the United Nations Truce Supervision Organization. It was guerilla warfare. Day and night attacks were perpetrated, people were killed, property destroyed, houses mined, travel endangered, and the entire country was put under alert.

These neighbors intended to harass Israel permanently, under cover of night and the armistice agreements, which had effectively immobilized Israel's Army. The Arab guerillas for the most part released prisoners trained by the Egyptian Army to carry death and destruction into Israel, began to penetrate deep into Israeli territory. They were the "Fadayin" units. No mistake could be made as to their identity and leadership—the Government-controlled Cairo radio system continually broadcast official communiques issued by Fadayin headquarters in Gaza on their attacks, killings, and minings. From 1949, the year in which the armistice agreements were signed, to

Amin-Al-Husseini, the Grand Mufti of Jerusalem, meets with Adolf Hitler during World War II.

the end of 1956, Arab attackers, including Egyptian-trained Fadayin, carried out 3,377 raids into Israel territory, killing 443 Israelis, and wounding and mutilating 963. No home was safe, no wife who saw her husband go to the fields to work or travel on one of the highways was sure of his safe return. It was only persistence, courage, and political maturity that enabled the people of Israel to continue normal life during this wave of organized terror and guerilla warfare.

This critical state of affairs incited Israeli reaction. The storm gathered, public pressure on the Israeli Government increased, people in village and town insisted that it was the primary obligation of a government to guarantee the security of the citizens. Israel struck back, sometimes with excessive vehemence, but only after severe and continual provocation. As a law-governed, civilized country, Israel did not want to disguise its defense through the use of guerilla fighters. The game played by the Arab countries, that of sending attackers, boasting about their feats over the radio, and, in the face of United Nations inquiry, denying responsibility, blaming the Arab refugees whose hatred "compels them to take vengeance," was foreign to Israeli policy. Israeli representatives to the United Nations continually repeated that an armistice agreement cannot be one-sided.

It was not taken into account, on observing the greater number of Arab casualties, that while the people of Israel were victims of the night, killed while pursuing their peaceful occupations, almost all Arab victims were soldiers engaged in battle, with all the means to defend themselves. Nevertheless, Israel was condemned for her defensive attacks under severe provocation.

The physical war of death and destruction was accompanied by a well-planned campaign of harassment on all other fronts. When Israel started to drain the Huleh marshes on the Syrian border, Syrian hostilities and continual complaints to the United Nations authorities began, holding up the work for years, causing international commotion. In time, Israel was permitted to finish the drainage of the marshes and add fifteen thousand acres to her arable land.

However, the entire world found itself directly affected as the Egyptian blockade of the Suez Canal, designed to stop Israeli ships or foreign ships which "dared" to drop anchor in Israeli ports, was perpetrated in clear violation of the 1888 Suez Canal Convention. As a result, almost all maritime nations rose in vocal protest. The acting United Nations Mediator, Dr. Ralph Bunche, stated at a Security Council meeting that "no vestiges of wartime blockades should be allowed to remain, as they are inconsistent with both the letter and the spirit of the Armistice Agreements." Israel brought the question of the Egyptian blockade before the Security Council on July 12, 1951. The Security Council adopted, on September 1 of that year, a resolution calling on Egypt to terminate its blockade practices. Egypt's refusal was adamant.

The blockade was only a part of the hostile measures taken against Israel's economy. A special Arab committee did its best to tighten the belt of economic boycott around Israel—not only within the realm of Arab sovereignty, but throughout the world—by denying business relations to any company which had any economic relations with

The Grand Mufti chats in Berlin with Arab volunteers serving in Hitler's Army.

Mourners view the bodies of Israelis shot down in an Arab ambush (1948).

In the midst of conflict, while Arab armies invaded Israel and Arab planes bombed Tel Aviv, food was distributed to Arab refugees in Jaffa.

Ralph Bunche affixes his signature to the Egyptian-Israeli General Armistice Agreement at Rhodes (February 24, 1949). In the foreground is Henry Vigier, personal deputy of Mr. Bunche.

Israel. According to official Israel sources this Arab boycott and blockade caused losses of approximately eighty million dollars.

The Suez Canal affair was accompanied by an even more flagrant divergence from the recognized rules of international law—the blockade of Eilat, the southern port of Israel, the country's outlet to the Far East and East Africa. Shore batteries placed on the tip of the Sinai Peninsula and on Tiran and Senafir, two isles at the entrance to the Aqaba Gulf from the Red Sea, closed the vital waterway to and from Israel's port of Eilat.

This was the complete circle of Arab hostility. Hostile acts against Israel have continued, without interruption, to this day. All Israel's appeals and proposals for a peace settlement, for negotiations, have been to no avail. Proposals made by Israel's representatives at the United Nations before the *Ad Hoc* Political Committee and proposals for non-aggression pacts emanating from the rostrum of the Knesset were not even considered. The Palestine Conciliation Commission, established by the General Assembly resolution of December 11, 1948, to aid the governments and authorities concerned in reaching a final settlement, made many efforts to fulfill its task, finally inviting the parties to a conference in Paris. Egypt, Jordan, Syria, and Lebanon refused to meet at joint sessions with Israel to discuss the "Comprehensive Patterns of Proposals" formulated by the Commission. The Commission had to hold two separate conferences. The Palestine Conciliation Commission felt that its proposals should be preceded by a solemn declaration on the part of both parties to "settle all differences, present or future, solely by resort to specific procedures, refraining from any use or acts of hostility," which would be tantamount to a non-aggression pact between the four Arab states and Israel. The Arab states declined, Israel agreed. The Paris conference was deadlocked.

The professed plans of renewed, all-out aggression against Israel were manifested daily, while preparations were started for a new attack on Israel, from all sides, by all the Arab states. A unified military command of Egypt and Saudi Arabia, Egypt and Syria, and Egypt and Jordan had all plans for an attack on Israel ready. In the words of the Commander-in-Chief of the Egyptian Army, General Amer, "the hour was coming close for the final battle for the destruction of Israel."

The unified Arab commands met, prepared for the attack, boastful and confident after eight years of planning and the acquisition of large stores of Russian arms ready for use in forward positions close to Israel's borders. Israel saw itself compelled to strike, to destroy the bases of the Fadayin whose continued attacks made the situation inside Israel almost unbearable, in order to forestall the all-out assault. On October 29, 1956, the Israeli Army attacked. After only one hundred hours of combat, the entire Egyptian Army concentrated in

Members of the Israeli delegation sign the General Armistice Agreement between Israel and Egypt. Seated left to right: Eliahu Sasson, expert for Arab affairs; Colonel Yigal Yadin (later to become Israel's Chief of Staff); Walter Eytan, Director General of the Israeli Foreign Ministry and chief of the delegation; and Rav-Seren Aryeh Simon.

Representatives of Syria and Israel sign the final Armistice Agreement in a tent at Mahanayim in the Galilee (July 20, 1949). Witnessing the ceremony on behalf of the United Nations are Henry Vigier and Brigadier General William Riley, Chief of the Truce Supervision Organization.

the Sinai Peninsula and the Gaza Strip was defeated. The Israelis captured five thousand prisoners and massive arsenals, freed the Gaza Strip, and opened the entrance to the Gulf of Aqaba, the free maritime lane to Eilat.

This successful military campaign proved again that, in Azam Pasha's words, "Israel could victoriously resist the whole Arab world," and marked a radical change in the border situation. The Fadayin, who, as the Arab representatives at the United Nations meetings explained, were perpetrating their acts of murder and destruction "on their own behalf," as individuals imbued with hatred toward Israel, as people who suffered personally, disappeared suddenly. The unexpected quiet on Israel's war-riddled borders seemed sufficient proof that the eight-year guerilla war was generated and directed by the governments of the Arab states. Israel had adequately illustrated its power to defend itself against any Arab aggression.

The danger of Arab aggression has not been reduced by the federations and mergers between Arab states. When Egypt and Syria decided to merge into the United Arab Republic, Syria was, in effect, turned into an Egyptian province. When, within a few days of its inception, the United Arab Republic included the medieval monarchy of Yemen under its rule and assumed a new title—the United Arab States—Egypt once again became the center of Arab nationalism. Immediately following this development Iraq and Jordan joined forces, but their union was dissolved by the Iraqui revolution of July 1958. Iraq has become an adversary of the United Arab Republic and a source of friction in the Arab world.

These political occurrences are bound to have a vital impact upon Israel, for Israel's location is so strategic and sensitive that it may well increase the danger of armed conflict if the Arabs attempt to achieve rights of passage and territorial unity through force.

The creation of the United Arab Republic and its subversion in Iraq has brought to light Egyptian imperialism and its desire to subdue and control all other Arab states. It has also destroyed the myth of a homogenic Arab nation which populates the Arab states. Of the millions of non-Arab nations now living under Arab rule (the Kurds, Assyrians, Maronites, and almost five million Copts in Egypt), only one group dared to deny allegiance to Arab nationalism—the Maronites in Lebanon, pronouncing themselves part of a Christian country, stated that they want no share in a process of unification which ignores the existence of non-Arab nations within the Arab states. The voice of this group of dissenters cannot be discounted in a valid appraisal of present and future developments among Israel's neighbors.

THE ARAB REFUGEE

The most tragic products of Arab aggression were the Arab refugees. These people were innocent victims of a well-planned scheme. The exodus of the Arab population was intended to show that the Arabs would never live under Israeli rule. Of course, it can be assumed that the evacuation was

In accordance with the Armistice Agreement, Jordanians and Israelis negotiate details of placing eighty thousand acres of land into Israel's possession, establishing the actual boundary with the help of maps traced originally at Rhodes.

Members of the Arab Legion stand at attention beyond the Mandelbaum Gate, the line dividing Jordan-controlled Old Jerusalem and Israel-controlled New Jerusalem.

also meant to allow the attacking, bombing, and shelling Arab armies freedom to kill and destroy without harming any of their own people. The masses of evacuees were assured of immediate return in the wake of the advancing, victorious Arab armies.

There are many documents which illustrate this policy of the Arab Higher Committee and Arab governments. A secret report of the British headquarters in Haifa, April 26, 1948, stated that: "An appeal has been made to the Arabs by the Jews to reopen their shops and businesses. . . . At a meeting yesterday afternoon, Arab leaders reiterated their determination to evacuate the entire Arab population and they have been given the loan of three ton military trucks as from this morning to assist the evacuation."

A. J. Bidmead, the British Superintendent of Police in Haifa, acting in accord with British policy at that time, assisted the evacuation in order to deliver an additional "argument" that Jews and Arabs cannot live together. The Near East Broadcasting Station in Cyprus, the outspoken promoter of Arab views, and arch-enemy of Zionism and Israel, commented on April 3, 1948: "It must not be forgotten that the Arab Higher Committee encouraged the refugees' flight from their homes in Jaffa, Haifa, Jerusalem, and that certain leaders have tried to make political capital of their miserable situation."

Arab refugees, repatriated to Israel, are greeted by Arab residents on their return to Acre. The number of Arabs in Israel has grown from 69,000 in 1948 to 212,000 in 1957.

The London *Economist,* October 2, 1948, gave publicity to an eyewitness British report: "During subsequent days the Jewish authorities which were in complete control of Haifa urged all Arabs to remain in Haifa and guaranteed their protection and security."

These are but a few excerpts. Many others are available to indicate where the responsibility for the Arab refugee problem must lie. One of them, that of Monseigneur George Hakim, the Greek Catholic archbishop of Galilee (in an interview printed in the Lebanese paper *Lada-al-Janub,* August, 1948), is of particular interest: "The refugees were confident that their absence from Palestine would not last long, that they would return within a week or two. Their leaders had promised them that the Arab armies would crush the 'Zionist gangs' very quickly and that there was no need for panic or fear of long exile."

The number of refugees who left their homes is far smaller than generally believed. When Sir Alexander Cadogan, Great Britain's representative to the United Nations, who fought against the Jewish State, brought this problem before a meeting of the Security Council on August 2, 1948, he maintained that there were "certainly no less than 250,000 Arab refugees from Palestine." At the end of August, 1948, the Secretary General of the Arab League placed the number at 582,248. On October 18, 1948, Dr. Ralph Bunche stated that the number of Arab refugees had reached 472,000. This number has mushroomed to 1,000,000 for, despite the many efforts of the United Nations Work and Relief Agency, no census of the refugees was permitted, no deaths registered. To quote a saying which became familiar in United Nations circles, "there is a place where man can achieve immortality—in the Arab refugee concentrations." The refugee concentrations have been a gathering point for Arabs from all the countries, seeking shelter and support which, meager as they are, still afford a higher standard of living than is provided within the Arab countries themselves.

The refugees' fate, whatever their actual number, became of concern to the United Nations and the State of Israel. The United Nations Works and Relief Agency, which provides these refugees with their basic needs, has, within these ten years, performed an outstanding act of humanitarianism.

Soldiers of Jordan's Arab Legion stand guard on the ancient walls of Jerusalem during the anti-Western riots by Arabs in January, 1957.

The annual reports of this Agency are written proof of efficiency in human care, indicating that the refugees are far better off, in many respects, than their brethren living in Arab countries. Medical care is frequent and efficient, the education standards are higher, and there is a greater chance for vocational training.

But, this does not comprise a solution to the problem. In spite of the resolution of the United Nations Assembly, which specifically offered all refugees the right to choose "repatriation or compensation," with the provision that the refugee be ready to live in peace with the State and its citizens, they continually express their hostility. A second resolution of the General Assembly, January 26, 1952, endorsed a program for the resettlement of the Arab refugees in the countries of their present abode allocating a sum of $200,000,000 for the implementation of this scheme.

This solution is fully endorsed by Israel. But it is opposed by the Arab states. An influx of one million Arabs, reared in hatred to Israel, resolved to destroy it, incited by Arab governments to an uncompromising attitude, would disrupt the whole fabric of the State of Israel, would become a powerful "fifth column," and could facilitate the liquidation of the State in a manner more effective than by force of arms. It is apparent that the Arab governments are interested not in a solution of the Arab refugee problem, but in its perpetuation, as their most forceful instrument in all their anti-Israel actions.

A representative of the United Nations Works and Relief Agency stated in 1952: "The Arab nations do not want to solve the Arab refugee problem. They want to keep it an open sore, as an affront against the United Nations, and as a weapon against Israel."

All Israel's attempts to discuss this problem within the framework of general peace negotiations, to initiate talks on compensation of refugees after the Arab states renounce their anti-Israel economic boycott, have had no effect on the Arab governments. The Arab population within the boundaries of Israel has grown from 69,000 in 1948 to 212,000 in 1957; the blocked accounts of the refugees in Israeli banks have been released; but the Arab governments remain unmoved. They have not hesitated to refuse even the smallest assistance to their brethren. They remain detached on their abundant, vast stretches of land. From

their billions of dollars of oil revenues, nothing has been given to assist the aged, to care for the sick, or to shelter people without homes.

Various commissions of investigation have visited the refugee camps. Many felt that the Arab refugee problem should be considered as part of the general world refugee problem, which arose in the wake of World War II. They suggested that the hundreds of thousands of Arab refugees should be regarded in the same light as the almost fifteen million refugees in India and Pakistan, the well over a million refugees in Indochina, and even the twelve million German refugees who have been absorbed into West Germany.

Within these ten years, Israel received almost half a million Jewish refugees from Arab countries.

Israeli border police and military personnel inspect the site where two Israeli watchmen were murdered by Arab Fadayin.

Many of them had to leave behind all immovable goods and even much of their clothing. The plight and expulsion of tens of thousands of Egyptian Jews is of later date. Their property was confiscated, in total value greater than all the properties left by the Arab refugees. The Israelis must weigh the Arab demands for compensation against that of the Jews who were deprived of their property in Iraq, Egypt, and Yemen.

As for the solution of the Arab refugee problem, in the words of a leading Israeli figure, Israel is "still waiting for Arab cooperation for attainment of this goal."

THE HISTORIC BACKGROUND OF THE DISPUTE

The present hostility toward Israel has been attributed to Arab nationalism, but historic facts

Rushdi Shava, appointed Mayor of Gaza by Israeli military authorities after the Sinai Campaign, officiates at a ceremony inaugurating the Gaza Municipal Council.

A general view of the United Nations Security Council chamber as a Syrian representative urges the Council to condemn Israel for erecting a bridge at the southern end of Lake Huleh (May 23, 1957).

An Arabic translation of Hitler's *Mein Kampf* was standard issue to Egyptian Army officers during the Sinai Campaign. This is the cover and frontispiece of one of the copies found on Egyptian prisoners of war.

An Arab refugee camp in the Gaza Strip.

Egyptian President Abdul Gamal Nasser and Syrian President Shukri Kuwatly ride through the streets of Damascus just before the two countries were linked in the United Arab Republic (February, 1958).

make this premise questionable. The first Arab leaders, those who alerted the Arabs to their rights for independence, have been genuinely sympathetic toward the desire of the Jews to rebuild their ancient home. Numerous documents written by the Arab leaders who pleaded the Arab cause at the Versailles Peace Conference after World War I, represent outspoken recognition of Jewish rights in Palestine, heightening, in contrast, the conservatism of the Balfour Declaration and the Palestine Mandate. For example, in 1919, the Emir Feisal (son of King Hussein of Hejaz), the father of Arab liberation, wrote, in a letter to Professor Frankfurter, a member of the Jewish delegation to the Versailles Peace Conference:

I want to take this opportunity of my first contact with American Zionists to tell you what I have often been able to say to Dr. Weizmann in Arabia and Europe.

We feel that the Arabs and Jews are cousins in race, have suffered similar oppression at the hands of powers stronger than themselves and by happy coincidence have been able to take the first step toward the attainment of their national ideals together.

We Arabs, especially the educated among us, look with the deepest sympathy on the Zionist movement. Our deputation is fully acquainted with the proposals submitted yesterday by the Zionist Organization to the Peace Conference, and we regard them as moderate and proper. We will do our best, in so far as

we are concerned, to help them through: we wish the Jews a most hearty welcome home. . . .

We are working together for a reformed and revived Middle East, and our two movements complete one another. The Jewish movement is national and not imperialist, our movement is national and not imperialist.

After stating that there is room for both movements, and the realization of both their national goals, Feisal turns toward the future:

People less informed and less responsible than our leaders and yours, ignoring the need for cooperation of the Arabs and Zionists, have been trying to exploit the local difficulties that must necessarily arise in Palestine in the early stages of our movements. Some of them have, I am afraid, misrepresented your aims to Arab peasantry, and our aims to the Jewish peasantry, with the result that interested parties have been able to make capital out of what they call our differences.

I wish to give you my firm conviction that those differences are not questions of principle, but on matters of detail such as must inevitably occur in every contact of neighboring peoples, and as are easily adjusted by mutual good will.

I look forward, and my people look forward to a future in which we will help you and you will help us, so that the countries in which we are mutually interested may once again take their place in the community of civilized people of the world.

This letter followed a previous detailed agreement in fourteen articles between Chaim Weizmann, representing the Zionist Organization, and the Emir Feisal, in which both parties pledged "the closest possible collaboration in the development of the Arab states and Palestine." This distinction between the Arab states and Palestine leaves no room for doubt that Palestine was at that time envisaged as the country of the Jewish State. Article II of the agreement of January 3, 1919, states:

Immediately following the completion of the deliberations of the Peace Conference, the definite boundaries between the Arab State and Palestine shall be determined by a Commission to be agreed upon by the parties hereto.

In a statement made by the head of the Syrian Delegation to the Versailles Peace Conference, Chekri Ganem, it is said:

Palestine is uncontestably the Southern portion of our country. The Zionists claim it. We have suffered too much from sufferings resembling theirs, not to throw open wide to them the doors of Palestine. All those among them who are oppressed in certain retrograde countries are welcome. Let them settle in Palestine, but in an autonomous Palestine connected with Syria by the sole bond of federation.

If they form a majority there—they will be the rulers. If they are in minority, they will be represented in the Government in proportion to their numbers.

These men saw not only the prospective Arab states, but the future Jewish State in Palestine, as well. They recognized the benefits to be derived from the existence of a Jewish Commonwealth. They saw, as Emir Feisal said, that there was room for both movements and the realization of their national goals but that there would assuredly be interested parties attempting to "make capital out of what they call our differences." Those parties were many, the Arabs who looked for partisan aggrandizement, as well as the British hoping to perpetuate their rule in the Middle East.

The geographical facts provide ample proof that there is room enough for both peoples. The area covered by the Arab states—Egypt, Iraq, Jordan, Lebanon, Libya, Saudi Arabia, Sudan, Syria, and Yemen (without the North African states, Tunis and Morocco)—is 2,999,150 square miles, while Israel has a territory of only 8,050 square miles. Could anybody assume that countries which possess almost three million square miles can be justified in demanding, as the price of peace, that Israel surrender two thousand square miles of her territory? In fact this is the crux of the problem. It could only be the hope that a diminished Israel would become inviable, and therefore destined to disappear, which is the father of such schemes for boundary revisions.

The basic approach to the problem of Arab-Israel relations must be founded on the expression of understanding between these two peoples reflected by the statements of the Founding Fathers of the Arab states. The Arab and the Jewish nations can bring back to the Middle East the prosperity and high cultural values it has known in the past.

Israel's Tenth Anniversary celebrations on Mount Herzl are opened by Speaker of the Knesset Joseph Sprinzak (April 25, 1958).

13 ISRAEL'S FUTURE

At the tenth anniversary of Israel's independence, the minds of the Israelis and Israel's friends turn not only to the past for an appraisal of the goals achieved, but also to the future.

On the holiest of days in the Jewish religion, the Day of Atonement— when every Jew is obliged to make his personal confession before the Almighty and himself—a prayer for the future constitutes the last sentence of the service, a promise to make the coming year a year of identification with Jerusalem, with Zion.

A review of the achievements of Israel's short history has become a national habit whenever an appropriate occasion calls for it. On the eve of each anniversary of Israel's independence it is customary for the highest officials of the State to sum up the passing year against a broad picture of all the years of Israel's existence, to point to the achievements, the goals which have not been attained, or faults committed. But this is only part of the Independence Day addresses. They usually also draw a picture of the future as envisioned by the authorities, based on the results of careful research by experts in many fields.

These official and semi-official pronouncements serve as a sufficient indication of what the Israelis are planning for the years that lie ahead. Among these projected plans, one of the most important is the further growth of the population. The State plans to admit another million people within the next ten years. The fact that a nation of less than 700,000 people in 1948 could have conceived of 2,000,000 citizens in ten years' time—a conception turned to reality—makes the new goal of an additional million in the next decade seem all the more possible.

The natural resources, only initially tapped, will become a growing source of the nation's wealth, income, and continuing march toward economic independence. Concentrated efforts will be made to increase exports, to expand industries, to curb imports. The balance of trade will become the most important concern of Israeli authorities striving to achieve a balance between imports and exports.

Greater agricultural cultivation, full exploitation of natural resources, and expansion of exports will be accompanied by an intensified effort to develop Israel's merchant marine. Plans toward the end make possible the evolution of a sea-going nation as foreseen by Israel's Cabinet Ministers on the eve of the Tenth Anniversary. The example of Norway, a country of three million people with a renowned merchant marine, offers hope to Israel —especially in view of the fact that within these years Israel has achieved first place among the Middle East nations with its expanding merchant marine and has every reason to believe that growth will be greatly accelerated.

Israel has direct access to great seas—through the Mediterranean to the Atlantic Ocean and through the Gulf of Eilat and Red Sea to the Indian Ocean. Whatever the fate of the Suez Canal as a link between the two oceans—Israel shall remain a gateway for world trade, either by direct sea routes or by trans-shipment of goods across its land. In the coming ten years, Israel's position as a natural crossroads between continents and oceans will be one of the most important factors in Israel's economic development and political position.

The belief of Israel's leaders that, left alone, Israel and the Arab states would have found a way to settle their differences long ago, will be justified in time. While no final peace agreements can be taken for granted while the "cold war" continues, as long as the Middle East remains the center of political competition between the Soviet bloc and the Western nations—there is still well-founded hope that some kind of a *modus vivendi* will evolve. Israel's greatest desire is to bring to an end all headlines dealing with bloody Arab attacks, aggressions, and the unavoidable Israeli counteractions.

Israel's hopes are based not only on its ability to defend itself against the attacks of any or all of the Arab states, but also on the conviction that, with the passing of years even her most violent foes will be compelled to recognize its permanent existence. Then, too, one must take into account

**President Yitzhak Ben Zvi and Prime Minister
David Ben Gurion review the Tenth Anniversary
military parade, Jerusalem.**

A unit of the Women's Corps in the parade in Jerusalem.

Bedouins practice for a camel rodeo to be presented as part of the Anniversary celebrations in Tel Aviv.

scientific development and the revolution in weapons of war which force upon the world a new evaluation of these two opposing factors in the Middle East.

The development of the ballistic missiles—the I.C.B.M. and the I.R.B.M.—will, in time, make land bases obsolete and so remove one of the main elements of Arab strength in international bargaining. Although Israel is only a State of two million people, while there are forty million Arabs, it is not numbers which will count in the next decade, but scientific capabilities, research, and technical progress. In war, as well as peace, one invention, one problem of ballistic propulsion solved, weighs more on the scales of international power and prestige than millions of people.

Israel has made tremendous strides in science and technology, and according to the desire and resolution of its leaders it is resolved to concen-trate its efforts and energies primarily on scientific development.

The dream of harnessing atomic energy for practical use is at the center of scientific research. There are many scientists in Israel who prophesy that the coming decade will find Israel's power needs supplied by the exploitation of atomic energy, an achievement which will certainly mark not only a revolution in Israel's economy, but also a revolution in the entire Middle East, since one of the main factors in this region's importance as a pawn in international politics will be reduced greatly if not wiped out completely. As power drawn from atomic energy replaces the power being derived from oil, a different political picture of the Middle East will emerge, and a completely different appraisal of its various countries will become imperative.

Atomic energy, harnessed for peaceful use, is

only a part of this concentrated Israeli effort to make use of brains where nature lacked abundance. Research into the most suitable and inexpensive methods of purifying seawater will, the Israelis hope, produce striking results and solve one of the most vital problems of agriculture—lack of water. With this end in mind, another grandiose plan is being evolved—a canal from the Mediterranean to the depression of the Dead Sea, 1,286 feet below sea level, could provide tremendous amounts of electrical energy for more factories and facilitate exploitation of natural resources.

And last but not least, the use of solar energy, already in its initial stages, constitutes another field of research, which can provide the country with cheap power and turn the burning sun of the Israeli climate into a boon to man and nature.

Israel's leaders recognize the importance of a ranking position in the world of science as not only a solution for the pressing needs of Israel and its growing population, but also, as aid for the many underdeveloped countries of Asia and Africa whom Israel would supply, as she has already started to do at the end of the first decade, with the fruits of her research and achievements.

These achievements will certainly play their role in the field of mutual relationship between

Yemenite Jews blow ancient *shofars* at the Anniversary ceremonies on Mount Zion.

Israeli soldiers in a torchlight procession at the Anniversary celebrations in Ramat Gan Stadium, Tel Aviv.

Israel and the Jews in the countries of the Diaspora. The great scientific development of Israel, its growing role in the world of science and research, will add new dimensions to the position of Israeli Jews among the Jews of the world. For students of political Zionism as well as for those who recognize only the spiritual bonds between Israel and Jewish communities the world over, this position which Israel shall attain in the world of ideas, of human progress, and of science will become the focal point of mutual adherence. The prophetic words "from Zion shall come the Torah" will be translated into modern terms when science and knowledge complement the Jewish spiritual and traditional values which Israel hopes to develop and strengthen in the second decade of its existence, to become the spiritual center of all Jewish communities throughout the world.

CREDITS

The authors and publisher are grateful to the following photographers, organizations, institutions, and picture services for permission to reproduce their photographs in this book:

A. D. Arielli, Isaac Berez, Birnefield, W. Braun, F. Csasznik, P. Csasznik, N. Daphnis, Frank J. Darmstaedter, H. Chaim Fine, Sam Frank, Eric Frankenheim, T. D. W. Friedmann, A. L. Goldman, Hans Kaufmann, Kougel, Kay Lawson, George Pickow, Hans Pinn, Louis Reens, Schleissner, F. Schlesinger, H. Sonnenfeld, L. Sonnenfeld.

Alexander Studios, American-Israel Gas Corporation, American Committee for the Weizmann Institute of Science, American Friends of the Hebrew University, American Fund for Israel Institutions, Attar, Bar-Ilan University, British Information Service, Carmi, Photo European, Gedalia, Hazel Greenwald-Hadassah, Rapho Guillumette, Histadrut, Inlani Photo, Israel Government Tourist Office, Israel Office of Information, Jewish Agency, Jewish Museum, Jewish National Fund, Keren Israel Institute for the Blind, Keystone Pictures, Z. Kluger, Mirlin-Yaron, Mizrachi, National Broadcasting Company, Orient Press Photo Company, P. I. P., Poale Agudat Israel, Religious News Service, Photo Sphinx, Sports for Israel, State of Israel Bonds, Technion, Trans World Airlines, United Charity, United Israel Appeal, United Jewish Appeal, United Nations Photo Service, Weizmann Institute, Wide World Photos, Photo-Studio Zaloman, Zionist Archives, Zionist Organization of America.

INDEX-

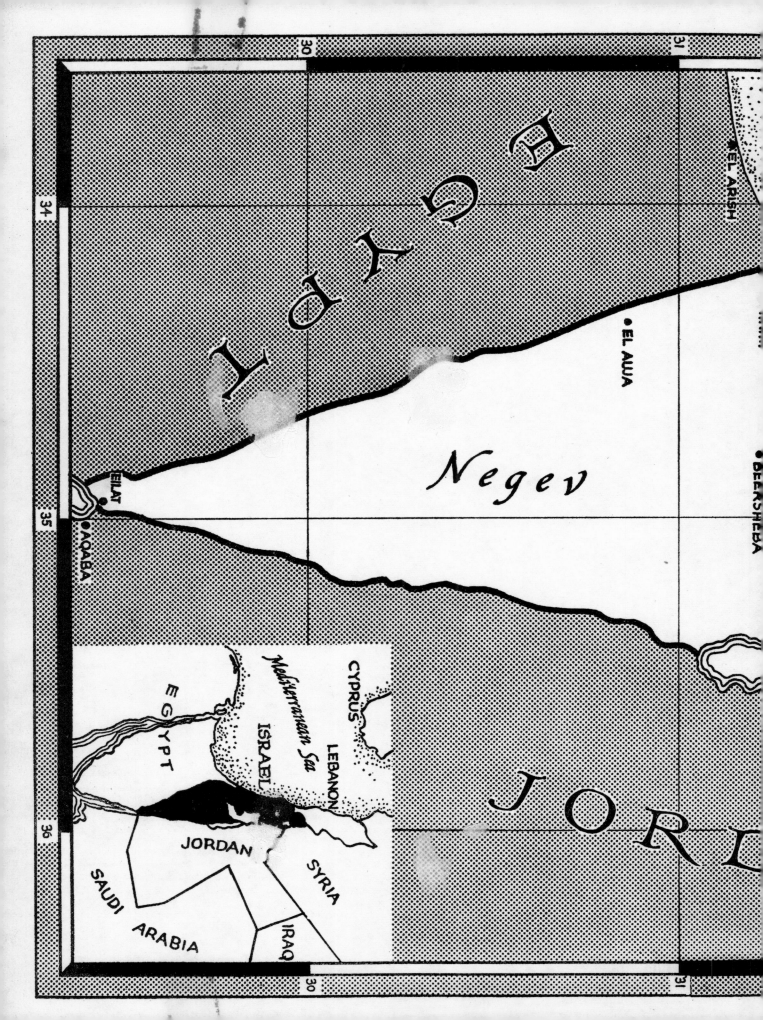